THE MODERN STATE OF JACOB

A REVELATION OF THE GOD WHO CHOOSES THE UNQUALIFIED

SAMUEL WHITEFIELD

ONE KING PUBLISHING

The Modern State of Jacob
By Samuel Whitefield

Published by OneKing Publishing
PO Box 375
Grandview, MO 64030

Email: contact@oneking.online
Web: https://oneking.online

CONTENTS

INTRODUCTION

The story of Jacob does not expose how you think about Israel. It exposes what you know about God.

The "God of Israel" is arguably the most prominent title God uses for Himself,[1] which means God chooses to reveal who He is through His relationship with Israel. And the name "Israel," first and foremost, does not refer to a nation; it refers to a person also known as *Jacob*. Accordingly, whenever you hear the title, "God of Israel," you should also understand it to mean "God of Jacob." And as Scripture bears out, God, then, is identified with Jacob more than any other biblical character.

If you do not understand God's relationship with Jacob, you have neglected God's chosen way to reveal Himself. As a result, you do not understand God as He is or as He has chosen to reveal Himself.

When God chose to refer to Himself as the "God of Jacob," He made a decision to reveal Himself through His relationship with Jacob. Through His choice, God is saying to us, "Go back and study My relationship with Jacob if you want to know who I am." But most of us have not carefully studied that relationship. If we study that

---

1. See the chapter "The Knowledge of Jacob's God."

relationship carefully, however, we discover that God's relationship with Jacob:

- Is incredibly offensive to human reason.
- Confronts us on a deep level with who God is and how He relates to people.
- Provides the template for God's relationship with Israel.
- Continues to drive world history.
- Exposes a deep issue that is at the root of the original rebellion of the satan and all sin after that point. This root is overlooked by most people but is far deeper, darker, and evil than most people realize. The satan wants this root to remain hidden, but God's relationship with Jacob exposes it.

But why call a book *The Modern State of Jacob*? The reason is simple: We now live in the first generation in history when God is confronting the whole world with the question of "Jacob" through the emergence of what we call the "State of Israel." The State of Israel is not a simple subject, but it forces us to face God's election of Israel and the implications of it. He wants us to understand this because He wants us to understand *Him*. It is part of God's self-revelation.

However, if we do not view Israel through the lens of Jacob, we will not understand the Modern State of Israel nor relate to it properly. More importantly, we will not relate properly to the people of "Israel" who bear Jacob's God-given name. And most importantly, we will not relate properly to God Himself.

The events of October 7th have changed our world forever. For the first time in history, an attempted genocide was live streamed on the internet. The perpetrators broadcasted their crimes proudly when the world's news agencies could not even comprehend what was happening. Within days, there were marches in the nations of the earth supporting the perpetrators of the genocide, and the world was on the brink of world war. It is impossible to fully comprehend what has transpired since October 7th, but the issue of "Jacob" is not going away. It will only intensify in the days ahead. October 7th confronted the nations and tested the Church again with the issue of Jacob. And the response in the nations has been shocking and bewildering.

The question is do we understand God's relationship with Jacob well enough to have His perspective of history and to participate in His purposes?

(The word *Israel* can be confusing because it can be used to describe a people, a kingdom or government, and a physical land. In this book, the word Israel will be used primarily to describe the people of Israel. In our time, the people of Israel are commonly referred to as *Jews*. While this is not precise, it is common usage, so the terms *Israel* and *Jews* are mostly interchangeable in this book. When you see *Israel,* think people unless the context clearly uses the term *Israel* to describe the land or government of the nation. Furthermore, the word *Israel* comes from a person first known as Jacob. As we will see, Jacob's story and his transformation to Israel previews the story of Israel, the nation, people, and land. So there will be points in the book where *Jacob* is used to refer to the people of Israel because the Bible refers to Israel as a person and a people, using the names Jacob and Israel.)

The Biblical Narrative Begins and Ends with a Controversy Over Jacob

God's election of Jacob is so important that it is a central theme from the beginning to the end of the biblical narrative of this age. The root of the temptation in Genesis 3 that led to human sin and the catastrophe that has followed began as a controversy over the issue of election, so there is a very real sense in which offense over divine election is at the root of evil in this age.

This offense not only begins the story of this age, it will also be found at the conclusion of this age. The prophets warn over and over again that the age will end with a great conflict over Jerusalem and the people of Israel:[2]

> *For the LORD has a day of vengeance, a year of recompense for the cause of Zion. (Isaiah 34:8)*

> *The clamor will resound to the ends of the earth, for the LORD has an indictment against the nations; he is entering into judgment with all flesh, and the wicked he will put to the sword, declares the LORD. (Jeremiah 25:31)*

> *Hear, you mountains, the indictment of the LORD, and you enduring foundations of the earth, for the LORD has an indictment against his people, and he will contend with Israel. (Micah 6:2)*

The land of Israel, the city of Jerusalem, and the people of Israel will become a global controversy that we cannot now fully anticipate. But we are warned the age ends with an unprecedented conflict around God's election of Jacob.

What is it about election that is so foundational it triggers the original conflict in Genesis and the last conflict in this age?

Furthermore, as we will see, the controversy over Jacob is not limited to the beginning and end of the age. It is a controversy that never goes away and constantly tests the nations. And periodically, it tests people in severe ways. Anyone who doubts this must face the long history of the nations' relationship to Israel and the horrors of the last century which include both the Holocaust and the events of October 7th. Both are gruesome evidence that the controversy over "Jacob" has not yet ended.

Because the Church has neglected God's relationship with Jacob far too often, the Church has resisted God and has been on the wrong

---

2. Note that throughout this book, unless otherwise stated, "Israel" refers to the people of Israel, not necessarily the land or the modern State of Israel. Obviously, there is a connection between the people, the land, and the State. But the term is being used to refer to the people in most cases. And the term is generally used interchangeably with the more modern expression, "the Jewish people."

side of God's relationship with Jacob. Instead of respecting and honoring divine election, the Church has been hostile in her behavior toward God's election of Israel.

God's relationship with Jacob exposes our offense with the issue of "election" because God's relationship with Jacob is much bigger than "Jacob." It is God's method of revealing how He leads history, how He chooses, and how He relates to those "chosen" and those "not chosen."

Though many have held to the doctrine of personal election commonly known as "predestination," they have failed to respect the greatest corporate example of election God has given in this age: Israel. This is an incredible blindness. On one hand, many can theologically debate God's ability to choose some for salvation, but then neglect or resist God's corporate election of a people for a divine purpose, which clearly has not been accomplished.[3] Much ink has been spilled in debates over predestination, and that is not the focus of this book. We will focus on the issue of election as it is demonstrated in God's interactions with Israel. We will look to understand why the issue of God's election of Israel is the thing that sparked the evil of this age, why it is the great test of the end of the age, how we should understand it, and *most importantly,* how it affects our knowledge of God.

It follows that, if you do not understand election, then you do not understand:

- The God of Israel (Jacob).
- The nature of sin.
- God's plan of redemption.
- The purpose of Israel.
- The origin of sin in the garden.

---

3. Acts 1:6–8; 3:19–21; Romans 11:2, 11–12, 15. See also what the prophets predicted which clearly has not come to pass: Deuteronomy 30:1-6; Isaiah 4:3–4; 45:17, 25; 54:13; 59:21; 60:4, 21; 61:8-9, 65:23; 66:22; Jeremiah 31:31-34; 32:40; Ezekiel 20:40; 36:10, 27-36; 37:25; 39:22, 28-29; Joel 2:26, 32; Zephaniah 3:9, 12; 12:13; Zechariah 12:10-13; Matthew 23:39; 24:30; Acts 1:6-7; 2:21; Romans 10:13; 11:26–27; Revelation 1:7.

- The Person of Jesus.
- The modern State of Israel.
- God's leadership of history.
- The end of the age.

In this book, we will primarily view the issue of election through the lens of Israel's unique and ongoing calling because it is a God-given tool to lead us into the knowledge of God. And it has been tragically neglected, and that neglect has had serious consequences. Once we begin to understand God's election of Israel, we will see that this issue is so core and fundamental that it affects every aspect of our lives.

The way we relate to Israel and even the leaders in our own congregations and church movements is enough to indicate we do not grasp election biblically. It is time to get understanding before it is too late.

PART I

THE GOD OF JACOB

1

THE KNOWLEDGE OF JACOB'S GOD

You cannot understand Israel if you do not understand Israel's God, and you cannot understand God if you do not understand Jacob.

God has a burning desire to reveal Himself, and He has designed the redemptive story to reveal who He is. All of history is like a painting, and when you gaze at the painting, you discover a divine Person who reveals aspects of Himself in every part of the painting. Sadly, many people study parts of the painting and discover information about God, or information about His redemptive plan, but miss the message of the "painting."

The stories of the Bible were not written down primarily as history lessons. These stories are primarily about the revelation of God because God reveals Himself primarily through His relationship with His creation. It is what a person *does*, not what they "say," that reveals who they are, and the same is true of God. This is why most of the Bible contains stories and not teaching. God has given us the Bible and the stories of His work in history so we can discover who He is.

God's desire for self-revelation and deep relationship with His creation is so great it compelled Him to become a person so that He can be known intimately. God's ultimate disclosure of Himself is found in the Person of Jesus.[1] And while Jesus is completely unique and the ultimate revelation of God, even in the God's revelation of Himself through Jesus, God is revealed in the context of relationship. God Himself dwells in relationship, something Christians typically refer to as the "Trinity," and God is revealed by how He acts in this relationship particularly through the interactions between the Father and the Son. And in the Hebrew Bible and the New Testament, God is also revealed by His relationships with humans.

The Scripture records key relationships between God and specific humans, so we can know God as He is revealed in these relationships. If you understand these people and God's interactions with them as they are described in Scripture, you can know God. Conversely, if you do not understand God's interactions with these individuals, you will lack crucial aspects of the knowledge of God. Furthermore, God's interactions with people through Scripture set the stage for the story of Jesus, so if you do not understand God's interactions with His people in the Hebrew Bible, you will not fully grasp who Jesus is. Furthermore, Jesus revealed God in His interactions with people, so you must understand those interactions to truly understand who Jesus is.

God's commitment to reveal Himself primarily through His interactions with people is so foundational that He refers to Himself in context to His relationships with humans.

While God's association with specific humans is very familiar to most of us, if you carefully meditate on the stories of Scripture and the implications of these stories, it is quite shocking. *The uncreated, unequalled, majestic God has chosen to take on the names of people whose actions can be scandalous—names we all know like Abraham, Isaac, and Jacob.* And in His interaction with these people God confronts our assumptions about Him and simultaneously reveals who He is and why He is completely different from us. Our religiosity causes us to overlook what the Bible plainly tells us about some of God's favorite people. When we do that, we miss the knowledge of God that He

---

1. Hebrews 1.

wants us to have. Have we fully grasped the revelation of God that He gives to us in His relationships with people? Or have we read these stories as history and perhaps focused more on the people in the stories than on what these stories say about God? God gave us these stories so we would know Him, but we are often to human centric that we study the people in these stories more than God Himself.

We face two challenges. On one hand, we are so familiar with many of the biblical stories that we do not always fully consider what those stories actually say. On the other hand, we are unfamiliar with the full meaning and implications of many of the biblical stories because we have opinions about them but have not deeply meditated on what those stories say.

Perhaps the best known example of God taking on the names of humans is the phrase the "God of Abraham, Isaac and Jacob," but this is just one of the relational titles used in reference to God. These titles are established in the Hebrew Bible, and when all the relational titles are compared, the results are very revealing:

- God is called the "God of Abraham" about eight times,[2] but half of those references come from Genesis 24 where Abraham's servant refers to the "God of Abraham." Outside that one chapter, the title is only used a few times and nearly all of them are in Genesis.
- God is only referred to as the "God of Abraham and Isaac" twice.[3]
- God is referred to as the "God of Abraham, Isaac, and Jacob" seven times.[4] Four of these references come from one encounter with Moses, so there are only three additional uses of the title. (The New Testament quotes this title five times.[5])

---

2. Genesis 24:12, 27, 42, 48; 26:24; 31:42, 53; Psalm 47:9.
3. Genesis 28:13; 32:9.
4. Exodus 3:6, 15–16; 4:5; 1 Kings 18:36; 1 Chronicles 29:18; 2 Chronicles 30:6.
5. Matthew 22:32; Mark 12:26; Luke 20:37; Acts 3:13; 7:32.

- God is referred to as the "God of Jacob" twelve times,[6] with most of those references being in the Psalms. When God is referenced by the patriarchs' names, Jacob is clearly the most dominant title, especially in Israel's reflection on God long after the days of the patriarchs.

However, these are not the primary relational titles God has used. There is one that stands far above the rest: *God of Israel.*

God is called the "God of Israel" at least 199 times.[7] (The New Testament quotes the title twice.[8]) Forty-nine of these references come from Jeremiah, and most of those references are God speaking of Himself. When God spoke to Judah about her judgment *and* her salvation, He spoke to her as the God of Israel. This was intentional because God was speaking to the people in a moment where they were being forced out of the land due to their sin just as Jacob was. They needed to understand they were dealing with the "God of Jacob" who is also the "God of Israel." They were in a "Jacob" moment, but God was committed to them just as He was to their father, Israel. He would lead them back into the land and transform "Jacob" to become "Israel" just as He did for the nation's father.

When God speaks about Himself, the emphasis is even clearer:

---

6. Psalm 46:7, 11; 75:9; 76:6; 81:1, 4; 84:8; 94:7; 114:7; 146:5; Isaiah 2:3; Micah 4:2.
7. Exodus 5:1; 24:10; 32:27; 34:23; Numbers 16:9; Joshua 7:13, 19–20; 8:30; 9:18, 19; 10:40, 42; 13:14, 33; 14:14; 22:16, 24; 24:2, 23; Judges 4:6; 5:3, 5; 6:8; 11:21, 23; 21:3; Ruth 2:12; 1 Samuel 1:17; 2:30; 5:7, 8, 10–11; 6:3, 5; 10:18; 14:41; 20:12; 23:10–11; 25:32, 34; 2 Samuel 7:27; 12:7; 23:3; 1 Kings 1:30; 1:48; 8:15, 17, 20, 23, 25, 26; 11:9, 31; 14:7, 13; 15:30; 16:13, 26, 33; 17:1, 14; 22:53; 2 Kings 9:6; 10:31; 14:25; 18:5; 19:15, 20; 21:12; 22:15, 18; 1 Chronicles 4:10; 5:26; 15:12, 14; 16:4, 36; 17:24; 22:6; 23:25; 24:19; 28:4; 29:10; 2 Chronicles 2:12; 6:4, 7, 10, 14, 16–17; 11:16; 13:5; 15:4, 13; 20:19; 29:7, 10; 30:1, 5; 32:17; 33:16, 18; 34:23, 26; 36:13; Ezra 1:3; 3:2; 4:1, 3; 5:1; 6:14, 21–22; 7:6, 15; 8:35; 9:4, 15; Psalm 41:13; 59:5; 68:8, 35; 69:6; 72:18; 106:48; Isaiah 17:6; 21:10, 17; 24:15; 29:23; 37:16, 21; 41:17; 45:3, 15; 48:1–2; 52:12; Jeremiah 7:3, 21; 9:15; 11:3; 13:12; 16:9; 19:3, 15; 21:4; 23:2; 24:5; 25:15, 27; 27:4, 21; 28:2, 14; 29:4; 8, 21, 25; 29:21, 25; 30:2; 31:23; 32:14–15, 36; 33:4; 34:2, 13; 35:13, 17–19; 37:7; 38:17; 39:16; 42:9, 15, 18; 43:10; 44:2, 7, 11, 25; 45:2; 46:25; 48:1; 50:18; 51:33; Ezekiel 8:4; 9:3; 10:19–20; 11:22; 43:2; 44:2; Zephaniah 2:9; Malachi 2:16.
8. Matthew 15:31; Luke 1:68.

- God refers to Himself once as the God of Abraham.[9]
- God refers to Himself once as the God of Abraham and Isaac.[10]
- God refers to Himself as the God of Abraham, Isaac, and Jacob four times, but it is all in one conversation.[11]
- God refers to Himself once as the God of Jacob.[12]
- God refers to Himself twice as the God of David.[13]
- God refers to Himself as the "God of Israel" *46* times.[14] And over half of these references (28) are in Jeremiah which, as we will see, is very significant.

The comparison is not even close. God sees Himself as the God of Israel. So the question is this: *Do you know God as He is revealed in His past, present, and future with Israel?* Have you discovered God's revelation of Himself summarized by these titles?

The God of Jacob

The people of Israel are defined by the person of Jacob, and the person of Jacob is defined by the God of Jacob.

It is easy to forget that Israel is a *person,* not simply a nation. Israel is Jacob. "God of Israel" certainly is a national title—He is most certainly the God of Jacob's descendants—but the title carries multiple shades of meaning. Even when it refers to the nation, its meaning comes from the person of Jacob. When God calls Himself the "God of Israel," it means His relationship to His people is defined by His relationship with Jacob.

---

9. Genesis 26:24.
10. Genesis 28:13.
11. Exodus 3:6, 15–16; 4:5.
12. Isaiah 2:3.
13. 2 Kings 20:5; Isaiah 38:5.
14. Exodus 34:23; Joshua 7:13; 1 Samuel 10:18; 2 Samuel 12:7; 1 Kings 8:25; 14:7; 2 Kings 9:6; 21:12; 22:18; 2 Chronicles 6:16; 34:26; Isaiah 21:10, 17; 29:23; 41:17; 43:3; 45:3; Jeremiah 7:3; 9:15; 11:3; 13:12; 16:9; 19:3; 24:5; 25:27; 27:4; 28:14; 29:8, 21; 30:2; 32:36; 33:4; 34:2; 13; 35:13, 17, 19; 37:7; 39:16; 43:10; 44:2, 7, 11; 50:18; 51:33; Malachi 2:16.

The people of Israel are the corporate embodiment of the story of Jacob. Their story is his story. *Jacob is the prophetic prototype of a story that has many painful twists and turns, but must end in a singular breakthrough that produces a unique glory.* And as we will see, this is not simply the essence of Israel. It is the story of humanity as well. If you do not know Israel, you do not know God as He has revealed Himself, and if you do not know Jacob, you will not understand Israel. Furthermore, if you do not know God as He has revealed Himself, the loss is immeasurable. Nothing can compensate for that.

Some would say, "Why do I need to understand Israel?" Or "I thought God was finished with Israel. He loves everyone." Or "All I need to know is Jesus." But you need to ask a more fundamental question. The fundamental question is not, "Do you want to know Israel?" It is, "Do you want to know God?" If you want to know God, you will not neglect the person and people He has uniquely chosen as a vehicle for His own self-revelation.

When you do not understand Israel, you do not understand the method God has specifically chosen for His own self-revelation. And you cannot understand Israel unless you understand the man for whom Israel is named.

Yes, every people group matters. There are no superior humans. God even told Israel they were the least of all people.[15] It's not about Israel as the superior people, but it is about the revelation of God that is given through His unique story with that people. And if you understand, respect, and engage in that story, you will come into the knowledge of God. If you neglect it or misunderstand it, you will suffer incredible loss.

The title "God of Israel (Jacob)" is even more surprising if you consider it in context:

- God's covenantal relationship with Abraham is foundational to His plan to redeem. Abraham demonstrated the path of faith and walked with God.

---

15. Deuteronomy 7:7.

However, God only referred to Himself as the God of Abraham a few times.

- God delivered Israel through Joseph, who became one of the central previews of the Messianic King. And the book of Genesis devotes more space to Joseph than anyone else, including Abraham, Isaac, and Jacob. But God is not known as the "God of Joseph."
- God's relationship with Moses has no real parallel. God talked to Moses face to face in a way that was not like the other prophets.[16] He gave Moses unprecedented power, and Moses proceeded over God's covenantal marriage to a people. God used Moses to set something in motion that continues to define the Jewish people. However, God is not known as the "God of Moses."
- God made an incredible covenant with David and chose Him to be the ancestor of the Messianic King who will rule forever. But He is not known as the "God of David."

We could name many others with whom God had a deep relationship. Many of these individuals seem more significant in the story of Israel than Jacob. Many were used by God in defining moments or were used to preserve Israel. Each of these relationships reveal aspects of who God is, and yet God chose another name to define Himself and His people. And there is much at stake in that choice. There is a reason that God amplifies the person of Jacob when He speaks about His relationship with His people.

Many of us probably spend far more time on the stories of Abraham, Moses, David, or Daniel than we do the story of Jacob, but God's description of Himself is screaming at us: *"If you want to know Me as I am, you must know Jacob. I am His God!"*

There is something about Jacob that is foundational to God's revelation of Himself. If we miss it, our knowledge of God will be limited and restricted. We will accidentally form a knowledge of God

---

16. Exodus 33:11; Deuteronomy 34:10.

shaped by faulty assumptions that is incomplete. When we lose the knowledge of God, we lose everything. However, if you pause and meditate deeply on the story of Jacob and the full implications of that story, it will bring you into a knowledge of God *as He is.* That knowledge will probably shock you and confront you because God's relationship with Jacob reveals that God is completely different than we imagine Him to be.

In the end, you will discover the story of Jacob is not simply about Jacob. First and foremost, his is a story about God. Then, it is a story of a people, the people we call "Israel." And finally, it is a story about all of us.

- To understand God, then, you must know Jacob.
- To understand the people of Israel past, present, and future, you must know Jacob.
- To know and understand God's dealings with yourself, you must know Jacob.

Many people are confused about God, Israel, and their own personal walk because they have not known *the God of Jacob.* So the story of Jacob does not expose how you relate to Israel. It exposes how you relate to God.

We Are All Jacob

When you are content with your own blessing with no sense of burden for Jacob, you demonstrate a lack of understanding that Jacob's condition is your condition.

The issue of Jacob is the issue of humanity. When you stare at Jacob, you are staring at a mirror because, in a sense, we are all Jacob. You were chosen by God as an elect, priestly creature and, like Jacob, have hurt other people and created conflict through your own sin and self-centeredness. You have sought your own destiny through your own wisdom rather than living in active faith in the God who brings about a destiny that is completely impossible for you to bring about in your own strength. But God graciously pursues you to transform you. He has secured your future. He has enjoyed you. He has not given up on you, and He saves you by His strength and does for you what you cannot do for yourself.

God not only reveals our condition through the story of Jacob, He uses Jacob's story to redeem creation. And He is not finished with that story yet. Whether you know it or not, your story is inseparably bound to the story of Jacob. Yet many people are content to receive blessing from God and give no consideration to Jacob. Our apathy over Jacob reveals a smug pride that is happy to participate in Jacob's salvation and blessing but is quite content to leave Jacob as he is in his own trouble with no concern for his future.

Somehow, we find it sufficient to receive the salvation that is made clear for us through the costly story of Jacob and his people, and to enjoy that salvation without any thought that Jacob must also receive his salvation and inheritance.

God's revelation of Himself has cost Himself dearly, most notably in the Person of Jesus. But God's revelation of Himself has cost many of His friends dearly. They suffered from the rage of the satan, the hostility of other people, their own sin, the exposure of their greatest sins, etc. When you read the stories of the Hebrew Bible, there is much suffering. The prophet Hosea is one of the most vivid examples. Daniel is another one. The men and women of Scripture suffered something in the flesh for the message that we now hold in our hands. Jacob and his people have suffered tremendously, and yet we seem content to receive a blessing from that suffering without contending the suffering of Jacob comes to the great salvation that God decreed it must come to.

God joined His redemptive plan to Jacob, and He will not break that commitment, which means we have an unbreakable relationship with Jacob. And when you overlook that, minimize that, or seek to be free of it, you rage against the very process chosen by the God of Jacob to reveal Himself and to transform you into His image. As we will see, Jacob's future is deeply connected to a people who take up Jacob's cause and agree with God's election of Jacob at the cost of their own lives.

2

MORE THAN A MAN

BECAUSE ISRAEL WAS DESIGNED by God as the context for His self-revelation, the issue of God is at stake in the story of Israel. And it is easy to forget that "Israel" does not begin as a land, a political entity, or even a people. It begins as a person typically referred to as "Jacob." So you cannot understand God unless you understand Israel. And you cannot understand Israel unless you understand the man for whom Israel is named.

When God named Israel after a man, he made a profound statement. The story of Jacob is the story of his descendants. Jacob's life is more than the life of an ancient patriarch. His is a prophetic life that gives incredible insight into God's interactions with humanity and also serves as a prototype and prophetic summary of the people who come from Him.

Jacob's life summarizes the history of his people.

In the prophets' oracles, they frequently referred to Israel as "Jacob" when addressing Israel's sins but referred to Israel as "Israel" when they spoke with prophetic confidence about Jacob's glorious end. The prophets understood Jacob was the pattern for his people, and as we will see, Jacob's life remains a prophetic prototype. You cannot grasp the long story of his family or even the modern State of

Israel unless you know Jacob's story. The long story of Jacob and his people gives us glimpses of "Jacob" and of "Israel" throughout history, but the age will not end until the people of Jacob become "Israel" forever.

God's glory is at stake in Israel's prophesied destiny, and until Jacob becomes Israel, the revelation God wants to give of Himself is incomplete.

Many people are very familiar with the basic facts of Jacob's story, and that familiarity causes us to completely overlook things God wants to speak to us about. You may know the story of Jacob, but that familiarity may have caused you to read it quickly and not really understand it. Reading Jacob's story carefully, you find that it is very offensive. The story confronts us because God does not relate to Jacob the way we would. And if we meditate on that confrontation, it will lead us into a knowledge of God we may not currently have.

Before we can see the full significance of Jacob's story, we have to begin by summarizing the story and noticing key details about Jacob and His God—details you may have overlooked before. We also have to read the story in the context of the book of Genesis because the author of Genesis carefully recorded Jacob's story with many links and details to other stories.

A Barren Womb

When God made a promise to Abraham, the entire promise depended on Abraham having a son, but that was the one thing Abraham could not do. His wife was barren *and* too old to conceive a child. Abraham's promise depended on God producing life from the dead in Sarah's womb, and God did. This story of a promised son who is like life from the dead becomes a very significant story as God's redemptive plan unfolds. Like his father, Isaac, Jacob was born to a barren woman, and his dramatic birth set his story into motion. From the beginning, Jacob was another miracle son whose life was like life from the dead.

Jacob's birth was an answer to Isaac and Rebekah's desperate prayer,[1] but instead of a single son like Sarah, Hannah, or Elizabeth had, Isaac and Rebekah were given *two* sons. Two miraculous sons were born for a specific, divinely ordained purpose. Neither Jacob nor Esau were "ordinary" sons. Both were God's answer to their parents' prayers. God frequently chooses a barren woman when He wants a deliverer,[2] but neither Jacob nor Esau were the kind of deliverer anyone expected. Esau made serious errors, and Jacob was also a broken man who was devious at times.

God intentionally gave Jacob to Isaac and Rebekah as an answer to desperate prayer. But He gave them two sons, Jacob and Esau. They were not the kind of answer to prayer that we would expect.

Though Jacob and Esau were an answer to prayer, they began a power struggle while they were in their mother's womb. And before the boys were born, the Lord told Rebekah why they were struggling:

And the LORD said to her, "Two nations are in your womb, and two peoples from within you shall be divided; the one shall be stronger than the other, the older shall serve the younger." (Genesis 25:23)

Both sons were a miraculous answer to prayer and both nations, Israel and Edom, were the result of a miraculous birth. God chose Jacob for a specific purpose, and that choice created incredible conflict because God chose the younger son—the one no one else would have chosen. God's choice even split the parents. Isaac preferred Esau, and Rebekah preferred Jacob. God intentionally set a conflict into motion that began with Jacob and Esau, continued with Israel and Edom, and continues to this day between Jew and Gentile.

The story of Jacob cannot be fully understood apart from the story of his brother, Esau. There are obviously similarities to the story of Isaac and Ishmael. In that story, Abraham preferred the older brother, Ishmael, and had to submit to God's choice of Isaac.[3] In the

---

1. Genesis 25:21.
2. For example, consider the stories of Isaac, Samson, Samuel, and John the Baptist.
3. Genesis 17:18.

same way, Isaac clearly preferred Esau even though Jacob was chosen. (And in both stories, the older brother is not rejected; he is simply not the one to carry the promise.) However, the stories are also different. Abraham preferred Ishmael because he had years of relationship with Ishmael by the time Isaac was born. And unlike Ishmael, Isaac was the miraculous son born to a barren womb.

There is something unique about Jacob's story. He is the chosen brother who is also a twin. He was not chosen in isolation. He was chosen in context to another to whom he was deeply attached. His election was, in a sense, attached to Esau, and Esau's future was also attached to Jacob's election. If Jacob's story is going to be successful, then it must involve the stories of both brothers. His election is not simply for his sake. It is "attached" to others.

Jacob was born clutching his brother's heal, and in the context of Genesis, the idea of grabbing at a heel is an allusion to the prediction in Genesis 3:15 that the seed of the serpent will bruise the heel of the seed of the woman:

"I will put enmity between you and the woman, and between your offspring and her offspring; he shall bruise your head, and you shall bruise his heel." (Genesis 3:15)

Jacob obviously is not the seed of the serpent, but the fact Jacob was grabbing at a heel in his birth was shocking and foreboding. Jacob was the chosen one, but even the chosen one will be infected by the ways of the serpent. God will have to transform and deliver the chosen one. Jacob will be both called and compromised. And the stories that followed illustrate Jacob is not the "perfect" choice. Yet God's honor is at stake in His ability to unfold His plan through this choice.

Divine Election

To understand Jacob, you have to understand the theme of "election" because it is one of the main themes of Jacob's story. The word *election* refers to God's decision to specifically choose a person or a people for a specific redemptive purpose, and that is the way we will use the word in this book. Election is God's election or choice of an individual or a people.

Theologians have written countless books on the subject of election, but they typically focus on how an individual person becomes part of the redeemed people of God. Yet the topic of election is a much bigger subject in the Bible. As we will see, the issue of election is a foundational part of the redemptive plan. And God frequently chooses someone who appears to be the "wrong" choice, and that choice nearly always causes controversy. That controversy, as it is plays out, reveals a knowledge of God that He wants us to have.

God sets up the controversy of election so we can know Him as He is. If we neglect this controversy, we lose apprehending the full knowledge of God.

As we will see, those who cooperate with God's plan of election are able to participate in God's blessing, even if they were not "chosen." Those who resist God's plan, even if they were chosen, end up cut off from the blessing God intended to give them. If you do not understand the place of election in God's redemptive plan, then you will miss aspects of the knowledge of God, will be vulnerable to pride, and will not fully participate in God's greater plan. You may even end up resisting God's redemptive plan, confident you are doing the right thing.

Much more is at stake in God's election than we have imagined.

Disqualified

As Jacob's story develops, we discover two things. The first is that most of us would not have chosen Jacob. For example, Jacob's own father, knowing the prophecy given about his sons, chose Esau over Jacob. Esau was clearly stronger, more physically impressive, and a great hunter. He was the kind of man people would expect to lead a nomadic family, which is why his father preferred him. Jacob, on the other hand, was his mother's choice. He seemed to stay close to home, and he knew how to cook. He was obviously not the most impressive brother. The second thing we quickly learn is that neither brother was actually qualified to lead the family. Jacob was devious and not qualified. But Esau, despite his human strength, had other major flaws.

One day, Esau was completely exhausted, and Jacob was making stew.[4] The scenario highlights the profound differences in the two men. One was a "man's man," and the other was a cook. And in his hunger, Esau desperately wanted something to eat, and Jacob saw an opportunity, so he seized it. In Genesis 3, the serpent used attractive food to steal something from Eve and Adam, and Jacob enticed his brother in a similar way. He used attractive food to steal what belonged to Esau. The pattern of the heel grabber was at work. But Esau "despised" his birthright when he chose food over it. Both brothers had serious flaws.

God had already declared Jacob would carry the promise, but Jacob tried to scheme and secure something that was already his because he could not trust the divine process. Furthermore, the birthright and the blessing were not the same thing. The birthright generally went with being the firstborn, and the blessing was attached to the one who carried the miraculous promises given to Abraham. Jacob was promised the blessing but not necessarily the birthright. Jacob wanted Esau's birthright, and Esau wanted Jacob's blessing. In the end, Jacob took them both.

Stealing the Promise

Genesis 27 tells one of the most troubling stories in the Bible. In the story, Jacob and his mother decided to deceive his blind, dying father so that Jacob could steal the blessing God had already promised him. The story is incredibly dramatic. Jacob's desire for the promise was right because God had already told Rebekah the promise belonged to Jacob. However, Isaac was committed to giving Esau the promise

---

4. Genesis 25:29-34.

because he thought Esau was the better choice. As we already mentioned, there are hints here of the Abraham story and Abraham's desire for his firstborn, Ishmael, to carry the promise even though Isaac was the chosen son.

Rebekah and Jacob worked together on a scheme to deceive Isaac because neither could trust God to miraculously fulfill the promise He had made about Jacob. And, once again, this scheme focuses on attractive food. It was an intense repeat of Jacob's scheme with Esau, and the deception involving food again pointed all the way back to the deception of Genesis 3. This was the way of the serpent, not the way of faith. Jacob was nervous the deception would not work, but his mother convinced him and agreed to take the blame. The family dysfunction was obvious. God had chosen a people who, like the rest of humanity, are not perfect. They are also infected with sin, but God has chosen them and would bring about deliverance through them.

Esau traded his birthright for a meal, and Isaac was tricked into trading the blessing he wanted to give Esau for food. Jacob did not have the same kind of skin as Esau, so when Jacob was sent into see Isaac, Rebekah did something bizarre: She covered Jacob with the skin from the goats to make his skin feel more like Esau's. Isaac was suspicious that the son before him was not really Esau. He was clearly concerned Jacob would try to trick him, so he questioned his son three times to determine his true identity. Isaac was suspicious about Jacob's voice, his skin, and how Jacob had managed to hunt an animal and prepare a meal so quickly. When Jacob was questioned by his father, he not only claimed to be Esau, but he declared God had helped him.

Jacob deceived his father and attributed his success to God's favor.

When Isaac blessed Jacob, he placed his hands on the skin of the goats that had died to provide a meal and a covering for Jacob. Isaac's hands did not bless Jacob directly; he blessed Jacob through the covering of the sacrifice that gave its life so Jacob could obtain this blessing. The symbolism was profound. Jacob devised a scheme to take what God had promised to give him, and because of the scheme, Jacob needed a sacrifice to get the blessing.

Jacob will not be blessed apart from sacrifice. Sacrifice will be required for Jacob to become Israel.

Jewish interpreters have long seen some kind of correlation between the scapegoat ceremony instituted on the day of atonement and the story of Jacob and Esau[5] because this story is much bigger than it may seem. In the scapegoat ceremony, some identify Jacob with the goat that is the Lord's and identify Esau with the goat that is sent away. But in this story, Jacob was sent away outside the land as soon as he was covered by the skin of the goat. This cannot be accidental. So there are layers of meaning here that are not immediately obvious. What is clear is that, because of Jacob's sin, the blessing will require sacrifice.

Irrevocable Election

After Jacob stole his blessing from his blind, dying father, a shocking thing happened: *God did not take away the blessing.* This is probably the most controversial part of the story. Not only did Jacob keep the blessing, while Jacob was fleeing the land as a result of his sin, God met Jacob and told him, "I am with you," in a very dramatic way:

> *And he dreamed, and behold, there was a ladder set up on the earth, and the top of it reached to heaven. And behold, the angels of God were ascending and descending on it! And behold, the LORD stood above it and said, "I am the LORD, the God of Abraham your father and the God of Isaac. The land on which you lie I will give to you and to your offspring. Your offspring shall be like the dust of the earth, and you shall spread abroad to the west and to the east and to the north and to the south, and in you and your offspring shall all the families of the earth be blessed. Behold, I am with you and will keep you wherever you go, and will bring you back*

---

5. For an example, see: Rabbi Jonathan Sacks, "Thinking Fast and Slow," *Chabad.org*, https://www.chabad.org/parshah/article_cdo/aid/4405768/jewish/Thinking-Fast-and-Slow.htm/.

to this land. For I will not leave you until I have done what I have promised you." (Genesis 28:12–15)

God told Jacob He would not leave Jacob until He fulfilled His promise to Jacob. Notice that God's honor was at stake in the Jacob story. God would not leave him. Though Jacob suffered for his sin, there was no mention of his sin here. God *would not leave* regardless of what Jacob had done. And God *would do* what He had promised in spite of Jacob. Jacob's sin set conflict into motion, but the outcome of the story was not dependent on Jacob—it was dependent on God.

God's honor was at stake in His faithfulness to an unqualified, scheming man who deceived his father and intensified the strife in his family in order to steal something God had promised.

This story confronts our view of how God relates to people. Most of us would disqualify Jacob at this point and move on. We would strip Jacob of the promise because of what he did. But God said He was with Jacob even while Jacob was in his sin. Jacob would suffer for it, but he would not be abandoned. The reason was simple. Jacob's birth was miraculous, and God chose him for a purpose, but God did not choose Jacob because of his performance and righteousness.

Jacob was not chosen on the basis of performance, and he was not rejected on the basis of performance. If you do not understand this, you cannot grasp Israel, the gospel, or the God of Israel.

Even when Isaac realized he had been deceived, he knew the blessing was irrevocable, and he did not try to undo it.[6] He knew Jacob had been chosen before he was born. And he was not chosen on the basis on what he did,[7] but perhaps in spite of it. This does not mean Jacob's sin did not matter. As we will see, Jacob suffered tremendously for his sin. And the Lord strongly disciplined him.

God's glory is not at stake in working through qualified, capable people. God's glory is at stake in accomplishing His work through people who are obviously disqualified and incapable. We are quick to

---

6. Genesis 27:37.
7. Romans 9:10-12.

disqualify people on the basis of their sin, but we do not realize that the story of Jacob and Esau confronts us with a simple fact: We are all unqualified. *We are all Jacob.*[8]

I Will Not Leave You

Jacob could not bear the tension of the Lord's promise, so he took what was his in his own strength, and it created immense family conflict which exists to this day. And that family conflict set the stage for Jacob's exile because he could not dwell in the land in peace and safety.

Like Adam and Eve, and prefiguring the story of Israel, Jacob was sent outside the land as a punishment for his sin. *However, in his sin and his punishment, he was not rejected.* What's more, in the mystery of God's sovereignty, Jacob's punishment ended up enlarging his family. Though he was still "Jacob" and not yet "Israel," the Lord was with him in his exile.

God's absolute commitment to Jacob was not simply about Jacob. Much more was at stake here than the future of Jacob:

> *"Your offspring shall be like the dust of the earth, and you shall spread abroad to the west and to the east and to the north and to the south, and in you and your offspring shall all the families of the earth be blessed."* (Genesis 28:14)

God's plan has always been to bless the families of the earth through Jacob. So God's commitment to Jacob was not simply for Jacob's sake. It was for *our* sake. Even today, God has not given up on Jacob. Why? For Jacob's sake *and* for the sake of the nations. God's promise to Abraham, and then Jacob, has been the predetermined way He will bless the nations of the earth. And God will not deviate

---

8. This obviously does not eliminate the responsibility of elders in the Church to take care of the Body. There are times when a person needs to be disciplined and removed from a position in the Body if they are truly dangerous. As we will see, this also does not mean sin is left unaddressed.

from His promise even when Jacob sins. That tells us quite a bit about God.

God has been so committed to blessing the people of the earth through Jacob that the prophets warned us the age will end with a massive crisis around the election of the people of Jacob.[9] The crisis will be so intense the prophets predicted God will judge the nations on behalf of the way they related to Jacob.[10]

The future of the nations is at stake in the future of Jacob. Once you realize this, you will contend for Jacob's transformation into Israel, knowing that Jacob's issues are not unique to Jacob. They are human issues. Therefore, the things that keep Jacob from being Israel are the things that keep you and me from being what God wants us to be. And yet God has been merciful to us, having extended the promise of transformation through the Person of Jesus. If you have received mercy from the God of Israel, you should contend with all your strength for Jacob to receive the very mercy you are enjoying because it is the mercy that flows from the God of Jacob.

God will not bring the nations into their fullness apart from saving Jacob. It simply does not make sense. It would make a mockery of the story to save a remnant in the nations who are like Jacob and not save Jacob himself.

The spiritual powers know that God has staked His plan of redemption on His work through Jacob and his family. They understand the salvation of the nations is at stake in the salvation of this one people, which is why the people of Jacob are constantly surrounded by controversy and antagonism. What may appear to be a commitment to only one people is instead God's commitment to a person and a people who have failed (just like all the other humans), but salvation only comes when the failed and disqualified are saved and qualified by God Himself as an ultimate statement that this is the only way humans are redeemed.

---

9. Psalm 98; Isaiah 13:8; 34; Jeremiah 30:7; Daniel 7:21-22; Daniel 12:1; Joel 3:1-16; Zechariah 12:2-3; 13:8-9; 14:1-4, 9, 11; Jeremiah 30:5-7; Matthew 24:15-30; Revelation 11:2; 12:13.
10. Isaiah 34:8; 49:26; 63:1–4; Joel 3:1–2; Zechariah 14:2–4.

If God gave up on Jacob, all humanity would be lost. And the fact God is that committed to the election of a completely disqualified person says a lot about God.

To try to "qualify" Jacob or make him appear more righteous obscures the knowledge of God in the story and what the story is telling us about God. The Scripture does not hide the sins of Jacob or many other prominent figures, and when we manipulate the facts of the story to obscure their sin, we open the door to deception because we distort what God wants to reveal about Himself. The story of the Bible is not the story of God picking the "best." It is the story of God picking unqualified humans, like us, who prove they are disqualified, and yet God sets His affection on them and transforms them through His strength, *not* their superior humanity.

So while at first glance it may seem shocking that God's response to Jacob's deception of his blind father is "I am with you." But this response is the basis of the gospel. God's choosing Jacob, His election of Jacob, was not based on Jacob's performance; therefore, Jacob was not rejected on the basis of his performance. If God's choice of Jacob depended on Jacob's performance, then God's choice of us would depend on a righteousness based on our ability rather than God's mercy. If God were to reject Jacob for his sin, God would need to reject us all. After all, what one of us has not sinned like Jacob? If the message of the gospel is God's gracious mercy toward those who have sinned against Him, what would it say if God completely rejected the one whom He chose because that one sinned?

After Jacob deceived his father, the entire gospel was at stake. *What would God do?* God boldly declared what He would do. His response to sin is simple: *He will cover sin and qualify the unqualified.* While it may offend us that God affirmed His commitment to Jacob amid Jacob's sin, it gives us tremendous hope. God's affirmation of his commitment to a sinful man in perhaps his greatest sin gives all of us incredible hope. If God had rejected Jacob because of what He had done, then perhaps God will reject us as well.

As we will see, our expectation that God would disqualify Jacob for his sin is the fruit of a root of self-righteousness that is hidden in our hearts. It is a root God wants to expose and remove.

3

JACOB MEETS HIS MATCH

WHEN JACOB LEFT THE LAND, he headed for the area where Rebekah's family lived. Jacob deceived his father to secure his promise, and he ended up suffering from a family member who would deceive him in a similar way.

When Jacob arrived in the land, he quickly fell in love with a woman named Rachel, who was his uncle Laban's daughter. Jacob was so in love that he agreed to work seven years for Laban in exchange for marrying Rachel. After working seven years, the time came for Rachel to marry, and in the marriage celebration, something shocking happened. Instead of giving Rachel to Jacob, Laban gave his older daughter, Leah, to Jacob.

Rachel was a beautiful woman, and Leah apparently was not. As a result, it seems Laban did not have many options for a marriage for Leah, so he manipulated Jacob into marrying Leah. Laban then blamed it on a custom that the older daughter must be married first. Jacob tricked his father to secure for himself what typically belonged to the firstborn. So it was not an accident that, when Jacob wanted Rachel, he ended up being tricked due to an issue over the rights of the firstborn. Laban was certainly not righteous, but Jacob was obviously suffering for his sin. The one who deceived his father was deceived by his relative.

Jacob's marriages are clearly an inversion of what happened to Jacob when he sought to supplant his older brother. Jacob had to work seven more years to secure Rachel as a second wife. Jacob's sin divided his own family, and Laban's deception left Jacob with division in his own family. For the rest of his life, Jacob would bear the tension of two wives and two family units in conflict.

Though Jacob loved Rachel, she could not have children.[1] Leah, on the other hand, was unloved by Jacob but clearly chosen by God,[2] and she became the mother of most of Israel, including the messianic line through Judah and the priestly line through Levi. In the end, the messianic line came through the one Jacob did not love, the one God chose, while the one Jacob loved remained barren. God did not choose the beautiful one. He chose the one who was mistreated by her father and unloved by her husband. Jacob ironically choose the youngest when God did not. Leah and Rachel both had great sons, but in the end, God chose Leah's son Judah over Rachel's son, Joseph.

Jacob suffered for his sins, but God remained committed to him and the purpose God had prescribed for him. In fact, Laban recognized God's blessing on Jacob and knew he was blessed because of Jacob.[3] This made Laban's relationship with Jacob especially devious. Laban recognized God's blessing on Jacob yet sought to take advantage of it.

Though Jacob's suffering under Laban was a clear judgment for his sin, God's eyes were on Laban because he deviously used Jacob's blessing for his own purposes. Jacob's blessing was for the sake of others, but it was not to be manipulated. God watched Laban and then warned him to stop.[4] It was a foreboding preview of the nations

---

1. Genesis 29:31.
2. For example, see Genesis 29:31. The fruitfulness of Leah and the significance of her children indicate the Lord chose her in a special way to be the mother of most of Israel including the line of the Messiah.
3. Genesis 30:27, 29.
4. Genesis 31:12, 24.

attempt throughout history to manipulate God's plan for Israel to the sake of their own personal benefit.

Jacob became a great household during his time with Laban, but he eventually left Laban to return to the land. After years of frustration, Jacob cried out against Laban's injustice in their final encounter.[5] Though Jacob had been devious, the treatment from Laban was also devious and unjust. You can hear the cry of Israel through the generations in Jacob's voice—both suffering for sin and being taken advantage of by the nations.

Jacob could not remain in exile forever. His blessing was tied to the land, and because of his election, he had to return to the land. Jacob was afraid of what he might suffer because of his sin, but as he set his face toward the land, he encountered angels.[6] God was with Jacob in his return to the land—not because Jacob had been righteous, but because God had chosen him. And God's plan was at stake in His ability to preserve and transform this unrighteous man who encapsulates the human predicament.

Jacob Wrestles

As Jacob entered the land, he experienced panic *and* divine assistance because his return confronted him with his most famous sin. He was going to have to face Esau again, but before he faced Esau, he encountered another "man":

> *And Jacob was left alone. And a man wrestled with him until the breaking of the day. (Genesis 32:24)*

Jacob was finally alone. It was just him and another man. And it was a night of wrestling. Jacob fought this man all night long. He sought advantage over this man. He sought to prove himself through a show of tenacity and endurance. In the wrestling, you can hear the

---

5. Genesis 31:36-42.
6. Genesis 32:1.

cry that has been in the heart of this younger brother since his childhood. He was older at this point but still determined to prove his strength. Esau was physically strong but lacked endurance. Jacob lacked the raw strength of Esau but made up for it with deviousness and tenacity. This night, Jacob demonstrated a strength of another kind.

All night long, Jacob refused to let go, and in this wrestle, we see the mystery of election. God clearly chose a man who was disqualified, and yet this man would not let his election go. He deeply longed for something he was not qualified to possess. Ironically, his strength was both a divine gift and his undoing. But his strength was displayed in his longing for a divine blessing. You can hear a longing cry from a young child who wanted to be his father's favorite.—a child who knew he had been given a divine promise and yet lived in Esau's shadow.

Jacob later learned he was wrestling with God. The symmetry is profound. God is the One who has been wrestling with Jacob these several years.[7]

Jacob was in a wrestle over his own election. He knew he had a divine promise, but he did not know how to walk it out. This narrative tells us that Jacob's real struggle was not his father, his brother, or Laban. His real wrestle was with a "man" whom he later calls God. Jacob had been wrestling with God. In his heart, he treasured the divine promise, but he was not sure of God's election or God's ability to fulfill what He had promise. Jacob desperately wanted what God promised him, so he used every means possible to get it. He struggled to trust God's divine leadership, so he fought for the promise that had already been declared for him. And his human wisdom only amplified his wrestle. Ironically, his wrestle demonstrated a commitment to the promise.

Jacob's wrestle was empowered by his own fear because he was afraid of facing the consequences of his sin. He was about to face

---

7. John H. Sailhamer, *The Pentateuch as Narrative: A Biblical-Theological Commentary*, ed. Gary Lee (Grand Rapids, MI: Zondervan Publishing House, 1992), 198.

Esau again, and he was terrified. Deep down, he knew that he could no longer save himself, so he sought an advantage, some kind of scheme or trick that would enable him to survive his encounter with Esau. He had escaped Esau in his exile, but he could not run away from his calling forever. He had to come back into the land and be the blessing he was made to be. But could Jacob live in the land, or would his sin find him out and bring about his destruction?

Jacob's blessing would have to come at the cost of his own brokenness.

Jacob's struggle was resolved with his brokenness. In his weakness, he prevailed. But notice that Jacob never surrendered his strength. He fought God to the very end. *God* was the One who broke Jacob's strength. The narrative tells us that Jacob wrestled God throughout the night, in the darkness, and Jacob showed no signs of reaching the end of his strength.

A long night of wrestling is an incredible feat, and the story leads us to believe Jacob had the ability to infinitely wrestle. However, the night of wrestling had to end. A new day had to dawn. The whole encounter summarized Jacob's life. He was chosen for blessing, but he had been wrestling in darkness ever since he was born. He grabbed Esau's heel as a child and then deviously fought to secure his promise. He suffered outside the land, wrestling with his father-in-law. He refused to give up. He was determined that his strength and his schemes would somehow one day secure his promise.

But it was all a long wrestle in the darkness.

What Jacob did not realize was that he was wrestling God. His real wrestle was not his enemies. Deep down, Jacob longed for his promise, but he was not confident that God would fulfill His promise to him because he knew he did not deserve his election. And he knew that his family, namely his father, was opposed to his promise.

Abraham's strength could not fulfill God's promise, and he was tested severely by Sarah's barrenness. Isaac's wife, Rebekah, had also been barren. Neither Abraham nor Isaac could fulfill their promise by their own strength. And now Jacob faced the same test. And he was ready to fight all night.

Jacob was wrestling against God. "Can God fulfill the promises He made to me? Or will I have to fulfill my own promises? Will God be faithful when I've demonstrated that I'm disqualified?"

Jacob had been in the darkness his whole life, fighting someone he could not see clearly, never realizing that he was warring against the One who had made the promise to him. However, at this point, Jacob had returned to the land. God had waited on Jacob a long time, and the time had come. God would not wait any longer. Jacob had to exit the darkness and come into the light. It was time for a new day— a "morning" to dawn.

Jacob, however, would not give up. Something would have to happen for Jacob to come into the light and become the blessing. So God ended Jacob's night by breaking his strength:

> *When the man saw that he did not prevail against Jacob, he touched his hip socket, and Jacob's hip was put out of joint as he wrestled with him.... So Jacob called the name of the place Peniel, saying, "For I have seen God face to face, and yet my life has been delivered." The sun rose upon him as he passed Penuel, limping because of his hip. (Genesis 32:25, 30–31)*

God suddenly broke Jacob's strength to end the struggle. The struggle did not end because of Jacob's maturity. If it were up to Jacob, the struggle would still be going. The struggle ended because Jacob had returned to the land, and God had decided the time had come to break Jacob's strength and bring him into blessing. Jacob's schemes were fighting against God's means of blessing, so there was only one option remaining. God would break Jacob's strength to transition him into his calling. Jacob had wrestled with God and received a blessing, but it came at the cost of a limp. For the rest of his life, he would bear the limp of his injury as a testimony of his wrestle with God.

Once Jacob's strength was broken, God gave Jacob a new name:

> *Then he said, "Your name shall no longer be called Jacob, but Israel, for you have striven with God and with men, and have prevailed." (Genesis 32:28)*

Ironically, Jacob's raw commitment to his promise was described as "overcoming." It's an incredible insight into the way God views his people. God had to break Jacob's strength and bring an end to his sin, and yet in Jacob's sin, God saw a longing for the divine promise. Jacob could not transform himself into a man of faith to receive the promise, so God did for Jacob what Jacob could not do for himself. And He then declared that Jacob had overcome even though Jacob's "overcoming" often looked like scheming. And in the end, Jacob's "overcoming" required God's divine act on Jacob's behalf.

God views our struggle and wrestle with Him very differently than we view it.

A Blessing to the Nations

When Jacob's strength was broken, he entered into his calling as one qualified and secured by God. God *had* to do it this way because Jacob's life instructs us in the fundamental issue of humanity. Like Jacob, we are called to be priestly and yet are devious and disqualified. The God of Israel remains committed to "Jacob" in his failure and qualifies "Jacob" even when that means breaking his strength.

When Jacob came to meet Esau, he heard that Esau was coming with four hundred men, and he was terrified that he would face Esau's wrath. Jacob immediately developed a scheme and sent his servants ahead of him with extravagant gifts for Esau. He also put his family in front of him—from those he loved the least to those he loved the most. He hoped this elaborate scheme would enable him to avoid the results of his sin years earlier.

However, as soon as Jacob's strength was broken, everything became completely different. First, Jacob went *ahead* of his family.[8] Before his encounter, Jacob was prepared to sacrifice his servants and his family to secure his own safety. After his strength had been broken, he understood his future was never in his own hands. It was in God's hands. So he changed his scheme, and he went in front of his family. Jacob had clearly changed.

---

8. Genesis 33:3.

Second, when Jacob met Esau, he experienced the shock of his life. Esau was eager to see him. Esau came to him and embraced him, kissed him, and wept.[9] Not only had Jacob been broken, Esau had also been transformed.

Jacob's encounter emphasized the emptiness of Jacob's scheming and the covenant faithfulness of God.

Esau met Jacob with four hundred men, but those men did not come to fight Jacob. Esau had brought them to protect and serve Jacob and make sure Jacob safely entered the land. The message is obvious. Once Jacob was broken by God, he could see his future was secured *by God*. His sins had been covered by God, and his enemy suddenly became his friend. The one he feared the most came to serve him.

Jacob also approached Esau as a servant seeming to realize that his life was now in God's hands and that his "promise" was not simply for his own benefit. It was a promise that enabled him to serve others:

> *He himself went on before them, bowing himself to the ground seven times, until he came near to his brother. But Esau ran to meet him and embraced him and fell on his neck and kissed him, and they wept. And when Esau lifted up his eyes and saw the women and children, he said, "Who are these with you?" Jacob said, "The children whom God has graciously given your servant." Then the servants drew near, they and their children, and bowed down. Leah likewise and her children drew near and bowed down. And last Joseph and Rachel drew near, and they bowed down. Esau said, "What do you mean by all this company that I met?" Jacob answered, "To find favor in the sight of my lord." But Esau said, "I have enough, my brother; keep what you have for yourself." Jacob said, "No, please, if I have found favor in your sight, then accept my present from my hand.... Please accept my blessing that is brought to you, because God has dealt graciously with me, and because I have enough." Thus he urged him, and he took it. (Genesis 33:3–11)*

---

9. Genesis 33:4.

God gave Jacob a graphic object lesson. Now that Jacob's wrestle was over, he could rest in God's provision. And God could transform Jacob's greatest enemy into a dear friend. God had given Jacob a promise so he could serve and bless others, not simply so he could be "chosen." His future and reconciliation with his enemies were secure in God's divine purpose.

The meeting with Esau is one of the most significant moments in the life of Jacob because it points to the end of Jacob's story. The end was not hostility between brothers. It was two brothers, both blessed. One was chosen for a covenant purpose, but in the end, they were reconciled together, each seeking the other's benefit. The story did not end with Jacob's deceptions or Esau's rage.

Jacob's brokenness ended his schemes, revealed God's faithfulness, and brought reconciliation with mutual blessing.

When Jacob met Esau, he bowed down and tried to give to Esau. This was profoundly different from their previous meeting. Transformed from his scheming and manipulation, Jacob was no longer a deceiver; he had become a servant. Instead of seeking what Esau had, he approached Esau as a servant with a gift, confident that he then had "everything."[10] This is a dramatic preview that the end of the great conflict over Jacob's election will be reconciliation, and those not chosen for Jacob's role will become part of the redemptive story.[11]

After Jacob was broken, he purged his family's idols, and the terror of God surrounded him.[12] As long as Jacob was "strong," he suffered. But once his strength was broken, God's manifest Presence protected Jacob. And then God came to Jacob again and blessed him:

> *And God said to him, "Your name is Jacob; no longer shall your name be called Jacob, but Israel shall be your name." So he called his name Israel. And God said to him, "I am God Almighty: be fruitful and multiply. A nation and a company of nations shall come from you, and kings shall*

---

10. Genesis 33:11.
11. Amos 9:11;
12. Genesis 35:2–5.

come from your own body. The land that I gave to Abraham and Isaac I will give to you, and I will give the land to your offspring after you." (Genesis 35:10–12)

For a second time, God renamed Jacob, and God declared the blessing of Abraham with this new name. This time there was no struggle. Jacob had crossed over.

The Conflict Continues

The story of Joseph demonstrates the issue of election continued to test Jacob's family. The challenge of election is not simply for those "not chosen." It even tests the chosen. Joseph was Jacob's favorite, and he was divinely chosen to be the leader of the family.[13] Joseph's "election" caused incredible family conflict because the other brothers would not tolerate it.

While Joseph perhaps flaunted his chosen status as a young man, the fact remained that he was chosen for a special purpose. And his brothers were deeply envious of him. The test is the same test Jacob faced yet different. Joseph's brothers were jealous of the one who was chosen, while the main theme of the Jacob story was Jacob's longing for Esau's birthright and his fear that he would not get the blessing God had decreed for him.

In Joseph's story, his brothers acted like Jacob and schemed against their brother to eliminate him. They developed a scheme that sold Joseph into slavery and then gave his cloak to Jacob covered in blood. In that moment, Jacob "lost" his most precious son, and the chosen son was "dead."

But Joseph's story demonstrated the purpose of divine election by passing through suffering and then being exalted so he could be a blessing to the nations (i.e., Egypt) and to Israel. Joseph's exaltation was not for his sake or his glory. It was for the sake of everyone else.

After his exaltation, Joseph faced his brothers again, and this time

13. Genesis 37; 50:20.

he tested them. These tests essentially revealed the heart of his brothers. In the tests, he saw that his brothers had then changed. They were willing to sacrifice themselves for another brother. And Joseph finally revealed himself to them, declaring that God meant everything that happened for good.

Next, Joseph was suddenly restored alive to Jacob. The son Jacob thought was lost turned out to be "back from the dead" as well as Jacob's provider and defender in a time of famine. Though Joseph had been sent to the Gentiles through human schemes, it was according to God's purpose because Joseph had been chosen to serve Jacob, his brothers, and the Gentiles.

Joseph's story is so significant that his story is given more space in Genesis than any other story. His story serves as a messianic prototype and perhaps the primary messianic prototype for the last season of time. And when Jacob blessed his sons, he used the image of Joseph to describe the messianic ruler who would come from Judah.[14] When Jacob did this, it hinted that the messianic seed who will come from Judah will experience:

- A controversial election.
- Family rejection and strife.
- Betrayal and suffering among the nations.
- Great suffering.
- Exaltation among the nations.
- A profound reconciliation.
- Power that God uses for the aid of Israel and the nations.

Though Joseph is elevated above the family, in another twist, Jacob prophesies that in the end it will be another son, Judah, who will be chosen to a special role that was foreshadowed in the life of Joseph. And yet in another twist, when Jacob blessed Joseph's son, he reversed the natural order and declared that the youngest would become greater than the oldest. Genesis closes with a prediction that

---

14. Genesis 49:8.

God's election will continue to surprise us and inevitably create conflict.

PART II

THE ISSUE OF ELECTION

4

THE KNOWLEDGE OF GOD IN HIS ELECTION

HAVING LOOKED at the story of Jacob, we are ready to dive into the full implications of it. As we said in the beginning, God named Himself the *God of Israel,* and Israel is not simply a nation. It is a person: Jacob. So if you want to know who God is, you must know Him as the God of Jacob who is revealed by His relationship with Jacob and the way He transformed Jacob into Israel.

The story of Jacob boldly confronts us with the issue of election because none of us would have chosen Jacob. We would have chosen Esau like Isaac did. Furthermore, after Jacob deceived his blind, aged father, we would have written him off as completely unqualified for his calling. Yet God came to Jacob afterward and said, "I am with you."

We are so familiar with the Jacob story we can overlook the fact that it is a surprising and, at times, shocking story. And it is intentionally that way because God wants to confront you and me through that story with the knowledge of who He really is. He is not like us in our natural thinking. If you do not allow the Jacob story to confront you, and you do not meditate on the story, you will miss aspects of the knowledge of God that He wants to give you.

The knowledge of God is *everything,* so it is critical that we meditate on the story God chose to connect to His name. If we do not, we will not know God as He is, we will misunderstand the way He works, and we can even end up resisting Him unknowingly.

The Controversy of Election

The story of Jacob confronts us with the issue of election. Election is a fundamental part of how God leads His Kingdom, and it is frequently controversial. The Lord chooses on the basis of His right to choose, and He frequently does not choose the one we expect or those whom we think are most qualified. Therefore, election frequently creates confusion and conflict.[1] That confusion and conflict are not ultimately about the person or people "chosen." The conflict is really an issue of the knowledge of God.

Our struggle with election is not really a struggle with the humans chosen. It is a struggle with the God who chooses.

God uses election to reveal Himself. Some people are offended by this, because they assume that, when God chooses one person, He rejects the rest. But this is not true. When God chooses someone, He chooses them *for the sake* of the rest. Election is not a zero sum game where one wins and everyone else loses. It is not God's way of rejecting the ones "not chosen." It's His way of bringing us into blessing. Once you agree with God's election and cooperate with it, you will discover that God uses the election to bring those not "elect" into blessing.

God's election is serious. God confronts us with His right to choose, and He requires us to respect it because, as we will see, offense at election is at the root of evil in this age.

Election always creates controversy, and the controversy forces a conversation that God wants to have with us.

---

1. There is a whole theological system that is known for an emphasis on election and pre-destination. The emphasis in this system related to election typically focuses on soteriology or how someone is redeemed. That subject is beyond the scope of this book. In this book, we focus on God's election of a person or people for a redemptive purpose and not precisely how individual salvation works.

Many of the Bible's best known stories include the offense of election. Consider just a few examples.

- God chose Abraham for a foundational role in the redemptive plan, but we do not have any indication Abraham was "better" than other options. The text simply says God chose Abraham[2] and guaranteed His promises to Abraham on the basis of His nature, not Abraham's goodness. Abraham was not presented as the "best human." He was simply the one God chose for a unique role in the story.
- God chose Isaac to be the carrier of the promise even when Abraham deeply loved Ishmael and asked God to choose Ishmael instead.[3]
- God chose Jacob over Esau and Joseph over his brothers. In each case, the choice was controversial.
- God chose Moses, who was never a slave, to deliver slaves, and this was one reason Moses faced so much resistance from the Israelite leaders. He was the "wrong choice" for a deliverer. He grew up in an Egyptian palace with Israel's oppressor. And when he decided to embrace his people, he killed an Egyptian and ran away for forty years. When God came to him and predicted He would make Moses the most powerful man on earth, Moses said, "No thank you," to his assignment.[4] Perhaps he even spoke Hebrew with an Egyptian accent.
- God chose Israel to be His people and bear His name while also describing them as the "least" of all people and a stubborn people.[5] He picked the people whom none of us would have picked. They seemed small and insignificant when God chose them at Mount Sinai, and to

---

2. Genesis 12, 15.
3. Genesis 17:18.
4. Exodus 3–4.
5. Exodus 33:5; Deuteronomy 7:7

this day, people reject, minimize, or ignore God's choice of Israel.

- David was another example. When Samuel the prophet came to anoint one of Jesse's sons, Jesse did not even bother inviting David to appear with his brothers. David was obviously an unlikely choice to his father and his brothers. Furthermore, there are clear hints in the text he may have been an illegitimate son, further making him "not the right choice."[6]

- Jesus was the most controversial choice. He came from a small place and a humble background. He was certainly not the logical choice to be the promised Deliverer and great King, and when He claimed to be God, many simply could not believe it.[7] Isaiah even predicted we would not naturally agree with God's choice.[8]

- The apostle Paul was hostile to the gospel when he first heard it. He was trained as a Pharisee and lived a very Jewish life,[9] and yet God turned him into the best known messenger of the gospel to the gentile world and the people who were oppressing his own people.[10]

These are just a handful of the repeated examples in the Scripture, where God chooses someone for a redemptive purpose, and they are clearly "the wrong choice." *But this is God's way.*

---

6. There are clear hints in the text that David is an illegitimate son. For example, Jesse did not call David when Samuel told Jesse to call all his sons. There is some reason Jesse is ashamed of him or at least does not include him with the other sons (1 Samuel 16:3–11). In addition, after his own act of adultery, David laments that he himself was conceived in sin which is likely a specific reference to his own conception not a general theological statement (Psalm 51:5). Poetically, Jesus as the "Son of David" lived with a similar accusation.

7. Matthew 13:55, 56; Luke 4:22; John 6:42; 7:27.

8. Isaiah 53:1–4.

9. Philippians 3:4–6.

10. Acts 9:15.

God Chooses the Unqualified

Jacob was born grabbing at his brother's heel, a troubling sign that he would be infected with the ways of the serpent who seeks to wound the heel.[11] And as the story progressed, Esau became a confident, strong man who was his father's favorite. Meanwhile, Jacob was clearly his mother's favorite and was scheming to take from Esau what his father wanted to give Esau.

None of us would have chosen Jacob. We would have chosen Esau.

Jacob then collaborated with his mother to deceive his blind, dying father to take what God had already told Jacob He would give him. And after Jacob stole the blessing, we would all consider Jacob completely unqualified and take the blessing away, but instead the most incredible thing happened: The blessing was not taken away. Instead, God came to Jacob and declared that He would be with Jacob and preserve him:

Behold, I am with you and will keep you wherever you go, and will bring you back to this land. For I will not leave you until I have done what I have promised you. (Genesis 28:15)

God did not change His mind about Jacob when Jacob stole the blessing, and God wants us to discover something about His nature in His response to Jacob. God wants us to slowly and deeply meditate on His way with Jacob. If we do not, we will not know God the way He has revealed Himself. *God named Himself the "God of Israel" so we would carefully consider the story of Jacob and discover who God is. When we do, we will also know how to relate properly to corporate Israel.*

The story of Jacob demonstrates Jacob was not qualified, and that was precisely the point. The one God chose was unqualified, *and* the one not chosen was also unqualified. If God only chose the "qualified," it would be a statement that some humans are superior in their nature and "deserve" what God gives them. However, the exact oppo-

---

11. Genesis 3:15.

site is true. In fact, God has committed Himself to breaking the strength of the ones He has chosen[12] to demonstrate that they were not called because of their superior strength.

When we are chosen by God, we may have pride in our calling, but the crucible of our calling quickly creates a context for humiliation when our sin and lack of qualification reveal we are not capable of accomplishing what we are called to do. And when this happens, we must have confidence in the power of God to transform us and accomplish through us what we cannot do on our own.

God Enjoys the Unqualified

God not only intentionally chooses the unqualified, but He enjoys them.

One of the most powerful parts of the Jacob story is that God *enjoyed* Jacob at every step. God was not forced to choose Jacob, nor did He endure Jacob. God did not overlook Jacob's sin, but He enjoyed Jacob even when Jacob was scheming, insecure, and afraid that God would not fulfill His promises.

Many people assume God only enjoys the "perfect" or the "mature," or God will only enjoy us at some point in the future when we become mature. Yet God enjoyed Jacob at every step of his journey. Just as a loving parent enjoys a toddler even though the little one is very immature, creates an incredible amount of work, and contributes nothing substantial to the family, God enjoys His people in every stage of their development.

God has a profound ability to enjoy people while simultaneously disciplining, enduring, and maturing them. His affections are much more vast and powerful than ours, so we struggle to believe He is as loving as He is. But He is most loving. As the story of the people of Israel unfold, this becomes especially apparent. For example, when God made covenant with Israel on Mount Sinai, He only gave one reason for the covenant: His own affection.

---

12. Leviticus 26.19; Deuteronomy 32.36, Psalm 46.10, Isaiah 57:10; Ezekiel 37; Daniel 12:7.

*And **because he loved your fathers** and chose their offspring after them and brought you out of Egypt with his own presence, by his great power. . . . (Deuteronomy 4:37)*

*It was not because you were more in number than any other people that **the LORD set his love on you and chose you,** for you were the fewest of all peoples, but **it is because the LORD loves you** and is keeping the oath that he swore to your fathers, that the LORD has brought you out with a mighty hand and redeemed you from the house of slavery, from the hand of Pharaoh king of Egypt. (Deuteronomy 7:7–8)*

*Yet **the LORD set his heart in love on your fathers and chose their offspring** after them, you above all peoples, as you are this day. (Deuteronomy 10:15)*

God set His affection on a people who had nothing to offer Him.

God did not choose Israel because she was "great" or had something special to offer Him. He choose Israel simply because He set His affection on her. Moses spoke these words to Israel when God made covenant with Israel in the wilderness. God made that covenant in the pattern of a marriage betrothal, and when you read His words in that context, they reveal God's nature in a significant way.

When God spoke to Israel about His affection, it was like a groom speaking about a bride at their betrothal. Can you imagine a groom saying, "I want to say a few words about my bride." And then continuing to declare, "You are the least of all women. You have nothing to offer me." To our ears, this sounds horrifying, but this is exactly what God said to Israel. However, imagine a groom following those words with, "I am not marrying you because I can get something from you. I have simply *set my affection on you.* I enjoy loving you, and that is the entire basis of our relationship." These are the most powerful words a man could speak, and this is exactly what God said to His Israel, His "bride."

Affection is one of the deepest realms of pleasure, and God

declared to Israel: "You are small, stubborn, and idolatrous. You cannot do anything for Me. I do not need you. But I have affection for you." *God chose Israel because of His own pleasure.* And He loved Israel because He had "set His heart in love" on her fathers. God chose Jacob because He loved Jacob. He chose you for the same reason. Our relationship to God is secured by God's affections and not our performance. God demonstrates that to us by choosing the unqualified and then enjoying them even when they demonstrate their failure and suffer for it.

This is especially revealed by God's perspective of Israel's time in the wilderness. Consider God's lament over Israel through Jeremiah:

"Go and proclaim in the hearing of Jerusalem, Thus says the LORD, 'I remember the devotion of your youth, your love as a bride, how you followed me in the wilderness, in a land not sown.'" (Jeremiah 2:2)

This statement is astonishing. Most people do not read the narrative of Israel's time in the wilderness and come to this conclusion. When God came down on Mount Sinai, Israel immediately fell into idolatry in the worship of the golden calf. There are repeated stories of rebellion and God's judgments on Israel. Israel was stuck in the wilderness for forty years because of her unbelief. All together, the stories of the wilderness are very painful to read. God expresses His anger multiple times and judges His people. Yet when He reflects on the time in the wilderness, His summary is stunning: "I remember the devotion of your youth, your love as a bride...." When we read the stories of the wilderness, they read like a tragedy. When God reflects on that time, His heart explodes with emotion because He views the failures of the wilderness through the eyes of affection.

There is no human way to read the stories of the wilderness this way. It is not a matter of interpreting the facts. It is an issue of the knowledge of God—the God who knows what He is doing and intentionally chooses the unqualified and delights in His choices and His people even when He has to mature and discipline them. Perhaps you are familiar with the God of Israel, but do you know *this* God?

Because God loved Jacob (Israel) just as intensely as He loved corporate Jacob (Israel).

God opened the book of Malachi with a similar statement:

"I have loved you," says the LORD.... "Yet I have loved Jacob." (Malachi 1:2)

This statement is especially powerful because the book confronts Israel's compromise. And the statement comes after the Babylonian exile, which was one of the most severe judgments Israel had endured. Amid compromise after a severe judgment, God's first statement to Israel was, "I have loved you."

God's affection for unqualified people can be very shocking. It is easy to assume that our frustration and anger at unqualified people are justifiable or that our self-righteous anger is an expression of the Lord's anger. God is not like us, however. We are born sinful and insecure, but He has a vast capacity for delight in the unqualified. He can simultaneously be filled with delight in an unqualified person, angry at the way that person hurts others, and discipline that person for their failures. God shocks us by loving those who are not worthy of His love and, in their sin or immaturity, may even be hurting others. The good news is, once we grasp God's intense love for the unqualified, we realize that *we are also the unqualified.* And if that delight is available for them, even when they oppress others, God's vast ocean of delight is toward us as well.

There is a place to correct the elect, and God certainly disciplines the elect so they can come into their calling, but when we accuse and reject the elect on the basis of their failure, we display a lack of the knowledge of God. It is hypocritical to reject the ongoing election of those God has chosen because of their failures and yet expect to receive mercy from God ourselves. Just as salvation is by God's grace and not our performance,[13] so too election is on the basis of God's desire and not our achievements.

---

13. Romans 11:6. See also Romans 3:28; Galatians 2:16; Philippians 3:9.

If you recognize God's election in Jacob but do not understand God's delight in Jacob, you will not understand God.

God Chooses on the Basis of His Desire

Jacob was chosen by God, and God demands we respect that choice because in that choice is God's revelation of Himself.

In the story of Jacob, we learn that the glory of God is at stake in taking the *unqualified* and accomplishing through them what they could never do themselves. Jacob's story begins with him grasping for a heel like the serpent and scheming to steal what God had promised to give him. Esau was stronger and more physically impressive, and God wants us to see that He prefers weakness to what humans find attractive. We are supposed to carefully study these stories to discover this is God's way. And this is the way He wants to deal with all of us. He wants to accomplish in each of us what we could never do in our own strength. Instead of raging against the one called, we should discover that none of us is really qualified. Everything we get from God is a good gift that is undeserved.

Most people confuse *callings* and *gifts* with *rewards*. We assume, if a person is chosen by God, that means their calling is a reward, and they are superior to other humans. In reality, God's election is not a reward. The Spirit chooses "as he wills."[14] God does reward us[15] for how we use the gifts He has given us, but those gifts are not rewards for our superior performance. They are gifts given by God. This is why we should not be disillusioned when a gifted or called person fails. Their gifts may be powerful and unique, but their gifts are not rewards. They can still sin just as easily as anyone else.

Understanding this can also liberate us when we feel we are not as gifted as others. Remember gifts and callings are not rewards. Your giftedness is not a statement of how mature you are or even how

---

14. 1 Corinthians 12:11.

15. Matthew 6:19–20; Romans 8:23; 1 Corinthians 9:25; 2 Corinthians 1:22; 5:5; Ephesians 1:14; 4:30; Colossians 1:5; 1 Timothy 6:18–19; 2 Timothy 4:8; Hebrews 11:9–10, 13–16; 25–26; 1 Peter 5:4; James 1:12.

much God loves you. He simply chooses on the basis of His desire and gives some things to one and other things to another. He rewards you for the way you use the gifts He has given, but He does not evaluate you on the basis of gifts you were not given.

Because of pride, we often resist God's choosing, and that pride clearly communicates, *"I would be a better choice,"* because no one is ever offended by a choice unless they think they are a better option. And this offense forces a conversation God wants to have with every person.

God's choosing is purely on the basis of His desire and His decision. He is the Creator, and He is free to do what He wants with what He has made. And when we resist His right to choose, we resist God's right to be God.

When you are offended by the one(s) God has chosen, He has one question for you, "So you think you are a better option?" Your answer to that question exposes a deep pride and self-righteousness that is at the root of all sin. God wants to confront that, and His election of Israel is one of the ways He confronts us.

Once we recognize election and determine to honor it, we can be quick to justify the elect one and emphasize the sins of the one not chosen. It is very common to try to "clean up" the story of the chosen people to prove they are more righteous and the ones not chosen deserves whatever they may suffer. But this is a gross misunderstanding of election. The point of election is that God is choosing *on the basis of His own desire in order to reveal Himself,* not that God is rewarding a righteous one and highlighting the sin of the other.

To exaggerate the righteousness of the chosen while exaggerating the sins of those not chosen is to assume that God chooses on the basis of human righteousness and clearly states some people are superior to others. This is patently false. It violates the whole gospel. The biblical narrative is *not* that the chosen are superior. It is that the chosen are transformed and empowered by God to do what God created them to do. And in recognizing that comes the revelation of how God also wants to transform and empower you to do whatever you are called to do.

The Bible is very graphic and often shocking in its descriptions of the lives and sins of the elect. It does not present them as better humans. Why does God choose these humans who are guilty of serious sins and, at times, seem to be among the worst of all people? God wants to confront us with His choice and the true nature of those chosen because it confronts us with who God is. Obviously, the elect also often show very positive traits worthy of imitation. But we cannot only emphasize the positive traits and completely overlook the reality and implications of their sins.

Those who rage against God's purposes seek to exaggerate the sins of those chosen as if they are worse humans. Rage grows as the elect are described as the source of all problems, and this turns into a festering hate. When it is passive, it simply wishes the elect would go away or chooses to make pithy statements like, "God loves everyone the same. There are no differences." This ignores the obvious fact that there are differences. We all have vastly different abilities, and God distributes different gifts and callings *as He wills*.

Offense over election nearly always exaggerates the sins of those chosen. And this indicates a deep issue that must be settled, or it can quickly escalate to stronger verbal accusations against the elect. In turn, this can easily lead to violence against the elect because, as we will see, offense at the elect is a bitter root.

Jacob had good *and* bad traits. His election was not on the basis of a superior righteousness. It was on the basis of the Lord's choice alone. That is why it *must* be respected. If we respect Jacob's (Israel's) election on the basis of their goodness, we completely violate what God is trying to communicate. We do not respect Israel's election because they are righteous or holy. If this is the basis of your respect for Israel, it is a humanistic one, and it is very fragile. We respect Israel's election because we respect God. We want Israel to become holy, and we know they will be because God has declared it,[16] but we

---

16. Genesis 17:8; Exodus 6:7; 19:5; Leviticus 26:11-12; Deuteronomy 30:1-6; Isaiah 4:3–4; 45:17, 25; 54:13; 59:21; 60:4, 21; 61:8-9, 65:23; 66:22; Ruth. 1:16; Song of Songs 2:16; 6:3; Jeremiah 7:23; 11:4; 30:22; 31:31-34; 32:40; Ezekiel 20:40; 36:10, 27-36; 37:25–28; 39:22, 28-29; Joel 2:26, 32; Zephaniah 3:9, 12; 12:13; Zechariah 2:11; 8:8; 12:10-13; Matthew 23:39; 24:30; Acts 1:6-7; 2:21; Romans 10:13; 11:26–27; Revelation 1:7; 21:3.

do not respect Israel's election on the basis of her condition at any time. Respecting God's election may even bring suffering from those who rage against the elect or even the elect themselves, but we respect election because we fear God.

As we saw when God chose Israel on Mount Sinai, He clearly said they were the least and most stubborn of all nations.[17] God did not choose Jacob on the basis of performance, and He does not reject Jacob on the basis of his performance. God said to corporate Israel exactly what is plain in the Jacob story. He told Israel, "I love you, but you are not superior; in fact, you appear worse than many other options. But I am revealing who I am in My choice, and My nature is on display in the calling of the unqualified."

Choosing One and Rejecting Another

When we make election a matter of choosing the "better" one over the "worse" one, we distort the whole matter of election and miss the point.

A wrong understanding of election not only distorts the nature of the election, it also distorts our view of those not chosen. After all, if the chosen are superior and more righteous, then the not chosen are clearly inferior and more evil. While we must avoid exaggerating the sins of the elect, we also cannot exaggerate the sins of the ones not chosen. The storyline of God is that His mysterious plan of election works for the sake of the election *and* the salvation of those not elect. That is the mystery of God's plan. If we think He is simply choosing the better one, we will vilify the one not chosen rather than recognize that God also wants their redemption. Those not chosen can face great challenges, but God's end goal for them is not rejection but salvation. God's choice of Abraham and then Jacob was not the rejection of everyone else. It was a choice for the sake of everyone else.

Our job is to stand with election without exaggerating the righteousness of the election *or* exaggerating the sin of the non-elect. Meanwhile, we must contend for the salvation of the non-elect

---

17. Exodus 33:5; Deuteronomy 7:7

because that is the purpose of election. In fact, the vast majority of people who will read this book are Gentiles who, in this plan, were not born part of the elect family. Yet through God's plan of redemption, readers like you can be adopted into the family of the redeemed through God's purpose with those chosen. If you then reject others who are not elect, it is the height of hypocrisy.

People can easily become so committed to Israel that they then turn against other peoples and treat them as second-class citizens. This is not the right response to election, and it is not godly. You have to bear the tension of unflinching commitment to God's election *and* an understanding that God's plan of election is designed to offer mercy for all. In God's leadership, His plan for the elect is designed to bring those "not chosen" into great blessing and into the family. To condemn the non-elect misunderstands the plan of election as much as rejecting the elect.

If you were born into the chosen people, you had absolutely nothing to do with that choice. So why would you reject those who are not chosen as if you were superior? You had *nothing* to do with your election. To adopt a place of superiority over the rest is to profoundly miss the purpose of your own election. And if you were not born as part of the chosen people, why would you easily accuse others who were not chosen? While it is good for you to come to respect God's election, that does not mean you are superior in any way to the rest.

5

ELECT FOR THE SAKE OF EVERYONE

BECAUSE WE SEE election through a human lens, we assume election is simply the exaltation of one and the rejection of another, but this is not the biblical view.

God's election is not exclusively for the sake of the one elected. It is for the sake of those not chosen.

From the beginning, Abraham was chosen as a blessing to "all the families of the earth"[1] because, when God elects someone, it is for the benefit of others. We rage against election because we are self-centered, and we want privilege and benefits for ourselves even though, in reality, the elect often suffer the most. Israel's story has been a story of suffering to this day, and the prophets warned of future suffering before the story is finished. In the words of Tevye from *Fiddler on the Roof*, "I know, I know. We are Your chosen people. But, once in a while, can't You choose someone else?" While election is a special thing, it is for the sake of others, creates controversy, and leads to suffering.

Moses' election caused him to experience incredible pain and rejection. David suffered much as the chosen king. The prophets

---

1. Genesis 12:3.

endured incredible suffering. And so it continues. When you consider the Person of Jesus, you see the most intense example of election. God chose Him to redeem creation, and that calling caused Him to be "marred more than any man"[2] and to become the servant (slave) of all.[3] His exaltation is directly tied to His willingness to embrace a humble place as the servant.[4]

Jesus is the ultimate example that election is not simply for the exaltation, glory, and comfort of the one chosen. It is for the sake of everyone else. We only think that election is for the sake of personal exaltation, glory, and comfort because that is what we desire. And our own sinful desires corrupt our view of election.

Once again, this is why the election of one is not the rejection of the rest. It is simply God's means of exposing the deep self-righteousness and pride in our hearts and of accomplishing His purposes. Because election is a means of blessing, once you being to cooperate with God's election, you receive the blessing of that election because God longs to bless you through His plan of election. When you submit to God's election, He does not exclude you. He brings you into His family through His purposes. When you reject election, you actually cut yourself off from the blessing.

This is illustrated throughout the Bible. For example, consider the stories of Rahab and Ruth. Rahab was a prostitute, and the Israelites were told to completely destroy her city. However, when she asked if she could join Israel, she was rescued and became a part of the family. Ruth was a Moabite, and descendants of Moabites were prohibited from coming into the temple for ten generations.[5] Yet Ruth made her famous statement, *"Your God will be my God and your people my people,"*[6] and she was welcomed into Israel. She became the great-grandmother of Israel's most famous king (David), and even

---

2. Isaiah 52:14 NASB1995.
3. Matthew 20:26; 23:11; Mark 9:35.
4. Philippians 2:5–11.
5. Deuteronomy 23:3.
6. Genesis 17:8; Exodus 6:7; 19:5; Leviticus 26:11-12; Ruth. 1:16; Song of Songs 2:16; 6:3; Jeremiah 7:23; 11:4; 30:22; 31:33; Ezekiel 36:28; 37:26–28; Zechariah 2:11; 8:8; Revelation 21:3.

though Moabite descendants were not to enter the temple for ten generations, he permanently altered Israel's worship sanctuary.[7]

Both Rahab and Ruth were listed in the genealogy of Jesus, further emphasizing the fact that, when you accept God's election, He uses that to bring you into His family and bring you into blessing.

To use a different example, consider a pastor. God gifts one to serve as a pastor, and the person leads the congregation. But their leadership is not for their own sake and their own privilege. They lead for the sake of the congregation. Their gift, calling, and election are given to serve the people. The same goes for a worship leader. They are gifted and chosen to lead worship for the sake of the congregation. While both a pastor and worship leader can, and should, enjoy their gift, that gift is not for their own sake. It is to serve the people.

The story of Joseph and his brothers perfectly illustrates the point. God chose Joseph for a purpose, and that purpose involved elevating Joseph among his brothers. Joseph's calling in the end, however, was for the sake of his brothers. He was not elevated simply so He could dominate his family. He was elevated so he could provide for his family in a great time of need. Joseph's election was for the sake of the family.

The Redemption of Those Not Chosen

We *must* avoid the binary idea that the elect are good, and therefore, the the non-elect are automatically evil. People commonly distort Bible stories to prove God picked the "better" person, but the Bible does not necessarily present things this way. The Bible is very honest about the failures of the elect and does so to confront us with the knowledge of God. We need to read the Bible as it is written to discover God as He is and be freed from our simple narratives of the good are chosen and those not chosen are bad.

---

7. 1 Chronicles 28:11-19; 2 Chronicles 8:14; 20:21, 28; 23:16-18; 29:25-27; 35:3-15; Ezra 3:10-11; Nehemiah 12:24, 45; 13:5-12.

The elect and non-elect are often tested by the distorted idea that God does not have a blessing for all. Those chosen and not chosen can be tempted to believe that being chosen is the only blessing. In reality, God intends to bless both. We should not relate to God on the basis of scarcity, where those chosen try to seize and protect what God has given them, and those not chosen seek to take what was not given to them. The Bible teaches us that God wants to bless all abundantly. We have to embrace His method and timing of blessing. The blessing may not be the same for everyone, but there is blessing for all. God's plan is not a zero-game sum only intended to bless a few. The exaltation of one does not mean the rejection of the rest. And once you embrace the plan, you discover incredible joy, fulfillment, and blessing in being exactly what God made you to be.

Jacob Wanted to be Esau

Election also creates tremendous pressure on the elect. Not only do they suffer, they often despise their own election once they realize it is not primarily for their own comfort and glory.

Jacob's struggle with Esau began in the womb. He was born grasping at Esau. And he made sure to get his blessing and Esau's birthright. When you read the story, it seems there are clear hints in the story that Jacob wanted to be Esau. Like their eponym, Israel's fundamental problem has always been to be someone else. Israel is called for a specific purpose and must be distinct from the nations, and yet Israel constantly wants to be like the rest of the nations and not bear the weight of her unique election.

Over time, the elect often despise their own election because of the pressure of their election and the pain of their failures.

God's Honor and the Nation's Blessing Are at Stake

Because God is committed to His election, we cannot experience the full blessing of God unless the elect are walking in their calling. This is true of every gift, and it is especially true of Jacob, which is why this age cannot and will not end until God has made Jacob into Israel, and Israel becomes a completely saved, holy nation. That condition will bring blessing we cannot imagine.[8] It is a blessing Paul described as "life from the dead."[9]

This forces a question: Do you delight in God's election and encourage the elect to fulfill their God-designed calling? Or are you content to see the elect fail or stumble in their calling? When we do not cooperate with God's election, which includes laboring to see the elect enter their calling, we all suffer incredible loss. The Church continues to suffer loss when we do not have an understanding of or respect for election.

We can hardly imagine how much is being held back because Jacob has not yet come into the fullness of his promises.

It has become common in Christian circles to say God used Israel in the past to demonstrate human failure and bring the Messiah, and there is no longer a distinct purpose for Israel. Distinction is now swallowed up in some kind of "equality." But this violates everything the Bible says about election. Israel was not chosen simply to demonstrate human failure. Man's failure was very apparent before God chose Abraham. Furthermore, Israel was chosen for a divine purpose, and God's honor is at stake in that purpose being fulfilled. The New Testament plainly states that purpose has not yet been fulfilled. Peter made it plain in the book of Acts that what the prophets said had not yet been fulfilled"

> *Repent therefore, and turn back, that your sins may be blotted out, that times of refreshing may come from the presence of the Lord, and that he may send the Christ appointed for you, Jesus, whom heaven must receive* **until the time for restoring all the things about which God spoke by the mouth of his holy prophets long ago.** *(Acts 3:19–21)*

And the author of Hebrews reminded his readers that Abraham,

---

8. Romans 11:12.
9. Romans 11:15.

Jacob, Moses, and the rest of Israel's heroes have not yet received their promises:

> *By faith Abraham obeyed when he was called to go out to a place that he was to receive as an inheritance. And he went out, not knowing where he was going. By faith he went to live in the land of promise, as in a foreign land, living in tents with Isaac and Jacob, heirs with him of the same promise.... By faith Jacob, when dying, blessed each of the sons of Joseph, bowing in worship over the head of his staff.... By faith Moses, when he was grown up, refused to be called the son of Pharaoh's daughter.... And all these, though commended through their faith, did not receive what was promised. (Hebrews 11:8–9, 21, 24, 39)*

The New Testament authors knew that God's plan for Israel was not finished and that God would make them into a holy, saved, glorious people capable of leading the nations by their priestly example. The idea that Israel was chosen when they were not qualified but "lost" their distinct calling because of their sin is the very opposite of the gospel. They were not chosen for their performance, nor are they cut off for their performance. To say that they were not chosen for their performance but then cut off for their performance is anti-Bible and anti-gospel. That idea is the product of a faulty, incomplete knowledge of God.

God's honor, not Israel's honor, is at stake in His ability to fulfill His purpose of election through Israel.

The Lord has brought us to the first moment in history when the whole earth is slowly being forced to stare at Jerusalem and reckon with the State of Israel. We are easily numbed by the news, and it is easy to overlook the moment we are in. Never in human history have the nations been forced to deal with Israel. The majority of the earth did not know or care about Israel in the days of Abraham, David, or Paul. But now, suddenly, the whole earth is slowly having to deal with Israel—a situation no one could have imagined even a few decades ago. We must recognize this as God's doing, not the result of mere human plans.

God is forcing the nations to face His divine election of Israel because it reveals something of who He is. Do you realize how unique the moment you are living in is? Do you know the God of election who has not forgotten His promise to Jacob? God is not content for Israel to remain Jacob, half scattered in the nations as Jacob was when he fled to Laban. He is ready for Jacob to become Israel. But He is looking for us to agree with His election. In the purposes of God, He will require us to agree with that election, not simply through mental acknowledgement, but through our prayers and our lives. Ultimately, God is going to require His people in the nations to be willing to give their lives for the sake of Israel's election. As we will see, the prophets plainly predicted that God would judge nations on whether they were willing to stand with the election of Israel at the cost of suffering, and Jesus also repeated this prediction.[10]

The controversy over Israel's election will rise in the days ahead because of how much is at stake in Jacob becoming Israel. So you must begin to understand election now.

The Question

Election confronts us with fundamental questions:

- It confronts our knowledge of man.
- It confronts our self-righteousness.
- It confronts our pride.
- Most importantly, it confronts our view of God.

The issue of election is certainly not limited to Israel. It is a part of every aspect of our lives. We are all created equal in value, but we are not the same. One is smarter than another. One is more athletic than another, and so it goes. The vast majority of what you have was

---

10. For example, the context of Matthew 25:31–46 indicates it is a clear reference to Joel 3:1–2.

determined by your birth. In other words, you were "chosen" to have the gifts you have. And you must know God does not evaluate people on what they were not given, but on what they were given. This is why Jesus predicted that many people we now consider great will not be great in the age to come. And many people we do not consider great will be great.[11] God does not evaluate you on whether you are "elect" or not in a certain way. He evaluates you on what you do with what He gave you.

Election confronts you daily. A person is chosen for a job or ministry over you. Or perhaps you are chosen over another. Someone has a gift or a gifting you do not have. Or even more challenging, someone less gifted is chosen instead of you for something you expected. The question is what do you do when you think you deserve something you do not receive? Do you rage against the one chosen? Do you gossip and let everyone know the one chosen is unqualified? Do you build a case against the one chosen until they ultimately fail and then whisper, "I told you so"? As we will see, this is the venom of the serpent who is also known as the "accuser."[12] What do you think God thinks of these petty games, especially when those who have received divine mercy try to tear down others out of envy?

God's opinion can be found in Malachi 1:

"But Esau I have hated. I have laid waste his hill country and left his heritage to jackals of the desert." (Malachi 1:3)

Many read this verse or Paul's quotation of it in Romans 9:13 and assume God always hated Esau:

And not only so, but also when Rebekah had conceived children by one man, our forefather Isaac, though they were not yet born and had done nothing either good or bad—in order that God's purpose of election might continue, not because of works but because of him who calls—she was told,

---

11. Matthew 19:30; 20:16; Mark 10:31; Luke 13:30.
12. Zechariah 3:1; Revelation 12:10.

"The older will serve the younger." As it is written, "Jacob I loved, but Esau I hated." (Romans 9:10–13)

Notice Paul was careful to point out that, when Esau was born, God never said He hated Esau. God's choice of Jacob was related to His "purpose of election." That purpose is accomplished by God picking Jacob when neither Jacob nor Esau had done anything good or bad. In other words, God's choice of Jacob over Esau for a specific assignment had nothing to do with Jacob's righteousness or Esau's sinfulness. God simply chose Jacob.

Paul quoted God's word to Rebekah from Genesis 25:23. God did not "hate" Esau before he was born, nor did He not tell Rebekah that He had rejected Esau. God simply gave Esau a difficult assignment: Esau would have to serve his younger brother. This assignment was challenging culturally and also difficult because of who his brother was. The physically "stronger" brother would have to serve the physically "weaker." It was a difficult assignment, but there is no mention that God had rejected Esau.

After quoting Genesis to describe the beginning of the story of Jacob and Esau, Paul quoted Malachi, the last prophet in the Hebrew Bible. In Malachi 1:2–3, centuries later, God said He hated Esau. There is obviously a big difference between what God said about Esau in the beginning of the Bible in Genesis and what He said at the end of the Hebrew Bible, and that difference is explained by the history that occurred between Genesis and Malachi. Paul expected his readers to know that history and use it to interpret his quotations. But if we do not know the long history between the Israelites and the Edomites, we can miss Paul's point.

Malachi's statement about Esau was made after the Babylonian invasion of Israel, which was one of the most catastrophic events in Israel's history. Babylon invaded Judah multiple times, eventually destroying the temple, carrying most people into captivity, and bringing an end to the kingdom of Judah. Babylon caused immense destruction and suffering. The prophets' messages were clear: The suffering inflicted by Babylon was the result of Judah's sin. Because

Judah persisted in rebellion, injustice, and idolatry, God brought Babylon against Judah as a judgment.

When the Babylonians came to destroy Jerusalem and take the Israelites as captives, the Edomites saw it as a great opportunity. They took advantage of God's judgment on Judah and saw it as a chance to take Judah's land and take Judah's inheritance for themselves. God hated Edom because they knew God had given the land to Judah, but they tried to take Judah's inheritance by taking advantage of Judah's judgment for her sin.

Malachi summarized God's response to Edom's sin, but a longer response can also be found in the book of Obadiah:

> *Because of the violence done to your brother Jacob, shame shall cover you, and you shall be cut off forever. On the day that you stood aloof, on the day that strangers carried off his wealth and foreigners entered his gates and cast lots for Jerusalem, you were like one of them. But do not gloat over the day of your brother in the day of his misfortune; do not rejoice over the people of Judah in the day of their ruin; do not boast in the day of distress. Do not enter the gate of my people in the day of their calamity; do not gloat over his disaster in the day of his calamity; do not loot his wealth in the day of his calamity. Do not stand at the crossroads to cut off his fugitives; do not hand over his survivors in the day of distress. (Obadiah 10–14)*

The first key to understanding Obadiah's prophecy is to understand that the Babylonian invasion was a divine judgment against Judah. The second key to understanding Obadiah's prophecy is to understand that Edom sought to take advantage of Judah's judgment for their own benefit.

When Judah was under judgment for her sin, the Edomites tried to take advantage of Judah's suffering. When the Babylonians invaded the land, they tried to take what they could from Judah's inheritance. Judah was deep in sin and compromise, so it was not an issue of Judah's righteousness. It was an issue of respecting God's election. The moment of judgment exposed the jealousy of Edom as they tried to take what God had allotted to Judah.

When Edom tried to take advantage of Judah's judgment, God one response: Esau I have hated. God did not hate Esau when he was born. Nor when he struggled with Jacob. He only hated him after he sought to take advantage of Jacob's judgment and seize Jacob's inheritance.

So here's the question: To what extent are we guilty of Edom's sin? In what ways have the nations sought the inheritance of Jacob? And have we not exposed a root of envy, at times in sophisticated ways, but speaking against the idea of any abiding, ongoing call on Israel? And furthermore, we need to soberly consider to what extent the root of Edom's sin is present in our theology. Whenever we craft a theology that the people of Israel no longer have any distinct inheritance because of their sin and failure, we are essentially behaving like Edom.

Over the last 2,000 years, many Christian theologies have often been based on the premise that Jacob is under judgment for his sin and, therefore, no longer has no unique inheritance. And then we take the next step of appropriating all of Jacob's promises to a predominantly gentile "church." Is this not the sin of Edom? And if it is, what will God say to that sin?

The issue is not whether or not Jacob has sinned. The issue is whether we think and act like God and contend for Jacob's redemption with a resolute commitment to Jacob's ongoing election regardless of his present condition. But our theologies expose our hearts. At best, we lack understanding of who God is, and at worst, we are nurturing a murderous root of envy to remain in our hearts. But even ignorance can be deadly because the long, painful history of the Church shows the ease to which we can become caught up in the sin of Edom. What may begin as ignorance can easily manifest itself as something much darker and much more evil.

The Scripture is very clear that we can share in and participate in God's blessing by being grafted into Israel's story through Jesus. However, sharing in the blessing is very different from condemning Jacob and seizing the blessing for ourselves with no distinct, ongoing place of distinction, choosing honor and blessing for Jacob. And this is the sin of Edom.

Jesus' Response to Sin

It is easy to be horrified by the story of Edom, but is this not what we do day in and day out when we rage against the one we think should not be elected? Do we intercede for others when they fail? Do we contend for the glory of God to be displayed through the eventual success of ones He has called? Or do we see their failure as an opportunity to advance our agenda?

For another example, how many of us would have responded to Peter the way Jesus did? Jesus called Peter to be an apostle, but he had significant issues when he was called. He was bold, brash, and arrogant. And then he denied the Lord three times in a massive failure. What would your response to that failure be? Would you have secretly delighted in the fact that Peter was no longer a "problem" among the apostles? Would you be glad to be rid of him or feel justified with your dislike of Peter now that his arrogance was shattered by his sin? Would you quote Jesus' own words that He will deny anyone who denies Him before men?

Or would you do what Jesus did? Jesus prayed urgently for Peter and then pursued Peter to restore him to his calling when he failed:

> *"Simon, Simon, behold, Satan demanded to have you, that he might sift you like wheat, but **I have prayed for you that your faith may not fail.** And when you have turned again, strengthen your brothers." Peter said to him, "Lord, I am ready to go with you both to prison and to death." Jesus said, "I tell you, Peter, the rooster will not crow this day, until you deny three times that you know me." (Luke 22:31–34)*

When Jesus spoke to Peter, He did not use the word for *prayer* that He typically used. He used a stronger word that means He fervently, urgently prayed for Peter Jesus only used this word on three different occasions, and each time the context was intense.[13] It can be translated "beg" or "plead." Jesus did not simply "pray" for Peter. He

---

13. Matthew 9:38; Luke 10:2; 21:36; 22:32.

intensely fought for Peter in prayer. Furthermore, Jesus did not fight that Peter would avoid his failure. Jesus knew Peter would fail. He fought that Peter would be restored and come into the fullness of his calling *after* he failed.

This kind of contending was the basis of Jesus' entire life. He did not come for perfect people. He came to serve those who were his sick, needy enemies—unable to help themselves.[14] In short, He came to transform the disqualified so they could be restored to their calling. So the question is: *Do you think and act like Jesus?* Or do you claim the name of Jesus and yet not adopt the way of Jesus?

Do you use your strength to help the unqualified understanding that Jesus, the only qualified One, gave His life for us to enjoy a life we are completely unqualified for? Do you take the same delight God does in serving those who are unqualified, realizing that any grace or calling you have is a gift from God that is completely undeserved?

Seeking to Benefit from the Failure of the Elect

If you do not understand election, you do not grasp God.

Perhaps God has chosen you in a specific way. It may be something that seems big or small to you. Can you trust God with your election? Or do you scheme like Jacob and treat other people as though they are disposable in your pursuit of your God-ordained "calling"? If you do not feel chosen, do you cooperate with God's purposes with full confidence that God's election is for your own good and blessing?

Jesus not only shows us the sufferings of the elect, He shows us how to walk if we are not elect. Jesus gave His life serving the calling of others. He suffered so that we can walk in our calling (election). This is what God is like. God serves the ones He has called. God actually delights in serving the calling of another. The fundamental question is this: Do you want to become like God? Or do you want to live in a self-centered way that tolerates envy toward the chosen?

---

14. Matthew 9:12; Mark 2:17; Luke 5:31–32.

This is not a small issue. The prophets strongly warn us that, if we do not settle our offense with election, we will get caught up in an end-time rage against the election of Israel. We have already seen repeatedly throughout history where even Christians got caught up in hostility toward the people of Israel because they did not understand and honor God's divine election. And we are not better than our fathers. If we do not know God as the God who elects, we will be woefully unprepared for the next storm and the final storm over Israel's election. And the consequences will be more severe than we can now imagine.

Of course, nearly every Christian immediately recoils at the suggestion they could get caught up in a rage against Israel. But read the history books. We are not automatically better than our fathers. God hated Edom because they sought to profit from the failure of Jacob. However, have we not done the same thing?

According to the New Testament, we have received great benefit from Israel's success and Israel's failures. Do we not seek to enjoy blessing from Israel's story and Israel's inheritance while Israel does not yet enjoy the fullness of their blessing? Are we not quick to embrace being "grafted into" Israel's blessings,[15] but assign all of Israel's sufferings to Israel? How is it that we expect to take the blessings that come from God's story with Israel and yet give Israel only the sufferings?

When we declare that we are grafted into Jacob (Israel) and able to enjoy blessings that we have received, in part, through Israel's failure and show no concern at all for the condition of Jacob are we not, in fact, dangerously near the sin of Esau? We seem quick to take Israel's spiritual inheritance for ourselves with little concern for Israel's condition. And, even worse, propagate theologies that entirely divest Jacob of any unique, future blessing.

God wants the nations grafted into the story of Israel. He has been very clear about that from the beginning.[16] But the blessing

---

15. Romans 11:17, 24.
16. For example, in God told Abraham all the families of the earth would be blessed in

does not come from stealing Israel's inheritance and appropriating it for yourself when Israel does not yet enjoy the fullness of that inheritance. Nor is it being content with a theology that ends Israel's story with Israel's failure, rather than in her dramatic transformation from "Jacob" into "Israel," enjoying the fullness of God's blessing and fulfilling her full purpose.

When we are content, even eager, to take Jacob's spiritual blessings which have come to us through Jacob's suffering with no regard for Jacob's condition, are we not guilty of the sin of Edom?

While every Christian is horrified by the suggestion they could be passive in the face of something like Nazi rage, if we do not face our present sins, are we not vulnerable? Nazi Germany was not an ignorant society. It was an educated, sophisticated, and advanced society filled with theologians. Germany was transformed into something grotesque and horrifying because the Church had not dealt with these issues. Why do we imagine that such a thing cannot happen in our day and time? Especially when the prophets, and Jesus Himself, warned us the conflict over Israel's calling is not yet over?

---

him and God called Jacob to become a company of "many peoples." See Genesis 12:3; 17:4–6; 18:18; 28:3; 35:11; 48:4.

6

RELATING TO THE ELECT IN THEIR FAILURE

BECAUSE ELECTION IS on the basis of God's choosing and not righteousness, it is inevitable that the elect fail. So then, how do we agree with God's election when the elect fail?

When the elect fail, the most common response is to criticize and accuse them, and point out their disqualifications. Often, the sins of the elect are exaggerated, which, as we will see, is a symptom of pride and envy. Envy can lead to people taking delight in pointing out the failures of those chosen. Sometimes, that delight is open. At other times, even among Christians, that delight is expressed in smug attitudes and whispering that is really gossip.

When the sins of the elect are exaggerated or eagerly broadcast to ensure everyone knows, it is a form of accusation and an indicator of pride. Accusation often consists of suggestive statements and whispers that produce questions in people's minds about another. Those questions produce premature judgments, as well as firm judgments, about other people. It also includes distortions of what is true, or wrong conclusions based on true facts. Accusation is a direct characteristic of the satan[1] who is called "the accuser,"[2] and we'll see in a future chapter why accusation is fundamental to his character.

Accusation is perhaps the biggest challenge individuals and the Church face. We are constantly under assault by accusation. There are accusations from ourselves in our own minds, accusations from others, and even accusations from our spiritual enemies.

Accusation emphasizes the disqualification of the elect in order to strengthen the self-image of those not chosen. We see this constantly with Israel and even in local congregations when ministry leaders fall. Of course, reasonable steps need to be taken when someone sins severely, and there are situations where discipline is needed, which can include permanently removing someone from a certain position or ministry. However, accusation takes delight in failure and emphasizes the disqualification of a person. In its most mild form, it simply seeks to see a person removed from the place God has chosen for them. In its more aggressive form, it seeks the elimination of the chosen altogether.

Though one may not have the courage to say it or take extreme steps, the desire to see the elect removed rather than transformed to fulfill their calling is essentially the same as the desire to eliminate the chosen. If the place God has designed for them is eliminated, then they are, at least in part, eliminated as a person. In the same way that Jesus said anger is equivalent to murder[3] because murder is simply a graphic outworking of anger, all accusation aims at the removal of the chosen person from their God-given place, which is essentially the desire for the elimination of that person. If they are not in the place God designed for them, they cease to be the person God designed them to be.

---

1. "Satan" is not a name. It is a function that translates to "accuser" or "opponent." Though this title is typically translated "Satan," in the original language, this enemy is called "the satan" because it is not a proper name. In this book, we use "the satan" instead of a proper name because this is what the Bible calls him. This is addressed more fully in this book in "Corrupted by Envy."
2. Zechariah 3:1; Revelation 12:10.
3. Matthew 5:21–22.

The elect can sin to such an extent in certain circumstances that they need to be removed for the sake of themselves or others, but this should be a painful process as Scripture clearly demonstrates this is not the norm. It is common that the elect endure discipline because of sin and failure, but this is designed to be a process that transforms the elect for their calling.

The Bible constantly confronts us with this. In nearly every story of one chosen, we are graphically told about their failures. Corporate Israel's failures are plainly told throughout the Bible. Most of the most famous characters have shocking failures that include pride, murder, and sexual sin. And even in their failure, their election remained. Of course, there are consequences for their sin, as there are for everyone, but we see consistently that God does not eliminate election because of failure. Instead, He demonstrates His glory by taking sinful, disqualified people and working something through them that they are humanly incapable of.

We must recognize that accusation against the elect, especially when they fail, is an expression of accusation which is the nature of the satan. It is an expression of his worldview.

Israel has constantly suffered accusation since the beginning. It is the default response of the nations because it is the response of the accuser who has deeply infected humanity with his sin. We must face the fact that the Church has been infected by his lies as well and often acted as an accuser, acting in his spirit and not the spirit of Jesus.

So how do we relate to the inevitable failures of the elect?

Accusation vs. Conviction

We must avoid accusation, but that does not mean we ignore the failures of the elect. We are called to walk with each other and address sin.[4] As we have seen, the elect are not "more special," so they need the same care and concern as anyone. They are real humans, and

---

4. Proverbs 27:5–6; Matthew 18:15–20; Galatians 6:1; James 5:19–20.

their redemption matters, so we should address their failures because we love them just as we do for anyone else we care about. (In fact, it could be said that many failures of the elect are intensified by a celebrity culture that glorifies the elect and fails to treat them as real humans who face the same challenges and have the same weaknesses as everyone else.) Furthermore, because election is for the sake of others, we cannot overlook the failures of the elect because everyone suffers when the elect do not take their place and fulfill their assignment. When they are in their God-ordained place, we all benefit. But when they are in sin, rebellion, or compromise, we all suffer.

If we honor the election of God in a biblical way, we will avoid accusation, and we can also play a part in God's conviction of those He has chosen. *Respecting those God has chosen means rebuking them when necessary so that they may enter into their calling.* Accusation says you have failed and no longer have a calling or a future. Conviction says you are not living up to your calling, but you must, and you will. If we do not speak godly correction (the key is *godly*) to those who are called, we do not truly love them because they need godly correction like everyone else.

A godly rebuke is not an accusation. It is not automatically a public, humiliating exposure of sin. It is a true word spoken directly to the elect in order to lead them to a good and successful end. If you rebuke the elect for any reason other than their ultimate success, you are entering into accusation. We do not rebuke people only to show they are wrong. We rebuke people in order to see them succeed. And we rebuke people with confidence that God can bring about a good outcome.

Israel's prophets were Israel's harshest critics, and some of their words were scathing. But their harsh critiques were not designed to destroy or humiliate Jacob, but rather to transform Jacob into Israel. Their prophecies ended with the profound promise that Jacob *will* become Israel regardless of how bad things may appear at any one time.

Is your critique of Israel aimed at exposing her sins and faults? Or is it given in the context of God's unbreakable relationship with Jacob, with the confidence Jacob will come into his calling?

The prophetic is a God-given gift that fights for the future of the elect even if it requires an uncomfortable confrontation. That confrontation may be unpleasant, painful, or even humiliating, but it is done with the good of the elect in mind. Some people love confrontation and exposing sin. But it is not "prophetic" merely to expose sin. Any second-rate reporter can do that. Read the prophets. They were often overwhelmed by their task, and they confronted people for the purpose of salvation and redemption. That goal determined the nature of their confrontation, and it should guide our confrontations as well.

When it comes to Israel or anyone else God has chosen, it is not prophetic to expose the depths of Jacob's disqualification. That is the spirit of accusation. Remember Jacob's disqualification came from the fact that he was *human*, which means his disqualification is your disqualification. How do you want your disqualification handled? That is the way you should handle Israel's sins.

Our story is intertwined with Jacob whether we are Jewish or not. Our stories are inseparable. Honoring election does not mean overlooking Jacob's sins. At times, it means confronting Jacob and working for his good and his salvation while honoring his election and avoiding the spirit of accusation and condemnation. This is the tension we must hold.

Divine Discipline

The failures of the elect are more than personal failures. Because of their calling, those they are called to serve also bear additional discipline. And added to that is the weight of knowing their failures impact many other people even more than the failures of others. Because of the weight of their calling, the elect endure additional discipline, and throughout their history, the people of Israel have endured divine discipline.

Israel has probably been the most publicly disciplined people throughout history.

We have to understand divine discipline through a biblical sense. Biblical discipline is not rejection. Discipline is designed by God to accomplish a divine outcome. When we read about Israel's discipline, even when the situation seemed hopeless, the prophets consistently predicted that God's discipline would not bring about the end of Israel but a glorious salvation we can hardly anticipate.[5] We cannot always tell how God will produce this salvation, but the prophets were very certain God would bring about that salvation even if Israel seemed like she would lose hope. If we view divine discipline through an unbiblical lens, we severely distort God's leadership of Israel. In fact, some have accused, disqualified, and rejected Israel on the basis of a distorted understanding of God's discipline. That is essentially what Edom did, and God responded with a severe rebuke.[6]

We must know that God has really strong opinions about how we respond to His discipline of others.

The Challenge of Election Is God's Way

God changed three peoples' names in the book of Genesis: Abram, Sarai, and Jacob. But the author of Genesis did not treat the name changes the same way. Abram was consistently referred to as Abram up to Genesis 17:5, when his name was changed to Abraham. From that point forward in the book, we never read Abram again. His name was Abraham. Period. The same was true for Sarah. She was referred to as Sarai until God changed her name, and then she was called Sarah, and Sarai was never mentioned again.

---

5. Deuteronomy 30:1-6; Isaiah 4:3–4; 45:17, 25; 54:13: 59:21; 60:4, 21; 61:8-9, 65:23; 66:22; Jeremiah 31:31-34; 32:40; Ezekiel 20:40; 36:10, 27-36; 37:25; 39:22, 28-29; Joel 2:26, 32; Zephaniah 3:9, 12; 12:13; Zechariah 12:10-13; Matthew 23:39; 24:30; Acts 1:6-7; 2:21; Romans 10:13; 11:26–27; Revelation 1:7.
6. This is the context of the book of Obadiah and part of the basis for the Lord's severe statements about Edom.

However, it was very different with Jacob. God changed Jacob's name to Israel *twice*,[7] and yet after his name was changed, the book of Genesis continued to use the name Jacob. In fact, after Jacob's name was changed, he was called *Jacob* approximately 76 times while the new name *Israel* was only used 43 times. So after God changed Jacob's name, the book of Genesis continued to refer to Jacob as *Jacob* nearly twice as often as it referred to him as *Israel*. When you read this in light of Abraham's name, the author of Genesis was obviously trying to make a significant point. And this point was not limited to Jacob's story as an individual. Particularly in the prophets, the nation that came from Jacob was addressed as *Jacob* at times and *Israel* at other times. For example, in the Hebrew Bible, the people of Israel were referred to by the name *Jacob* over 400 times. And in the prophets, this was especially symbolic because they used the story of Jacob as a foreshadowing of Israel's past, present, and future.

The point is clear: We have to bear with the fact that Jacob *is* Israel and is also *not yet* Israel. That is the controversy of election. Jacob was chosen by God even while he was still Jacob. He was Israel because God's plan to bring Jacob to glory would succeed. It could not be stopped. In that sense then, Jacob was Israel, but not yet Israel. We must respect Jacob because Jacob would become Israel while bearing with Jacob while Jacob was not yet fully Israel. And as history unfolds, we have seen, and continue to see, Jacob *and* Israel. Israel is not simply Jacob because God has chosen Jacob and secured his calling. And yet Jacob is clearly not Israel.

As we have seen, this is offensive, and God demands we respect it because it is not about Jacob. It is about Israel. Furthermore, this is a snapshot of our own condition. If we have been transformed by Jesus, we can already see glimpses of our future glory. Yet we live in fallen bodies, and so we continue to be Jacob. Israel's national condition is our personal condition, so when we mock Jacob for being Jacob, we are, in fact, ridiculing our own condition. But when we respect Jacob as Israel, God will respond to us, and this respect for His election will

---

7. Genesis 32:28; 35:10.

actually bring about our transformation. If we give mercy to Israel, we will receive mercy. But if we refuse to give Israel mercy, mercy will not be given to us:[8]

> Because of the violence done to your brother Jacob, shame shall cover you, and you shall be cut off forever...But do not gloat over the day of your brother in the day of his misfortune; do not rejoice over the people of Judah in the day of their ruin; do not boast in the day of distress. Do not enter the gate of my people in the day of their calamity; do not gloat over his disaster in the day of his calamity; do not loot his wealth in the day of his calamity...For the day of the LORD is near upon all the nations. As you have done, it shall be done to you; your deeds shall return on your own head. (Obadiah 10, 12–13, 15)

As we have already seen, mercy does not mean overlooking sin. But it does mean that whatever is spoken or done is done out of a desire to see Jacob come into the fullness of his unique calling. It is not to be done for the purposes of humiliation, disqualification, or envy.

The handling of Jacob's name was a prophetic statement about Jacob's condition. And it was an indication to us that the battle over Jacob's election and his future was not settled in the book of Genesis. It is a battle that will continue until Jacob becomes Israel. And as the Hebrew Bible developed, the prophets gave more definition to what that meant, generally summarizing it as a day when *all* Jacob (Israel) is righteous and holy, living as a blessing in the earth and glorifying the name of Abraham and his great God.[9]

As the book of Genesis closed, Jacob blessed his sons and gave prophecies over them. This section highlighted the challenges of election even within the family of Jacob. For example, when Jacob

---

8. See also Genesis 12:3; Matthew 5:7; Romans 11:17–24; James 2:13.

9. Deuteronomy 30:1-6; Isaiah 4:3–4; 45:17, 25; 54:13: 59:21; 60:4, 21; 61:8-9, 65:23; 66:22; Jeremiah 31:31-34; 32:40; Ezekiel 20:40; 36:10, 27-36; 37:25; 39:22, 28-29; Joel 2:26, 32; Zephaniah 3:9, 12; 12:13; Zechariah 12:10-13; Matthew 23:39; 24:30; Acts 1:6-7; 2:21; Romans 10:13; 11:26–27; Revelation 1:7.

blessed Joseph's sons, Jacob predicted the younger son would be greater than the older. Joseph tried to correct his father, but Jacob was firm. The younger would exceed the older.[10]

When Jacob blessed his sons, there was another surprising twist related to Joseph. Joseph's story is the longest story in Genesis, and he was the best candidate for the promised deliverer in the book of Genesis. As the book came to a close, we began to discover that Joseph would not be the ultimate deliverer because, though he saved his people, they were left dwelling outside the land and awaiting the fulfillment of the promises.

Because Joseph was such a dominant figure in Genesis, if he was not the deliverer, then surely the deliverer would come from him. After all, he was uniquely chosen from God and exalted above his family. But when Jacob prophesied, there was another twist to the story. Jacob's prophecy predicted that the ruler of the family would not come from Joseph but from Judah. In his prophecy, Jacob described Joseph but then applied that description to a seed who would come from Judah.[11]

All of this is simply the beginning. From Genesis forward, the controversy of election continued:

- God chose Moses to lead Israel out of Egypt. Not only was Moses *not* the oldest son, Moses *never* lived as a slave. He was raised as an Egyptian in the palace and grew up with the oppressor rather than the oppressed. Furthermore, he ran away when confronted with Israel's crisis. His Hebrew probably had an Egyptian accent. When God offered him unprecedented power and commanded him to deliver Israel, he refused. He also refused to speak to Pharaoh, so God had to speak through Aaron. Yet God was stubbornly committed to Moses' calling.
- David was chosen as Israel's most famous king. When

---

10. Genesis 48:14–21.
11. Genesis 48:8–10.

Samuel came to David's father, Jesse, to anoint one of his sons as a king, however, David was so unlikely a choice that Jesse did not even ask him to meet the prophet. No one expected David to be king. He was given the lower-class job of being a shepherd. A good case can be made that David may have even been an illegitimate son. But he was God's choice, nonetheless.

This pattern is not limited to the Hebrew Bible. In the New Testament, we find the same thing:

- Jesus was obviously not what anyone expected the Messiah to look like, and He lived His whole life with that controversy. Even when He healed people and demonstrated unusual power many people struggled with the idea that He was the chosen One.[12]
- Peter was an arrogant disciple who denied Jesus three times when Jesus was arrested. Even Peter thought these denials disqualified him. But Jesus intentionally went to Peter and made him the first prominent leader in the church in Jerusalem, and Peter continued for decades as a prominent leader.
- Paul was enraged by the early followers of Jesus and tried to persecute the movement. Yet he was chosen by God to be the leader who became the most visible and perhaps the most influential early leader. What's more, Paul was a devout Jew who kept the law perfectly and knew Scripture deeply. He was a brilliant Jewish scholar who should have served among his own people by any reasonable measure. And yet he was sent to the Gentiles, a people whom he likely had despised much of his life.

The stories could go on and on and on. God repeatedly chose

---

12. Matthew 13:55–47; Luke 4:22; John 6:42.

someone we think was not the right person, and then He put His glorious redemptive power on display in His work through that person. That work requires we respect His choice, and that choice is "irrevocable."[13] The glory of God's leadership is when we agree with His exaltation of a person whose exaltation ends up serving *our* benefit. God's exaltation of one is not His rejection of the rest. It is simply His way.

If we resist His way, though, we become captive to self-righteousness, pride, and envy, and we end up harboring the sin of envy. Yet if we cooperate with His way, we end up receiving incredible blessing.

"Fascinated" by the Elect

Offense over election is typically the biggest challenge relating to election, but there is another challenge: an unbiblical fascination with the elect which produces all kinds of unhealthy dynamics. People fascinated with the elect often elevate the elect to a place God never gave them. This very elevation sets the elect up for possible failure because God never designed humans to be worshipped. How many humans have self-destructed simply because they were worshipped by other humans, which is not something the human frame can handle? (Note the word *fascination* has a range of meanings, so I'm using it here to speak of *unbiblical* fascination.)

Those fascinated by the elect tend to overlook or minimize the sins of the elect in the name of respecting God's election. This can happen in a cultish way with certain groups or leaders, but it more commonly happens when people defend the elect in everything they do and avoid mentioning clear sins simply because they want to honor God's election.

Whenever we are "fascinated" with someone on the basis of their election, we are on the path to idolatry.

Fascination leads to idolatry, and when we idolize someone, it becomes too painful to face the fact that our idols have failures. As a

---

13. Romans 11:29.

result, we overlook the failures of our idols so that we do not have to face our own idolatry. We often prefer to live with a distorted belief in ideal, perfect humans simply to avoid the painful reality that our beloved "idols" are not flawless. When we avoid the sins of the elect, it is a profound deception, and it is not the biblical way to honor election.

Fascination can express itself in a number of ways. Some people develop a sense of identity through their association with the elect, and they do not want to lose that sense of identity. For example, this happens frequently when gentile Christians begin to recognize the ongoing calling of the Jewish people and then begin to adopt a Jewish life, hoping to be accepted by Jews. When people deeply crave the attention and affirmation of the elect, it becomes idolatrous, unhealthy, and unbiblical. However, they simply need to live as Gentiles who express biblical love, honor, and respect for the calling of the Jewish people. Others obtain real benefits from their relationships to the elect. These benefits may be financial or may be emotional. In either case, they develop an unhealthy relationship with the elect because they do not want to risk losing a relationship and the benefits that accompany it.

We have to be aware of unbiblical fascination with anyone chosen, including Israel, because it leads to idolatry and unhealthy relationships that actually hinder the elect.

If we truly love the elect, we will contend for their calling, which includes bringing godly, humble rebukes when necessary. If we do not biblically rebuke those God has called when it is necessary, we are selfish and ungodly. It is selfish because the only reason we do not is to avoid the shattering of illusions about the elect, the pain of difficult conversations, the potential loss of relationships, or the possible loss of a perceived status that comes with our relationship to the elect. It is also ungodly because, when we do not rebuke those in their sins, we show we truly do not care for them. If a friend never speaks to a friend caught in a sin, it demonstrates a lack of true concern. Furthermore, if we ignore sin, which brings destruction, in the elect and our other relationships, it is likely we will ignore sins in our own lives.

Many do not want to bear conflict with the elect or lose the perceived benefits of their fascination and identification with the elect, and so they are content to look the other way and allow them to persist in their sin.

The prophets are perhaps the best example of dealing with the sin of the elect. The prophets could be harsh critics of Israel, and some of their rebukes are scathing. However, the prophets did not rebuke Israel to disqualify her. They rebuked Israel because they believed in Israel's election. What's more, their rebukes were connected to an affirmation of Israel's ongoing election and predictions that Israel would eventually come into that calling. Their rebukes can seem incredibly harsh, but they were deeply rooted in Israel's election, and their rebukes were given to provoke Israel to fulfill her calling.

Biblical Respect

Fascination with the elect and the idolatry that accompanies it create an impossible situation where the elect can never truly live up to what is being expected of them. This can lead to two disastrous outcomes. It can lead to a delusion where we pretend that a certain people are more "perfect" than they are in order to preserve our "idols," or something shatters our idolatry, and we become hostile to the elect out of the pain of our own disillusionment.

This can happen when those who "love" Israel discover Israel is not perfectly righteous and, at times, sins just like other people. When this new information is too difficult to bear, a person can often become anti-Israel and become as vocal in their criticism of Israel as they were in their support of Israel. In reality, all they discovered is that the elect are not "better" humans, and they are not intrinsically righteous. They have discovered what God said about Israel from the beginning, but if they do not have a biblical framework for election, they will not be able to bear the tension between respect for election and the reality of the sin of the elect. We must live in that tension, though. It is in that tension that we discover who God is.

We must respect the election of God and, like the prophets, speak plainly to the elect, being willing to rebuke them in order to bring them into their calling.

We are called to live out a biblical response to election:

- We respect election because we respect God, not because the elect are superior.
- We avoid fascination (idolatry) with the elect. We recognize they are humans just like us. They were chosen on the basis of God's desire and not their performance. We respect God's choice, but we do not elevate the elect in an unbiblical way.
- We are not surprised by the sin of the elect.
- We understand that God's glory is at stake in the fulfillment of His election through His strength and His ability to work through those who are demonstrably unqualified.
- We are willing to address the sins of the elect because we care about them as individuals and we care about their corporate calling. We rebuke the elect with confidence in God's ability to bring a good outcome, and rebukes are not simply criticisms or exposures. They are intentional and, sometimes, painful words designed to bring the elect into the fullness of their calling.
- Rebukes most often come in the place of relationship or recognized positions of leadership. The knowledge of sin does not give us an open door to rebuke everyone personally.

7

A GLIMPSE AT THE GLORIOUS FUTURE

THE BOOK of Genesis gives us profound glimpses of the glorious future when the sin of envy is resolved and God's purposes for election unfold. Throughout the book, there are several instances where one is chosen, and it causes incredible conflict. Most of these stories revolve around brothers, where the act of choosing creates incredible conflict.

Thank goodness, conflict is not usually the end of the story. If you carefully read the key stories of conflict between brothers, these stories also give us a glimpse of a glorious reconciliation and mutual blessing. This glimpse of the glorious future grows as the book develops. If you miss this glimpse of the glorious future, the book of Genesis can seem hopeless, which both exposes the sin of envy and gives a peek at its resolution.

The story of Cain and Abel is a disastrous story of brotherly conflict, and it leaves us feeling hopeless. Sin took dominion over Cain, and he left no room for his relationship with Abel to recover. The conflict ended with Abel's death. But after that, things took a different turn.

The Isaac and Ishmael story is another painful story of God's election of one brother over another. Even Abraham longed for

Ishmael to be the chosen son, but God was adamant. The chosen son must be born miraculously from a dead womb, so Ishmael was not chosen to carry the promise, but it is important to notice that Ishmael was never rejected by God or Abraham. He remained a part of the family even after Isaac was born. Ishmael was only forced out of the family when he rejected Isaac, and that rejection created conflict.[1]

While we do not have time to fully explore the subject of Ishmael, the story gives us profound hints that God was going to do something redemptive in spite of the immense family conflict that had ensued. God named Ishmael, "I hear you," which was a meaningful name to give a child who became the leader of a people group. Just as Israel was connected to Jacob's story and his name, Ishmael and his family were connected to this name.

Furthermore, the first two appearances of the Angel of the Lord in the entire Scripture are both to Hagar over the issue of Ishmael. Ishmael was given a mixed prophecy that included both trouble and promises.[2] Even after Ishmael was forced out of the family, when Abraham died, Isaac and Ishmael stood together side by side at Abraham's grave, which pointed to a future reconciliation between the two brothers.[3] Interestingly, there were several key Jewish figures named Ishmael throughout Jewish history, further demonstrating that there have been Jewish readers who understood Ishmael was not a "rejected" son. He simply was not the one chosen to carry the seed. The story is not about the rejection of Ishmael; it is about God's election of a younger son and the subsequent conflict that choice caused. But the story ends with reconciliation.

We have already looked at Jacob's story in depth, and it is similar to Isaac and Ishmael yet much more intense. God picked the younger son that we would not have picked, and this time the younger son took actions to obtain his calling, which caused division in the family and suffering for himself. However, like the Ishmael story, God never

---

1. Genesis 21:9; Galatians 4:29.
2. Genesis 16:11–12; 21:18.
3. Genesis 25:9.

said He rejected Esau. He simply said Esau had a difficult assignment: Esau would need to serve his younger brother.[4] This assignment was challenging, but he was not rejected. And when Jacob and Esau met a long time after their great conflict over the blessing, we find a shocking thing: *Esau brought a small army to protect Jacob and serve his calling.*[5] And Jacob brought gifts for Esau. Both brothers came to give to each other. In this meeting, there was no conflict, only love, affection, and mutual blessing.

After their reunion, the brothers went separate ways, but the author of Genesis was "careful to note that their parting of ways was beneficial to both. It was because of their great wealth they had to part company."[6] Considering the struggle over the blessing which escalated to Jacob's great act of deception and Esau's desire to kill Jacob, the story ends in a shocking way, and it is intended to be a picture of the redemption of Israel and the nations. The end of the story will include Jacob (Israel) coming back into the land in fullness and the nations coming into their own blessing as they also bless Israel.

There is another hint at this reconciliation in the story of the Exodus. After Israel left Egypt, Moses sent out twelve spies into the Promised Land to assess the situation. Of the spies, only two stood in faith: Joshua and Caleb. They are two of the heroes of the Exodus story, and decades later, Joshua led the conquest of Canaan, and Caleb received an inheritance in the land.[7] But what is especially fascinating is that Caleb seems to come from an Edomite ancestor who became a part of Judah,[8] so this is another glimpse of Esau agreeing with Jacob's election, being reconciled to Jacob, and becoming part of the redemptive story.

---

4. Genesis 25:23; Romans 9:12.

5. Genesis 33.

6. John H. Sailhamer, *The Pentateuch as Narrative: A Biblical-Theological Commentary*, ed. Gary Lee (Grand Rapids, MI: Zondervan Publishing House, 1992), 204.

7. Numbers 13; Joshua 14:6–15.

8. For example, see Meredith Faubel Nyberg, "Caleb, Israelite Spy, Son of Jephunneh," ed. John D. Barry et al., *The Lexham Bible Dictionary* (Bellingham, WA: Lexham Press, 2016).

Amos built on this theme with his prediction that the restored kingdom of David would include the remnant of Edom:

> "In that day I will raise up the booth of David that is fallen and repair its breaches, and raise up its ruins and rebuild it as in the days of old, that they may possess the remnant of Edom and all the nations who are called by my name," declares the LORD who does this. (Amos 9:11–12)

The nations of Israel and Edom eventually became enemies, but Amos predicted there would be a reconciliation under a restored kingdom of David that includes Edom in the kingdom. And the apostles quoted Amos in Acts 15 when they saw a large number of Gentiles embracing the God of Israel through Jesus.

> "And with this the words of the prophets agree, just as it is written, 'After this I will return, and I will rebuild the tent of David that has fallen; I will rebuild its ruins, and I will restore it, that the remnant of mankind may seek the Lord, and all the Gentiles who are called by my name, says the Lord, who makes these things.'" (Acts 15:15–17)

There are many passages in the Hebrew Bible that describe the Gentiles coming to the God of Israel, so it is interesting the apostles chose this passage. When the apostles quoted Amos, they broadened the scope of the passage. Amos named Edom, but the apostles applied the prophecy to the "remnant of mankind," enlarging the prophecy to go beyond the people of Edom. This demonstrates how the apostles understood Amos's prophecy. It was about more than the restoration of relationship between Israel and Edom. It was ultimately about the restoration of relationship between Israel and a remnant of all the Gentiles. The warm reconciliation that Jacob and Esau experienced is a picture of a future reconciliation between Israel and the nations.

The final story over a divisive election between brothers is the longest story in the book of Genesis, the story of Joseph and his brothers. Once again, God chose a brother who was not the family firstborn, and it created immediate conflict and nearly resulted in murder. The brothers were hesitant to murder Joseph themselves, so they ended up selling him into slavery. But even in this, they clearly followed the way of Cain to get rid of the chosen one. They even told their father the chosen son was dead. It was a strange twist on Jacob's story. Jacob deceived his father to secure his place as the chosen son. And then Jacob was deceived by his sons in their attempt to eliminate the chosen son.

After a very intense conflict over election, the chosen one was kicked out of the family and went his own way. But after many years, something shocking happened. The elect son was suddenly elevated far above anything that he or his brothers would have imagined. And at the same time, a great crisis came, and his family needed urgent help to survive the crisis. They needed the help that only the elect brother could give.

When Joseph first met his brothers, they did not recognize him, and he forced them to go through many tests, demonstrating his brothers had changed significantly since they had wanted to kill him. And the story leads to an incredible moment of reconciliation, where Joseph and his brothers wept profusely and were rejoined. The previous two stories show us brothers being reconciled, but the Joseph story goes much further. They did not reconcile and then stay apart. They reconciled and came back together. And that is where the story becomes very interesting.

Joseph declared that the hostility of his brothers toward his election actually served a divine purpose:

And now do not be distressed or angry with yourselves because you sold me here, for God sent me before you to preserve life. (Genesis 45:5)

Joseph could see God's sovereign hand in the conflict over his election. In fact, Joseph plainly understood the purpose of his election. It was not about exaltation for his own glory. He had been exalted *for the sake of others.* Joseph used his exaltation to ensure his family was taken care of, and he became an immense blessing to his own family and to the Egyptians. There was obvious affection between Joseph and his family. Joseph was exalted for the sake of the rest. And when he was exalted, the others were not offended by it. They were grateful for it because they came into blessing through God's plan of election.

The Joseph story gives us perhaps one of the most complete glimpses of the conflict, purpose, and blessing of election in the entire Bible. In addition, the story may be considered the best prototype of the role of Messiah, the One chosen and exalted from Israel to serve and be a blessing to both Israel and the Gentiles.

At the close of the book of Genesis, we have a somber sense that this is just the beginning of the conflict over election.

8

THE MAJESTY AND MYSTERY OF DIVINE SOVEREIGNTY

THE SUBJECT of divine election is directly connected to the mystery of divine sovereignty.

The subject of God's sovereignty is a vast and glorious subject, and there are various ways the term *sovereignty* can be used by theologians. But we are going to focus on sovereignty as God's absolute leadership of history. God is very bold through the Scripture that He is the One leading history. Even in some of the most painful and shocking moments in history, God openly declares that He sits enthroned above it all, all history serves His purposes, and history is going toward His divinely determined end.[1] Even in moments when it seems like history is out of control, God is difficult to find, or evil is "winning," God is especially adamant that He is in control of history. And He is not shy about this point. On the contrary, He is very confrontational about it because to believe otherwise is a failure to know Him as God.[2]

When we believe that anyone other than God determines the direction

---

1. Genesis 12:2–3; Psalm 33:10-11; 86:8; 103:15–16; 113:5–6; Job 42:2; Isaiah 2:22; 14:27; 40:15; 44:6–7; 46:9-10; Jeremiah 29:11; Daniel 2:20-21; 4:35; Acts 17:26; Revelation1:8 .
2. Job 38–41; Psalm 33:10-11; 115:3; 135:6; Isaiah 45:5–13; 46:9-10; Jeremiah 18:1–11; Daniel 2:20-21; 4:35; Romans 9:20–21.

of history, it is not simply an errant belief; it is a wrong view of God. It is a definition of God that is out of sync with God's description of Himself. It is a step toward defining God based on our own understanding rather than God's revelation of Himself.

The issue of God's sovereignty includes questions of how people come to salvation or how the human will relates to God's will. Those are important questions, but they are out of scope for this book, and we will not consider them here.

God's sovereignty is majestic *and* mysterious because God created many creatures that have some ability to choose and even resist Him. God's sovereignty includes two very bold claims:

- He is leading history toward His God-ordained outcomes. The whole phenomenon of biblical prophecy depends on this truth. Furthermore, even when people resist Him, they ultimately serve His purpose in the end.
- Humans and evil spiritual powers actively resist God, and in the process, their sin causes many to suffer and destroys His good creation. God holds people accountable for this sin and predicts He will judge sin because of the injustice and destruction that sin causes.

God essentially declares: "You can resist Me if you choose. Know, however, that I will always get what I want in the end. Your sin hurts creation, and I will judge it. But My will and My desire for creation are inescapable. You will ultimately serve my purposes." That statement is impossible for us to fully grasp, and *that is exactly the point.* The sovereignty of God is clearly declared in Scripture, and yet it is both majestic and mysterious. It is majestic because it confronts us with the nature of God. Who is this Person leading *all creation* to serve His purposes? And who is this Person who can cause everything to accomplish His purposes, even the decisions of creatures who are trying to actively resist Him?

Peter illustrated the point perfectly in Acts 3:

And now, brothers, I know that you acted in ignorance, as did also your rulers. But what God foretold by the mouth of all the prophets, that his Christ would suffer, he thus fulfilled. Repent therefore, and turn back, that your sins may be blotted out. (Acts 3:17–19)

Peter called certain men to repentance who had participated in Jesus' death and simultaneously told them they did exactly what God predicted and wanted. So which is it? Did they sin and need to repent? *Yes.* Did they accomplish the will of God? *Yes.* They resisted God in one sense, and yet their resistance accomplished God's divine purpose. So which is it? Is it God's perfect will or man's sinful rebellion? *Yes.* And this is not an isolated instance. Throughout the Hebrew Bible, God claims that evil empires are His agents advancing His purposes *and* that He will judge them:[3]

Woe to Assyria, the rod of my anger; the staff in their hands is my fury! Against a godless nation I send him, and against the people of my wrath I command him, to take spoil and seize plunder, and to tread them down like the mire of the streets. But he does not so intend, and his heart does not so think; but it is in his heart to destroy, and to cut off nations not a few; (Isaiah 10:5–7)

When the Lord has finished all his work on Mount Zion and on Jerusalem, he will punish the speech of the arrogant heart of the king of Assyria and the boastful look in his eyes. (Isaiah 10:12)

"Therefore thus says the LORD of hosts: Because you have not obeyed my words, behold, I will send for all the tribes of the north, declares the LORD, and for Nebuchadnezzar the king of Babylon, my servant, and I will bring them against this land and its inhabitants, and against all these surrounding nations. I will devote them to destruction, and make them a horror, a hissing, and an everlasting desolation. (Jeremiah 25:8–9)

---

3. Isaiah 10:5–12; 25–34; 29:3–5; 47:1–3; Jeremiah 25:8–9; 27:6–7; 50:18; 51:24; Ezekiel 38:14–23; Habakkuk 1:5–6.

Then after seventy years are completed, I will punish the king of Babylon and that nation, the land of the Chaldeans, for their iniquity, declares the LORD, making the land an everlasting waste. I will bring upon that land all the words that I have uttered against it, everything written in this book, which Jeremiah prophesied against all the nations. For many nations and great kings shall make slaves even of them, and I will recompense them according to their deeds and the work of their hands." (Jeremiah 25:12–14)

You will come from your place out of the uttermost parts of the north, you and many peoples with you, all of them riding on horses, a great host, a mighty army. You will come up against my people Israel, like a cloud covering the land. In the latter days I will bring you against my land, that the nations may know me, when through you, O Gog, I vindicate my holiness before their eyes. "Thus says the Lord GOD: Are you he of whom I spoke in former days by my servants the prophets of Israel, who in those days prophesied for years that I would bring you against them? But on that day, the day that Gog shall come against the land of Israel, declares the Lord GOD, my wrath will be roused in my anger. (Ezekiel 38:15–18)

"And you, son of man, prophesy against Gog and say, Thus says the Lord GOD: Behold, I am against you, O Gog, chief prince of Meshech and Tubal. And I will turn you about and drive you forward, and bring you up from the uttermost parts of the north, and lead you against the mountains of Israel. Then I will strike your bow from your left hand, and will make your arrows drop out of your right hand. You shall fall on the mountains of Israel, you and all your hordes and the peoples who are with you. I will give you to birds of prey of every sort and to the beasts of the field to be devoured. You shall fall in the open field, for I have spoken, declares the Lord GOD. (Ezekiel 39:1–5)

"Look among the nations, and see; wonder and be astounded. For I am doing a work in your days that you would not believe if told. For behold, I am raising up the Chaldeans, that bitter and hasty nation, who march through the breadth of the earth, to seize dwellings not their own. (Habakkuk 1:5–6)

You went out for the salvation of your people, for the salvation of your anointed. You crushed the head of the house of the wicked, laying him bare from thigh to neck. Selah (Habakkuk 3:13)

God has the ability to lead all history toward His desired ends even though heavenly and human beings constantly make decisions to resist Him. And even when we resist God, it does not have to be final. We can turn in repentance and be forgiven.

Peter understood this because his greatest personal failure had brought him into his calling. He was called to be a pastoral leader in the Church, but he was too arrogant and strong to serve the people. After the humiliating failure of denying Jesus three times, Peter's arrogance was broken. Ironically, this failure transformed him. Then he could be a gentle and compassionate leader capable of "feeding the sheep." Accordingly, when Jesus came to Peter to restore him, Jesus did not simply forgive Peter. He called Peter to fulfill His assignment once Peter's arrogance had been broken.[4]

Paul spoke in a similar way in Romans when he boldly said that even Israel's failures had brought about profound blessing for the world.[5] The reason was simple: God had already decreed that Israel would be a blessing to the nations. Israel is a blessing when she walks before God in righteousness *and* when she fails because her calling is to be a blessing to the nations. God's sovereignty is so intense that even Israel's failures bring about blessing for the nations because that is Israel's calling. And Paul also reminded the Romans to not be arrogant because Israel's "failure" would not be the final word. If God can sovereignly use Israel's failure, how much more can God fulfill Israel's promises and bring about a glorious end to Israel's story?[6] The story is simply not finished yet.

The issue of sovereignty is not vague in Scripture. It is perfectly stated and yet impossible to comprehend. *And that is the point.* A

---

4. John 21:15–17.
5. Romans 11:11–12, 15.
6. Romans 11:15.

biblical study of sovereignty should lead you to worship just as it did the apostle Paul:

> Oh, the depth of the riches and wisdom and knowledge of God! How unsearchable are his judgments and how inscrutable his ways! "For who has known the mind of the Lord, or who has been his counselor? Or who has given a gift to him that he might be repaid?" For from him and through him and to him are all things. To him be glory forever. Amen. (Romans 11:33–36)

If your understanding of God's sovereignty has not yet led you to worship and wonder, *you have missed the point.* If you are lost in an analysis of data and a search for answers that your mind can comprehend, you are trying to bring God down to your level and form a God in your own image that you can manage and explain. But we are dealing with Someone divine whom we cannot fully grasp. His sovereignty is something we can describe and wonder at but not fully comprehend because He is God.

This subject is far more important that you may realize because many of us have a distorted, limited view of God. We believe the future of the world is in the hands of spiritual powers or humans which in fact God sits enthroned above it all. Until you realize that, you have a very distorted view of reality.[7]

Sovereign Election

The subject of divine sovereignty forces us to face some of the most difficult questions about divine election. As we have already seen, God often elects a person we would not choose. When God does this, we can search in vain for some reason for God's election. We want to see "why" God chose this person. This search for "why" is a symptom of a deeper issue. It is a symptom of our humanism.

---

7. For more on this, see the book, *Have You Been Blinded? Facing Your Assumptions about God's Leadership.*

We assume God must choose people on the basis of their qualifications and what things they have to offer; therefore, when He chooses someone, we keep looking for things that demonstrate why God chose that person. Even when a person like Jacob or David demonstrated great failure, we search for positive qualities that led him to "deserve" God's election. We make a case that they were a good choice in spite of their weaknesses and were deserving, therefore, of God's choice. Our desperate search for some reason for divine election is pure and simple humanism and self-righteousness.

Because of our human insecurity, we cannot face the fact that we have nothing to offer God, and He desires us simply because He desires us. We, on the other hand, are transactional. We choose relationship with people based on the benefits we hope to receive. We give something to help another looking for something in return. We choose relationship with other people based on what they can give in return. And when they are not helpful to us in some way, we let the relationship go.

We cannot imagine God choosing without having some benefit in mind. We cannot imagine a God who chooses the disqualified. When we see virtues emerge in the lives of those chosen, we immediately assume these virtues were the basis of God's choosing rather than recognizing that perhaps these virtues were the result of God's choosing instead. Perhaps God has now prepared this person to serve His divine purpose, and this is the reason for their visible virtues.

Our humanism is so deep, we assume every honor and exaltation must be deserved in some way. And this causes us to stumble over the issue of election.

God's election is *sovereign*. He does it because He does it. He does not look at humans transactionally, looking for the "best option" to advance His purposes. He can advance His purposes through His enemies who oppose Him. He looks and He chooses whom He chooses. And then He enjoys working with the disqualified and working His work through them. The virtues we think are the basis of His choosing are really the expression of His work through the person that He already chose on the basis of His desire, not on the basis of that person's supposed "virtues."

God obviously enjoys rewarding His people for their response toward Him.[8] Rewards are a major theme in the Bible, and we do well to study the subject. It means a lot to God when people respond to Him. But we cannot confuse election with rewards. When we do, we inevitably end up in humanism. And the truth is our thinking is much more humanistic than we want to acknowledge.

God uses election to confront our humanism. The search for "reasons" for election, therefore, is in vain. God does not want to prop up your humanism. He wants to shatter it. And election is one of the ways He does that.

For example, there are some beautiful traits that emerge in Jacob later in his life, and many people use that to make an argument that Jacob was a "good choice." But this misses what the Scripture itself tells us. As we have seen, Jacob was born grabbing at his brother's heel in a clear allusion to Genesis 3. Paul explained the election of Jacob very simply:

> *And not only so, but also when Rebekah had conceived children by one man, our forefather Isaac, though they were not yet born and had done nothing either good or bad—in order that God's purpose of election might continue, not because of works but because of him who calls—she was told, "The older will serve the younger." (Romans 9:10–12)*

The "purpose of election" was demonstrated when Jacob was called *before* he could do anything good or bad. In other words, God did not look for qualities in Jacob that made him worthy of his election. To suggest that is to propagate a humanistic way of thinking. Jacob had nothing to offer God. God simply chose him because God is God and He wanted to choose Jacob.

This is why God demands we respect His choices. If God had

---

8. Matthew 5:11-12; 6:19–21; 10:41–42; Luke 6:35; 1 Corinthians 3:8; Philippians 3:14; Colossians 3:23–24; Hebrews 11:6; 2 John 1:8; Revelation 22:12.

chosen Jacob based on some virtues in Jacob, we would only have to respect the choice when Jacob demonstrated those virtues. But God did not choose on this basis. Therefore, we must respect God's election when Jacob does "good" *and* when Jacob does "evil."

For example, many say we should respect Israel for a number of reasons. Some of the reasons include the many good things that God has brought through the Jewish people. And, yes, we should acknowledge those things as gifts of God given to us through the story of Israel. However, these "good things" have nothing to do with why we respect God's choice of Israel. We respect God's choice because we fear God. If Israel does nothing good, we are still required to respect the choice because we fear the God who chose her.

If we only respect or love Israel because of the good she does or the benefits we receive, we are being transactional with Israel. Transactional relationships are always fragile because, at some point, you may question whether the benefits of the relationship are worth the cost. This is why many marriages fail. At some point, people decide the benefits of the marriage are not worth the costs. But God is not transactional, and He wants to shatter our transactional thinking.

God is looking for a people who will respect His election of Israel, and the other ways He elects, because they respect Him, not because of the benefits that accrue from their respect of that election. Jesus "respected" our election in the sense that, instead of leaving us in our condemned state, He gave His life and permanently scarred His body so we could walk in our election. What's more, He is looking for a people who think like Him—a people who so deeply agree with God's divine election they are willing to give their lives to see the "disqualified" walk in their election. He is looking for a people who are willing to lose their lives to honor His election rather a people who want to honor election only for the sake of blessing and benefits. Unfortunately, much "support" for Israel is based on this premise. But it is transactional and hollow. And the Jewish community knows it, which is why so many of them feel that, if there is any trouble, their gentile "friends" will abandon them.

If a marriage shows us what it means to honor covenant, then prostitution shows the true nature of transactional relationships. Each side seeks the lowest price for the maximum benefit. And this is where you inevitably end up if you "honor" election primarily for the sake of your own perceived benefits. Of course, God will bring benefits through His plan of election because His plan always produces blessing. But we do not respect election on the basis of benefit. We respect it because we respect God.

Divine sovereignty and election are deeply connected.

The failure to respect sovereign election is at the heart of Christianity's failures with regard to the Jewish people. The tragic and, at times, horrifying history between the institutional church and the Jewish people was only possible because of a failure to respect sovereign election. For example, some theologians propagated an idea the Jewish people had been "replaced" (rejected) because of their failures. This completely ignores the whole foundation of divine election. God never chose Israel based on her performance; instead, He clearly stated the opposite.[9] He placed His affection on Israel when she was a small, stubborn people committing sin with a golden cow idol.

If God did not choose Israel on the basis of performance, why would He reject Israel for performance? To say this is a denial of the very heart of the gospel.

At times over the last 2,000 years, the Jewish people have been ignored, tolerated, and even persecuted because of a lack of respect for divine election. In reality, respect for God's election of Israel is not based on the benefits that honoring the people of Israel may bring. And respecting God's election of Israel has nothing to do with whether or not Jewish people have embraced Jesus.

Respecting God's election of Israel is about one thing: respecting God on the basis of the fact that He is God and it is His choice.

While the failures of institutional Christianity must be faced and acknowledged, the book of Genesis also gives us profound hope. Our rejection of God's election can be healed. The same brothers who

---

9. Deuteronomy 7:7–8; 9:4–5.

raged against Joseph were ultimately saved by him and came into blessing through their submission to God's election. Like the story of Jacob's family, our story does not have to end with offense. It can end with blessing and reconciliation.

Jesus made this point in Matthew 24:30 when he referenced Zechariah 12:10–12 to predict that His Jewish kinsman would be reconciled to Him in the end, and we can take this principle as a great hope for the future. Just as Jesus will not always be rejected, Christianity's rejection of Israel's unique election will not ultimately last. God will bring about repentance and profound transformation. Gentiles will joyfully agree with and cooperate with God's divine election of Israel.

9

THE CHALLENGE OF SOVEREIGN ELECTION

WE NOW COME to another great challenge of sovereign election: *At times, those chosen by God seem to advance God's purposes through their sin.* If we do not face this, we can easily get offended with God's election.

Let's summarize what we have already said about sovereignty:

- God leads history, and He will get what He wants.
- God leads history through the actions of sinful humans. Humans sin and even oppose God, and yet God uses it to accomplish His purposes.
- God cares about sin, so even when it accomplishes His purposes, He still judges humans for sin and calls them to repent for their sin.
- God elects on the basis of His own decisions. He does not choose people because they are virtuous. The one He chooses, like everyone else, will sin, and even their sinful choices can and will advance God's purposes—not because of who they are, but because their God-ordained purpose functions on the basis of God's choosing and not their ability.

This part of God's leadership may be even more controversial than God's election, but it is demonstrably true. And it is part of Jacob's story.

Jacob was chosen by God before he was born, yet the story of Jacob obtaining this blessing was dramatic and suspenseful all the way to the moment of blessing. We know from the beginning that Jacob would receive the blessing and that the blessing must be given to him by Isaac because the blessing flowed through Isaac's line. Yet Isaac did not want to give Jacob the blessing. Instead, Isaac was determined to give the blessing to Esau. Based on the biblical chronology, Jacob was well over age 40 when Isaac blessed him. So even though the story can be read quickly, Jacob had waited decades for his father to change his mind and give him what God had already declared belonged to him. This is why the blessing encounter in Genesis 27 was so tense and why Rebekah finally decided to act decisively in deceiving her husband.

When we read Genesis 27, we already know Jacob must receive the blessing. But the question is *how?* Isaac was determined to give it to Esau. Isaac seemed to be dying, which meant time was running out. If Jacob did not act, what would happen? Should Jacob stand by quietly and wait for God to act the way David would wait for God to deal with Saul? Or should Jacob or Rebekah confront Isaac about the word God had already spoken? Perhaps they had already confronted Isaac, and Isaac had already refused to listen to them.

Even the fact that Isaac was blind in the scene pointed to divine sovereignty. Isaac was clearly "blind" to what God wanted or had chosen to refuse what God clearly wanted. So it seemed as though God had blinded Isaac so Isaac could not do the very thing he was committed to because, if Isaac had not been blinded, he would not have blessed Jacob. Even in the blessing, Isaac questioned Jacob because he was suspicious Jacob might try to take what Isaac wanted to give to Esau. He knew there was conflict in the family over the blessing. In the end, his blindness was what accomplished God's purpose.

When Isaac questioned how Jacob had so quickly prepared a

meal, Jacob claimed it was a result of divine favor. Jacob blamed his deception on God:

> But Isaac said to his son, "How is it that you have found it so quickly, my son?" He answered, "Because the LORD your God granted me success." (Genesis 27:20)

The dramatic flow of the story makes it appear as though Jacob's sin was almost necessary to secure his blessing. And yet Jacob suffered for his sin, demonstrating it was, in fact, sin. This is the challenge of God's sovereign leadership over history and how He uses our sinfulness. Jacob sinned, and yet it almost seemed his sin was necessary to fulfill what God had spoken. So God stood by Jacob's election though He also disciplined Jacob for what Jacob did, and Jacob's sin created trouble in his own family.

Furthermore, in all his deceptions, it is abundantly clear that Jacob really, really wanted what God had given him. He valued it differently than Esau did. Esau wanted the blessing, but Jacob longed for it. There was something so deep in Jacob that he would literally do anything to secure the promise that was made to him. This desire expressed itself in sinful and devious ways, and God had to break Jacob's strength, but even in his sinfulness, we see God had put a longing deep in Jacob's heart that would be necessary to endure what was required to obtain and maintain the promise. Jacob and the people of Israel, even in sinfulness, clung to a divine promise. That tenacity is the very thing required to steward the promise.

While Jacob fought for the promise, though Esau desired it, Esau also "despised" his birthright[1] and was willing to trade it for soup. Esau also chose wives who were outside the family. God would be perfectly right to elect even if Esau deeply desired the birthright, but in the story, we find that Esau did not long for what had been given to him with the tenacity Jacob did. So it was not as though Esau was

---

1. Genesis 25:29-34.

perfectly qualified and God took something from him and gave it to Jacob. Neither brothers were qualified.

In the end, Esau was blessed and content with what God had given him. He was glad to see Jacob receive the blessing that Jacob was destined to receive. Esau's reconciliation with Jacob gives us a prophetic glimpse of the future when the nations have abandoned their offense over God's election of Jacob:

> This view of the reconciliation between Jacob and Esau, Israel and Edom, is an important element in the future hope of the later Prophetic Books. It is a picture of the ultimate fulfillment of God's promise to Abraham: "In your seed all the families of the earth will be blessed" (12:3). Such a view seems firmly rooted in the theological structure of the ... narrative.[2]

The reconciliation of Esau and Jacob pointed forward and made a strong point that the offense at election was a temporary situation that causes sin and rage both in those not chosen and in those chosen. But it was not the end of the story. God would resolve the offense. This gives us the hope necessary to boldly confront our offense, and other's offense, over election.

God's election is not an issue of "justice." It is an issue of God's right to be God and choose as He wishes. He is under no obligation to justify His choices to us. Neither the chosen nor the unchosen deserve God's choosing.

Theologian John Sailhamer summarized the account of Jacob the following way:

> The point is not that the struggles were necessary for the accomplishment of the will of God, but rather that God's will was accomplished in spite of the conflict.... The point of the narrative is to reiterate the portrait of Jacob that has been central throughout these stories. That portrait is of a man who planned and schemed for what

---

2. John H. Sailhamer, *The Pentateuch as Narrative: A Biblical-Theological Commentary*, ed. Gary Lee (Grand Rapids, MI: Zondervan Publishing House, 1992), 192.

appeared to be his own gain, but who in the end actually accomplished God's purposes.... The writer's purpose is not to approve these human plans and schemes but to show how God, in his sovereign grace, could still achieve his purpose through them.[3]

The elect also face their own offense of God's leadership when they acknowledge that God leads them into their own suffering to accomplish their assignment. As we have already seen, Joseph, as one chosen by God, plainly acknowledged God's leadership of history in his own suffering. Again, Sailhamer comments:

In his words of explanation and comfort to his brothers, Joseph returns once again to the central theme of the narrative: though the brothers were responsible for Joseph's being sold into Egypt and though they intended "evil," God was ultimately behind it all and had worked it out for the "good." As he told his brothers, "God sent me before you to save life," and, "God sent me before you to preserve for you a remnant in the land and to save your lives." ... Joseph's words pull back the narrative veil and allow the reader to see what has been going on behind the scenes. It was not the brothers who sent Joseph to Egypt—it was God. And God had a purpose for it all. We have seen numerous clues throughout the narrative that this has been the case, but now the central character, the one ultimately responsible for initiating the plots and subplots of the narratives, reveals the divine plans and purpose behind it all. Joseph, who can discern the divine plan in the dreams of Pharaoh, also knew the divine plan in the affairs of his brothers. Through it all he saw God's plan to accomplish a "great salvation."[4]

This interaction between sovereignty and humans is simply more than we can grasp humanly speaking, which is why it led Paul to worship in Romans 11:33–34. *This is the mystery of sovereignty. The elect,*

---

3. John H. Sailhamer, *The Pentateuch as Narrative*, 185, 200.
4. John H. Sailhamer, *The Pentateuch as Narrative*, 223.

like everyone else, can actually advance God's divine purpose through their sin. And yet God does not endorse that sin because sin is a reflection of unbelief.

Jacob both sinned and accomplished God's purpose. And God gives us His story with Jacob to force us to grapple with His leadership. It can be extremely offensive because we tend to disqualify the elect when they sin. We assume that the elect cannot advance God's purposes when they sin. Yet they can. Because any human can advance God's purposes through their sin. It is simply more controversial when the elect sin because it seems as though their sin contributes to their God-ordained exaltation. We will still suffer for their sin, but in the mystery of God's sovereignty, He will accomplish His work through obedience *and* disobedience. This does not mean sin is okay. It means God's sovereignty over His creation is so strong that sin cannot break it.

As offensive as this may seem, it is deeply tied to God's commitment to partner with humanity. God will accomplish His work through human partners even though those partners are sinful. So, in one sense, this is the only option God has. If He only worked through perfect partners, He would not have any. Therefore, He does work through sinful partners, and we repeatedly see that these partners are disciplined for their sin, clearly demonstrating God does not excuse sin, but He still accomplishes His work through it.

We are invited to look into God's story in the past, present, and the future and see how God uses sin, failures, and successes to advance His purposes and transform His people. He is typically much, much more merciful than we would expect Him to be, and when we are offended at His "mercy" toward the elect, it exposes something in us, namely a lack of awareness of just how much mercy we have received.

When God uses the sin of the elect to advance His purposes, it is an expression of His mercy. He is not giving people what they deserve. God's leadership in this way is only offensive to us if we do not view ourselves through the lens of mercy. The truth is God has given us extreme mercy. We have not received what we deserve. Thus, if someone else receives what they do not deserve from God, why should that offend us? We have received abundant mercy, and that abundant mercy should cause us to *delight* when God gives undeserved mercy to another and advances their calling through their failures rather than cutting them off for their failures.

Offense over election demonstrates a blindspot. If you truly believe you have received undeserved mercy, it will not bother you to see God give others undeserved mercy.

PART III

THE ROOT OF IT ALL

10

IT ALL BEGINS WITH ENVY

IT IS NOW time to answer some foundational questions:

- Why is election so offensive?
- Why does God demand we respect His election?
- Why did the first sin outside the garden revolve around envy?
- Why is the anger and offense between Jew and Gentile (elect and non-elect) presented as the fundamental human conflict in the Bible?
- Why do so many of the stories of Genesis (and the rest of the Bible) revolve around a conflict based on envy?
- Why does God repeatedly seem to choose the younger brother or the one we feel is less qualified?
- Why does the Bible begin with stories of envy over God's choosing and also warn that the age ends with rage against Israel's election?

It is time to see why election and envy are so foundational in the biblical story. The reason is quite simple: *Envy is at the root of sin in this age.* This may be a surprising idea, but if you do not understand this, you will miss much of why God cares so much about election. And you will also fail to realize that, when we dismiss divine election, we are unwittingly cooperating with the satan. This is especially important because it has become common to dismiss the election of Israel as a mere artifact from the past and conclude that God now "loves everyone" and that "love" means He does not continue to choose and elect some for unique purposes. This idea sounds right to many people, but it is completely wrong.

God uniquely chose and gifted Israel for the sake of the nations. God's *love* for the nations was connected to His election of Israel. So why would He then, thousands of years later, "love" the nations by eliminating His unique election of Israel?

People endlessly repeat the idea that love for all peoples means there is no unique election of a people, and yet the idea that love means there is no unique election is obviously false because the subject of election is not limited to Israel. It is a pervasive part of all our lives. For example, in every congregation, we can see people chosen and gifted for a certain task. Some are gifted to lead and to teach. Others can lead music. There are numerous gifts in the congregation that are given, not on the basis of what people deserve, but simply on the basis of God choosing—or electing:

> *Now there are varieties of gifts, but the same Spirit; and there are varieties of service, but the same Lord; and there are varieties of activities, but it is the same God who empowers them all in everyone. To each is given the manifestation of the Spirit for the common good...All these are empowered by one and the same Spirit, who apportions to each one individually as he wills. (1 Corinthians 12:4–7, 11)*

The truth is we are equally valued but obviously not equal in gifting and function. To say otherwise is ridiculous. Do all have the same spiritual gifting? Do all have the same assignment in the Church? Obviously not. Do all have the same intellectual or athletic ability? Of course not. People are made differently. God uses these differences for certain redemptive purposes, but these differences do not mean that God loves the gifted and does not love others.

The dismissal of God's unique election of individuals and peoples for a redemptive purpose has an evil origin. Most people who hold to this idea believe it because it sounds right, and they are not necessarily trying to consciously oppose God. But the rejection of divine election is a deep deception, and it is time to expose the deception and see why election, envy, offense, and conflict are so prominent in this age.

When you read the beginning of Genesis very carefully along with other Scripture, a clear picture emerges very quickly. We find that the conflict over election began before the well-known family conflicts of Genesis. It began in the very beginning of the beginning.

We Must Begin at the Beginning

In the ancient, cultural context of the biblical world, customarily, the eldest son would become the leader of the family. It was normal and expected, and this is one reason why God's election in the Hebrew Bible was often so controversial. God not only chose "unqualified" people, He frequently chose those who were not the firstborn. If you do not live in a culture that prioritizes the firstborn, it can be difficult to understand just how controversial this was. God loves to choose the weak over the proud and the strong.[1]

God frequently chose the younger one who was less mature and experienced to carry the weight of the family. And the sinfulness of this age was set into motion when God overturned the expected order at the very beginning of creation.

In Genesis 1, we find an account of God's creation. In this account, there is another creative act that is not explicit, and that is the creation of the spiritual powers. These are powerful and majestic spiritual beings that are commonly referred to simply as *angels*. The title *angel* is a bit simplistic because it means "messenger" and

---

1. 1 Corinthians 1:27-29.

describes a function, but we will use that term because it is commonly used to describe glorious, spiritual creatures who serve (and oppose) God's purposes but do not have physical bodies like humans. We will use that term interchangeably with the term *spiritual powers,* which is another way the Bible references these creatures.[2]

There is little debate on when the powers were created, and we will not spend much time on that. God does not give us much information about them, but they were created before the earthly creatures described in Genesis 1–2. Some believe there are hints to their creation in Genesis 1, but that is beyond the scope of our study.

Let's look at a clear reference to the powers in Genesis 1:

Then God said, "Let us make man in our image, after our likeness. And let them have dominion over the fish of the sea and over the birds of the heavens and over the livestock and over all the earth and over every creeping thing that creeps on the earth." So God created man in his own image, in the image of God he created him; male and female he created them. (Genesis 1:26–27)

Some assume "Let us make" refers to the Trinity, but the language is not the language of one God in multiple Persons, but it is the language of multiple persons. We know this because the verb *make* in verse 26 is plural. In context, most scholars agree God is speaking to the spiritual powers He has already made and involving them in His

---

2. In the Hebrew Bible, the spiritual powers that are typically referred to as "angels" by most Christians are called "elohim" (אֱלֹהִים.) In many Bible translations, this word is translated as "gods" because the word describes a powerful spiritual being. The word can be used in a singular way to describe God as the ultimate spiritual being and many people are familiar with God being called "Elohim." However, biblically this word is also used to describe other kinds of powerful spiritual beings because it is not a proper name but a word used to describe a powerful spiritual being. "Spiritual powers" is a way of translating "elohim" in English. These creatures are not uncreated and all powerful like God, but they are spiritual beings and many seem to have a dimension of power which is different from what humans were given. Biblically God is described as the "Elohim of (all) elohim" (See Deuteronomy 10:17; Psalm 136:2; Daniel 2:47; 11:36.)

stewardship of creation. The Hebrew Bible also calls these powers, "sons of God,"[3] because they reflect the image of God to some extent. In verse 27, we are told God "created," and the verb *created* is singular, indicating there is only One who can create from nothing. So God invited the "us," or the heavenly powers, to be involved in His creation, but He alone can create from nothing. Again, this is apparently because *make* is plural in verse 26 while *created* in verse 27 is singular.

Job also described these heavenly powers rejoicing as God created:

"Where were you when I laid the foundation of the earth? Tell me, if you have understanding. Who determined its measurements—surely you know! Or who stretched the line upon it? On what were its bases sunk, or who laid its cornerstone, when the morning stars sang together and all the sons of God shouted for joy?" (Job 38:4–7)

The main point we must recognize is that, by the time humans were created, God had already created majestic and glorious spiritual powers. The book of Hebrews summarizes the assignment God gave these creatures:

Of the angels he says, "He makes his angels winds, and his ministers a flame of fire."... Are they not all ministering spirits sent out to serve for the sake of those who are to inherit salvation? (Hebrews 1:7, 14)

These creatures appear periodically in the Scripture, and when they do, people are nearly always terrified. Their appearance can be majestic, intimidating, and even terrifying. They seem to inhabit another realm of power, might, and intelligence from the realm we inhabit. When humans encounter their might and glory, they immediately feel inferior, which is key to understanding the creation account.

---

3. Genesis 6:2; Job 1:6; 2:1; 38:7; Psalm 29:1; 82:6.

For a minute, let's imagine what it would have been like to watch God create. Regardless of how you read Genesis 1:26, at some point, God created spiritual beings and gave them incredible power and beauty. They displayed a measure of the glory of God, and they were not bound by the restrictions of a physical body or the earth realm. They could operate in the heavens and on the earth, and travel between the two. They were terrifying and yet glorious. They were so impressive that it explains why they were called the "sons of God" in the Hebrew Bible. An ancient reader of Genesis would recognize these creatures as the "elder brothers" of creation.

But God did not stop after He made these creatures. He kept going. After forming the heavenly realm and the creatures that inhabit it, God put His focus on the earth. And then He began to form earth creatures day by day. He made truly impressive and intriguing creatures. Some could swim the seas. Others could soar through the sky. Yet others were bound to the land. Each had a glory all its own. When God was finished making every creature, He decided to make one last creature.

God started with some dust from the earth, which is the most humble thing imaginable. It is lowly, without any beauty, and lacks any of the glory of the heavenly realm. God took the dust and made one last creature that he called "man." And then there was a shocking surprise: This creature did not have the glory the angels were given, and yet this "man" bore the image of God in a unique way.

The Youngest Will Be Exalted

There are some things immediately apparent in Genesis when you read them in context. First of all, we have to recognize that humans are the *last* creature formed in the creation account. Because we are humans and naturally self-centered, we can easily miss this detail. We assume God saved the best for last, but in the culture of the Bible, the order puts man in a *lower* place than the rest of creation.

Remember the spiritual powers are described as the first sons of God in the Hebrew Bible. In fact, they are the only ones called this in the Hebrew Bible.[4] Culturally, in the world of the Bible, the eldest are the ones given superior privilege because they have greater responsibility for the family. As we have already seen, God frequently inverts this social order to make the point He can choose whomever He wants.

Both the angels and humans bear the image of God to some extent in the biblical account, but the angels are essentially the first-born in this narrative. They are the eldest. And human encounters with angels clearly demonstrate they are more powerful and wise than humans. Yet it is clear that this human was destined for a place of honor that was very different from what was given to the angels.

The creation of man is the first major inversion in the biblical story. The one who comes last and is not as qualified as the ones created earlier is elected to become the exalted one. In context, it is unthinkable.

David expressed his own wonder at this inversion in Psalm 8. He marveled that humans, created lower than heavenly beings, were given dominion:

> *What is man that you are mindful of him, and the son of man that you care for him? Yet you have made him a little lower than the heavenly beings and crowned him with glory and honor. You have given him dominion over the works of your hands; you have put all things under his feet. (Psalm 8:4–6)*

Daniel also described the exaltation of the saints by comparing them to the stars. In the ancient world, the heavenly powers were compared to stars, so this was a statement of God's intention to exalt the lower, dirt creature to a place like the heavenly powers:[5]

---

4. This is why it is so shocking for redeemed humans to be described as "sons of god" in the New Testament (Matthew 5:9; Luke 20:36; John 1:12; Romans 8:14–17, 19, 23; 9:26; 2 Corinthians 6:18; Ephesians 1:5; Galatians 3:26; 4:5–7; Philippians 2:15; 1 John 3:1–2; Revelation 21:7.) This phrase was used to describe spiritual powers in the Hebrew Bible, but it is assigned to redeemed humans in the New Testament, indicating the future of redeemed humanity is much greater than we may imagine.

5. See also Proverbs 4:18; Matthew 13:43; 1 Corinthians 14:40–42; Revelation 1:20; 2:28.

And those who are wise shall shine like the brightness of the sky above; and those who turn many to righteousness, like the stars forever and ever. (Daniel 12:3)

Imagine the angels watching creation unfold. Day by day, they watched God create and form new types of creatures. As God told Job, they "shouted for joy"[6] as God's creation was revealed. Each creature was unique and had a beauty of its own, but as expected, none of these creatures matched the glory and majesty of the heavenly powers. Then came the last creature. This last creature, man, was much more humble in essence than the angels. And yet it quickly becomes clear that God had inverted the expected order. He has chosen or *elected* this humble, dirt-based creature to be exalted to a place that is, in some ways, greater than that of the heavenly powers. This creature would become God's companion in a unique way. The humble creature had been chosen over the powerful creature. The ones who were the pinnacle of creation would now be put under a creature that was not qualified for the exaltation God had determined they would have.

The "younger" would be exalted over the "elder." The "weaker" had been chosen over the "stronger." The "humble" creature had been chosen over the "glorious" ones.

The glorious heavenly creatures who were made first and who appeared to be the natural rulers of creation were given a slightly different assignment to become:

"... ministering spirits sent out to serve for the sake of those who are to inherit salvation." (Hebrews 1:14)

The angels were called to serve the exaltation of a creature who did not appear qualified for the role for which they had been chosen. They were called to use their power and majesty to serve and exalt a humble creature. Imagine being given this assignment. The angels

---

6. Job 38:7.

were called to serve a creature who had been chosen to be exalted over them because this creature needed their help. The weaker needed the help of the stronger so that the weaker could be exalted above the stronger. *It was a massive inversion.*

The Bible is written in a deeply integrated way that requires meditation, and stories that come later in the Bible help you interpret previous events. In Genesis, family conflicts over divine election are a major theme, and the stories that follow creation are part of an unfolding narrative in which later stories help interpret previous events. In Genesis, the younger brother is repeatedly chosen over the elder, and this creates family conflicts that involve controversy, envy, strife, and even murder. Because the spiritual powers are the "elder brothers" of creation, we are expected to use the stories of conflict over election after creation to interpret the inversion of Genesis 1–3 and the beginning of sin and conflict.

There are two very interesting aspects of the relationship between the spiritual powers and humans in the book of Genesis. First, it quickly becomes apparent that humans bear God's image in a way the angels do not. This gives us a profound insight into the nature of God because it tells us the lowliness of the human frame can convey the knowledge of who God is in a way that the angels simply cannot. They seem to be too too majestic to fully display who God is. This is the beginning of the revelation that God is humble and lowly, a genuine servant.[7]

Second, God's design for the angels to serve the calling of the man has a profound beauty that is easy to miss if we simply see it as angels have to serve humans. God asked the spiritual powers to use their power and strength to serve the calling of a weaker creature and enable that weaker creature to be exalted to their place. This assignment required humility from the angels. And yet the assignment also has a profound beauty because God, as the most majestic of all, had already determined that He would lower Himself to the lowest place to serve the calling of the human. God asked the angels to do

---

7. Isaiah 42:1; 53:11; Matthew 20:28; John 13:12–15; Philippians 2:6–7.

precisely what He Himself would do. Because we are sinful, we do not think this way, but God does. In God, majesty and power exist to serve the weaker and exalt the weaker to places they cannot reach on their own. This is why God is a servant and loves serving. And He expects the same from His creation because creation was formed to display His image. If we do not display service and humility, we do not display His image.

The assignment God gave to the angels was not simply an assignment of service. It was an invitation to the angels to become like God and to bear His image according to the capacity He had given them. God, as the most powerful, chose to give His life and strength to exalt man, this humble creature, and He invited the angels to become like Him by serving man's calling. Though humans are chosen in that inversion, angels were also destined for greatness.

When God calls us to humility and to serve the purpose of others, it is a command to become like Him.[8]

When the spiritual powers serve their God-given assignment and help the younger brother or dirt creature come into his calling, they display the nature of God, and they are transformed into His image. However, when the powers refuse to cooperate with God, the opposite happens. Instead of growing in new dimensions of the knowledge of God, they become grotesquely disfigured and no longer display the glory they were meant to carry. Their self-centeredness distorts their very being, and they become God's opponent because they chose their own exaltation over divine humility.

Exposing the Arrogance of Our Envy

When we understand the creation in its biblical account, it exposes the arrogance of our offense at God's divine election.

---

8. For example, if you are Jewish, you are called to use your privilege (Genesis 12:3; Psalm 67:1–2; Isaiah 49:6; Philippians 2:6–8) for the sake of others. This is the reason Isaiah describes Israel and Israel's Messiah as God's "Servant" (Isaiah 42; 49; 50; 52.) And if you are gentile, you are also called to use your gifting for the sake of others, including for the sake of God's unique calling on the Jewish people.

When humans encounter angels, they are frequently intimidated and overwhelmed by the glory these creatures have been given.[9] And yet humans have been given a destiny the angels marvel at.[10] It is an incredible inversion! Among all the creatures mentioned in Genesis, we are the creatures who were chosen by God for a unique role that we are completely unqualified for. We are the younger brothers who have been chosen for a redemptive purpose over the older brothers.

When we become offended that someone else is chosen above us, it is incredibly arrogant because, even if we were the least of all humans, we would still be part of a race of disqualified, lowly creatures who have been chosen for exaltation on the basis of God's desire and not our own qualifications. We were made last of all and then given an exaltation that shocked the powers.

It is unbelievable arrogance to be exalted above majestic, glorious creatures and then be offended that someone else may be given a small additional exaltation we were not given. We have already been given something that is impossible to fully comprehend,[11] and we should be filled with unending gratitude for the kindness and glory God has freely given to us rather than offended and bitter that someone else might get something we may not receive.

When we view the glory of our inheritance[12] in context to the biblical narrative, *any* and *all* offense at election is an incredible display of arrogance and envy. It is a human expression of an ancient offense that set into motion the first sin in the age.

---

9. Daniel 8:17; 10:7–8; Luke 1:11–12, 30; Acts 10:3–4.
10. 1 Peter 1:12.
11. Romans 11:33-36; 1 Corinthians 2:9-10.
12. Romans 8:18; 1 Corinthians 2:9-10; 2 Corinthians 4:16-18; Philippians 3:20-21.

11

CORRUPTED BY ENVY

THERE IS much that the creation account does not tell us, but what it does tell us is very intentional. One of the most shocking parts of the creation account is that some of the spiritual powers who were created "fell" or rebelled against God. Some of the elder brothers of creation who were made as sons of God became His enemies instead. The Bible does not describe the rebellion of the sons of God in detail, but it gives us some very clear clues as to what happened. Many people wonder why the Bible does not give us more information about the fall of the satan and the powers, and there are several reasons for this.

First of all, we are not to be fascinated by the fallen powers. They want to pull humans into their rebellion, and they often use intrigue and mystery in an attempt to fascinate us. The Bible tells us what we need to know but avoids details because we are not to be captivated by them. This is why endless theories about the rebellious powers are unbiblical and unhelpful. We do not need to know more about them than what God has told us.

Second, the fall of the satan and everything that accompanied it was a deep betrayal that resulted in the death of every human ever born. The satan was created with great glory to partner with God and instead chose to destroy God's creation out of envy. It is hard for us to grasp how deep this betrayal was. It was so deep we are never given the satan's name. "Satan" is not a name. It is a title which means "adversary" or "opponent." For example, there is one passage where God is described as a "satan" or opponent when He confronts Balaam.[1] In Hebrew, this enemy is called "the satan," which means "the adversary." He is *the* adversary among the spiritual powers. ("Lucifer" is not his name either. That comes from a Latin form of the word for "morning star" that has become traditionally associated with "the satan" even though Jesus is also called the morning star.[2])

Satan's betrayal of his divinely given, and glorious, purpose was so deep that his name is not even given to us.

We are given very little direct information about the rebellion of the powers because that story does not deserve to be told. However, we are given enough information to understand the root of their rebellion so we can repent and avoid the same sin. There are details we do not know, but there is a clear progression in the text that is designed to give us the information we need.

The Beginnings of the Rebellion

Before the creation of man, no mention of any rebellion or conflict in the spiritual realm is made. We have already noted that sons of God are always spiritual powers in the Hebrew Bible, and the book of Job tells us that the sons of God shouted for joy when God began creating:

> *"Where were you when I laid the foundation of the earth? Tell me, if you have understanding. Who determined its measurements—surely you know! Or who stretched the line upon it? On what were its bases sunk, or who laid its cornerstone, when the morning stars sang together and **all the sons of God shouted for joy**?" (Job 38:4–7)*

---

1. Numbers 22:22.
2. Revelation 22:16.

Notice *all* the sons of God shouted for joy when God began His great work of creation in the earth. And as we have seen in Genesis 1:26, God invited the spiritual powers to join Him in His work of creation just before man was created. The book of Genesis confirms this because, day by day as God created, we are told His creation was "good."[3]

God even made "sea monsters" and saw that they were good:

God created the great sea monsters and every living creature that moves, with which the waters swarmed after their kind, and every winged bird after its kind; and God saw that it was good. (Genesis 1:21 NASB)

This is especially significant because the word used here (תַנִּין) is a word that is used throughout the Bible.[4] It is typically translated as sea monster, dragon, or serpent, but later on in the Bible, this word is used as a reference to the satan. However, when God created everything in Genesis, we are told that *everything was very good:*

And God saw everything that he had made, and behold, it was very good. (Genesis 1:31)

Based on the biblical account, right up to the creation of man, there is no mention of any rebellion in the cosmos.[5] But once man was created, and God's purpose for man became apparent in Genesis 2, we suddenly encounter the rebellion of the powers in Genesis 3.[6]

---

3. Genesis 1:4, 10, 12, 18, 25, 31.

4. Genesis 1:21; Exodus 7:9–10, 12; Deuteronomy 32:33; Job 7:12; Psalm 74:13; 91:13; 148:7; Isaiah 27:1; 51:9; Jeremiah 51:34; Ezekiel 29:3; 32:2.

5. Some scholars speculate about other theories of how and when the rebellion of the powers happened, but those theories are out of the scope of this book. Our goal is to understand the message the Bible is telling us based on a plain reading of the text. So we will examine what is plainly and intentionally stated in the text.

6. In Genesis 3:22, God spoke to the spiritual powers that He addressed in Genesis 1 again, and this time, He declared that humans had become like the powers, having knowledge of good *and* evil. Remember some read this as the Trinity, but in context, it is best read as God addressing the same spiritual powers that He spoke to in Genesis 1:26. In Genesis 1:26, the powers were invited to partner with God, but in Genesis 3, the

We are not given all the details, but it is obvious something happened. Some of the sons of God who shouted for joy according to Job 38 instead betrayed God and became His enemies. And the composition of Genesis read in light of later Scripture puts the rebellion between Genesis 2 and 3. These sons of God created in glory were instead condemned to destruction:

> God has taken his place in the divine council; in the midst of the gods he holds judgment.... I said, "You are gods, sons of the Most High, all of you; nevertheless, like men you shall die, and fall like any prince." (Psalm 82:1, 6–7)

Based on the biblical account, this rebellion happened sometime after the creation of man, and that timing is important for interpreting what happened. Up to Genesis 2, everything we are told about creation is glorious. But after God described man's role in Genesis 2, suddenly a rebellion appears.

When you consider the flow of the text, the message is straightforward:

- Spiritual powers were created before the creation of man.
- God continued to create what we call the "earthly" or "physical" realm. It has a beauty to it but is lower in majesty than what we call the "heavenly" or "spiritual" realm.[7]
- God's creation was "good," and all the sons of God rejoiced in what God had made in the heavens and on the earth.
- God finishes His creation with one last creature who is so humble this creature is made of dirt or dust.

---

powers were addressed as knowing good and evil, indicating some of the powers were then evil.

7. The way we think about these divisions is not necessarily biblical. Many people assume a framework of separation between spiritual and physical realms that is more rooted in ancient Greek thinking than the biblical paradigm. Biblical reality is much more integrated than the Greek understanding of reality.

- God began to describe a unique purpose for this last, humble creature. This creature was uniquely made in God's image. God's purpose for this humble creature included dominion over the earthly realm as he ruled on God's behalf. This description also contained hints that the human was destined for exaltation as a unique partner of God's. Genesis began by giving more space to the purpose of man than it did the heavenly creatures, and that alone tells us a lot about the focus of the biblical narrative.

- After man's purpose was unveiled, an evil spiritual power suddenly appeared. This power clearly rebelled against God. And this creature came into the garden to destroy the humans. There was no mention of this creature or his rebellion before God spoke about the calling of man.

Envy Produces Murder

In Genesis 3, a devious, deceptive serpent approached Eve in the garden, and the details in the encounter are significant. First, the Genesis 3 account is a literal account, but this person was clearly more than a snake like we know and understand snakes. For example, this creature spoke to Eve, and she was not surprised in any way by his initiating or carrying on conversation. Animals did not talk in the Bible,[8] and there was no reference to them speaking in the past. So this intelligent, talking serpent was clearly different from a typical animal.

Secondly, Eve was a wise creature made in the image of God for a unique calling, and she was accustomed to interacting with God when He walked in the garden. She was not a simple creature or an animal. She was a very intelligent creature made in God's image to

---

8. Obviously, Balaam's donkey spoke, but the whole point is that this was not normal. It was bizarre and shocking. It was very different from Eve's encounter (Numbers 22:28–30.)

rule the earthly realm. She and Adam were told to take dominion over the animals, so there was no reason for her to submit to a typical beast. When she interacted with the serpent, she considered him to be a wise creature whose counsel should be taken seriously. The consideration she gave to the serpent clearly demonstrated he was a spiritual power who appeared to be wise, intelligent, and trustworthy. Because of how Eve interacted with the serpent, we can conclude she was used to interacting with these kinds of spiritual powers and considered them to be trustworthy. She did not need to ask, "Who are you?" as humans frequently do later in the biblical story when they encounter angelic beings.

The serpent came to Eve with a clear agenda, and when we carefully consider his words, it reveals quite a bit about him. The serpent began by questioning God's goodness, and he questioned it in a very specific way. He questioned the limitations God had given Eve. The core of the temptation can be summarized this way: "God has put limits on you. But you can transcend those limits. He wants to hold you back. He wants to limit you to a certain place. But you can choose another place. You can be exalted above the place God has restricted you to. You can become like one of the gods[9] or spiritual powers." The test was about whether or not Eve would accept the place God had given her. Or whether she would choose to exalt herself in her own way to become something other than what God made her to be.

We can already see whispers of an offense, an offense that will become clearer as the story unfolds. The serpent tried to seduce Eve with a test over her purpose, design, and God-given limitations. When we mediate on the serpent's temptation, it seems the serpent himself was offended with limits that had been set for him, and he

---

9. The word *God* is a complex word in Hebrew. It can be used to reference "God" as a unique Person who is superior to all other powers, but it can also be used as a reference to spiritual powers who are clearly not in the same class as the one ultimate God. English translations handle this different ways, but a literal translation of the Hebrew would be *God* when we are speaking of the one true God that is in a category of His own and *gods* when we speak of spiritual powers who are like God because they are powerful, spiritual beings, but they are not God. The word *god* in Genesis 3:5 is plural and can be translated *gods* or *spiritual powers.*

clearly desired an exaltation beyond whatever place God had given him. We already know that God had given humans a place He did not give the spiritual powers, even though they were humble creatures created last. So it is obvious in the serpent's temptation that he was harboring an offense. He did not want to submit to God's sovereignty over his own purpose, and he did not want anyone exalted above him. He came, then, to infect humans with this same discontent.

The serpent then introduced the lie: "God knows, if you eat this forbidden fruit, it will enable you to exalt yourself to become like a god. You are currently just a human. But you can break free of the place God has put you. You do not have to live within the constraints God declared for you."

Out of the mouth the heart spoke,[10] and the serpent's words exposed his own internal conflict. He obviously wanted to rise "above" what was appointed for him and had rebelled in an attempt to break through the restriction God had placed on him. In some way, he had rejected the place God had given him, and he came to Eve to spread the venom of his own offense at the place God had given him. But he also came with something even more devious in mind.

Eve exposed the serpent's devious agenda with her response to his temptation to eat the forbidden fruit, "But if we eat the fruit we will die." The serpent dismissed Eve's concern, but he knew that she would die if she ate the fruit. This is a critical part of the encounter. The serpent did not come to get Eve to join his rebellion. This was not a simple case of, "Join my team. Work with me. I will give you a greater privilege than what God has given you." The serpent was not recruiting Eve or Adam to become part of his "kingdom." He was not here for partnership. He could have tempted Eve and Adam with a number of temptations, but the serpent had one clear agenda in mind: *death.*

The serpent tempted the humans with the same poison that had infected his own soul: the desire to be be exalted to a place that was not appointed for them. But he did not invite the humans to rule with

---

10. Proverbs 4:23; Matthew 12:34-35; Luke 6:45.

him; he wanted them to be destroyed. If his goal were partnership in rebellion against God, he would have chosen another temptation because immortal humans clothed with God's glory would have been much more useful and powerful partners than humans in decaying bodies destined for death. But the serpent did not have any interest in the future of the humans. He went after the only temptation he knew would destroy the humans and leave them unable to fulfill their divine election to be exalted above the powers.[11]

Once humans were dead, the serpent assumed they would never be able to be exalted above him or the other powers.

The serpent was incredibly devious because he tempted Eve with the idea that she could become "like one of the gods."[12] And ironically this *was* her destiny. The serpent knew God would exalt the humans and they would rule the spiritual powers with Him. This is why the serpent used this deception. He knew his offer would appeal to Eve because it was a perversion of her God-ordained future. With the promise of her calling, he seduced her into committing an offense that would kill her and, according to his understanding, leave her unable to fulfill her calling. The serpent infected Eve with his offense by offering her a different version of her destiny than God had in mind.

Offense and accusation often grow when we are discontent with our God-ordained destiny and instead want to live out a God-ordained purpose our way.

Theologians have wrestled with the question of why the serpent targeted Eve, and there are likely multiple reasons, but the serpent's

---

11. The satan's agenda is confirmed throughout Scripture, even at the very end of the Bible in the book of Revelation. In Revelation 12, John sees an apocalyptic vision of Israel as a woman with 12 stars on her head, and the satan is trying to destroy her. Just like in Genesis, he is not trying to lead the elect to join his team. He wants to destroy them.

12. Many English translations translate the serpent's temptation to become *like God,* but the word *elohim* is a plural word that can also be translated *gods.* Contextually in Genesis 3, the temptation is more likely to be "become like one of the spiritual powers" or "gods," not necessarily becoming equal to the one God who sits enthroned above all the powers.

purpose gives insight into one reason why he targeted Eve and not Adam. In Genesis 3:20, Eve is called the "mother of all the living," and the serpent knew that Eve had been given the unique ability to form and create new humans. Because his agenda was the destruction of all humanity so they could never fulfill their predestined purpose to rule, he targeted the human who had the ability to form and create new humans.

God held Adam and Even completely responsible for their rebellion, but the story is very clear that they were seduced and deceived. They knew enough to resist and did not, but they did not suddenly fall into rebellion on their own. This serpent shrewdly and intentionally led them to the death. He had a very strong motive and a very clear objective. He knew exactly what would happen if he succeeded, and he risked everything to destroy the human. In the process, he became the greatest mass murderer in all history. He was a murderer from the beginning:

He was a murderer from the beginning, and does not stand in the truth, because there is no truth in him. When he lies, he speaks out of his own character, for he is a liar and the father of lies. (John 8:44)

The serpent's murderous nature is the fruit of his envy, and when you read Genesis 3 in its full biblical context, the serpent's offense is clear. Envy had taken root in his heart, and he did not want to see the human exalted to a place over him. He could not bear the idea that the "younger" sons of God were chosen for something he had not been chosen for. So there was only one possible option. He would have to destroy the human. He knew humans would die if they ate the fruit.

The satan came to Eve with one purpose: *to become the greatest mass murderer in history.* And he succeeded. He brought about the death of every human who would ever be born. When we read this encounter in light of the rest of Genesis, it becomes even clearer. When a person is offended by God's choice of the other brother, their envy produces a spirit of murder. Whether it is an actual murder in

Cain's case, a desire for murder in Esau's case, or the desire to destroy a person without committing an actual murder as in the Joseph story, envy produces murder in Genesis. And Genesis 3 is the origin of murder, which tells us it is also the origin of envy.

Before we continue, we need to pause and look at the second sin in Genesis–the second story of offense over election that also ended in murder.

12

ELECTION, BLESSING, AND THOSE NOT CHOSEN

THE BOOK of Genesis was carefully written to teach us about the conflict, nature, and purpose of election. It began in Genesis 3, but it is typically done through stories about brothers where God chooses the one whom we would not have chosen. This, of course, immediately causes family conflict.

Our response to election is not ultimately a response to those chosen. It is a response to the God who elects. Therefore, our offense or agreement with election is an offense or agreement with God Himself.

We have looked at the first sin in the garden, and before we continue, we need to look at the first sin outside the garden. When you read the stories together, the message of Genesis becomes even clearer. What's more, it gives us insight into the relationship between the one chosen and the rest. The first sin outside the garden is found in the story of Abel and Cain. This is not precisely a story of election because we do not see Abel sovereignly picked for a divine purpose, but Abel's sacrifice was "chosen," so we see the trace of the conflict over election. Since Abel was the younger brother and Cain was the elder, we can look at their story as another one of the main inversion stories in Genesis, where the one who is chosen by God is not the firstborn.

When we read this story in context, it helps us better understand Genesis 3 and the subsequent stories after Genesis 4:

> In the course of time Cain brought to the LORD an offering of the fruit of the ground, and Abel also brought of the firstborn of his flock and of their fat portions. And the LORD had regard for Abel and his offering, but for Cain and his offering he had no regard. So Cain was very angry, and his face fell. The LORD said to Cain, "Why are you angry, and why has your face fallen? If you do well, will you not be accepted? And if you do not do well, sin is crouching at the door. Its desire is contrary to you, but you must rule over it." Cain spoke to Abel his brother. And when they were in the field, Cain rose up against his brother Abel and killed him. Then the LORD said to Cain, "Where is Abel your brother?" He said, "I do not know; am I my brother's keeper?" (Genesis 4:3–9)

Not Being Chosen Is Not Rejection

There are several foundational issues in this story we must notice before we continue. The first is found in God's response to Cain, "Why are you angry? If you do well will you not be accepted?" In other words, God's acceptance of Abel was *not* His rejection of Cain. God also wanted to receive Cain, delight in him, and bless him. God "had regard" for Abel, but that did not mean He had nothing for Cain.

Just because one is chosen by God for a specific purpose does not mean the others are rejected.

The enemy twists our thinking so that, when a person or a people are chosen, we assume their selection is our rejection. But God does not operate this way. We have already seen that He chooses the elect for the sake of the whole, so He has everyone in mind when He chooses. Furthermore, He desires all and has blessing for all. Everyone does not get the same thing, but there is blessing for those not chosen, and God wants you to enjoy that blessing. This truth is emphasized in the Cain and Abel story because, even after Cain sins in the murder of his brother, God was surprisingly willing to protect Cain.[1]

Our acceptance before God is not tied to whether or not we are chosen. For example, Gentiles who have received incredible blessing from God's election of Israel do not have to become Jewish to receive a blessing from God. We can love and serve the Jewish people as a chosen people, knowing that God enjoys us in our gentile condition. Our job is not to become another people. That is not the path to blessing. In fact, Paul warned believers not to try to take on another people's identity.[2] Instead, we are to rejoice in the identity we have been given. As we honor the election of another, we discover profound blessing is available for us through God's election of someone else. God's selection of one is not a rejection of another. He simply has something different, and He *enjoys us* just as He made us. After all, we had no choice in being chosen or not. The Bible demonstrates that, if God did not choose us for a certain purpose, He has something else in mind for us, which is still important to Him.

God told Cain to do well because he would be received by God and there would be a blessing for him. God's favor toward one did not mean there was no favor for another.

One of the great deceptions in our heart is that life is a zero sum game. If you win, that means I lose something. If you receive honor or privilege, that comes at my loss. We see the success of others comes at the cost of our success, but this is not true. This thinking is the fruit of envy, and it flourishes when we have a distorted view of God. A true view of God recognizes that God made everything to flourish. Your flourishing and my flourishing may not look exactly the same, but I do not lose anything if you succeed, even if you succeed much more than I ever do. Because of envy and selfish desire, we cannot celebrate the successes of others if we think their successes might come at our own expense. This is the fruit of the serpent's venom. It is a distorted view of reality. You know you have conquered envy when

---

1. Genesis 4:14–15.
2. Romans 12:3-5;1 Corinthians 7:21-24.

you can genuinely celebrate other people's achievements as much as your own.

The lie that God's creation is a zero sum game, with limited blessings only available to those who conquer others and exalt themselves, is the very lie that seduced the serpent, and it is very fertile ground for our own envy.

This is the opposite of God's thinking. God elects but does not reject those not elected. In fact, the very act of election is God choosing how to administrate His Kingdom instead of us fighting each other for roles in the Kingdom. God's election is a kindness to us. Instead of a brutal conflict over Kingdom roles, God graciously chooses us and gifts us differently so we can enjoy and serve each other, confident that our place in the Kingdom comes from God's giving, not our own "victories" over each other.

This is displayed most ultimately in Jesus who:

- Gladly laid down His life so that even His enemies could come into the fullness of their calling.[3]
- Challenged His followers that the greatest person is the one who seeks to be a servant and who is not like the people who seek to triumph over others and dominate them.[4]
- Told us that the highest expression of love is the willingness to give our lives for our friends—to lay down our opportunities and futures so others have a chance to pursue the fullness of their own lives.[5]
- Evaluated John the Baptist as one of the greatest of all human beings.[6] John was a prominent, influential national figure who yielded his influence for the sake of Jesus. John was willing to let his influence and prominence fade when he was about thirty years old. John's disciples were bothered by Jesus' prominence, but John delighted in

---

3. Romans 5:8–10.
4. Matthew 20:25-28; Mark 10:42-45; Luke 22:25-27.
5. John 15:13.
6. Matthew 11:11.

Jesus' success even though it came at his expense. John famously rebuked his disciples with powerful words about Jesus' success, "Therefore this joy of mine is now complete. He must increase, but I must decrease."[7]

Sin Is Crouching

God told Cain, "And if you do not do well, sin is crouching at the door. Its desire is contrary to you, but you must rule over it." There is a lot of meaning in this verse that is not immediately apparent in the English translation. The NET translation helps communicate the verse a bit better:

"Is it not true that if you do what is right, you will be fine? But if you do not do what is right, sin is crouching at the door. It desires to dominate you, but you must subdue it." (Genesis 4:7 NET)

God addressed Cain's offense at his brother and told him to do what was right so he would be blessed. You can see God's genuine concern and love for Cain. God also warned Cain that, if he did not respond well, sin was "crouching at the door." This phrase is loaded with meaning as the NET translators explain:

The Hebrew term translated "crouching" (רֹבֵץ, *rovets*) is an active participle. Sin is portrayed with animal imagery here as a beast crouching and ready to pounce (a figure of speech known as zoomorphism). An Akkadian cognate refers to a type of demon; in this case perhaps one could translate, "Sin is the demon at the door."[8]

"The door" is also likely a loaded reference. Remember that in a previous chapter God sent Adam and Eve outside the garden and set

---

7. John 3:29–30.
8. Biblical Studies Press, *The NET Bible First Edition; Bible. English. NET Bible.; The NET Bible* (Biblical Studies Press, 2005).

an angel to guard the way to the Tree of Life. *Door* can also be translated "opening," and with that image in mind, it is possible God gave Cain a warning about a creature who was just outside the opening of the garden, seeking to trap Cain just as he trapped Cain's parents.

Regardless of what the door refers to, Cain was warned that there was a creature, here called sin, that is a crouching beast. Sin sought to dominate Cain, but Cain *had to* subdue him. Remember this story occurred just after the serpent deceived Eve, so this beast was obviously the same person. He was no longer a veiled serpent. This time he was called "sin" and was described as a crouching beast. The beast that deceived Cain's mother was now after him.

This is the second obvious attack of the satan against humans, and we must carefully notice his strategy. In the garden, he was very subtle with Eve because she had not yet fallen. Now, the temptation was more open. He was coming for Cain in a more overt way. He was not seducing Cain with a forbidden pleasure. He had come to exploit Cain's offense at his brother. And Cain knew what happened in the garden. He knew this tempter was a beast. And he knew this beast produced death.

This was the second great sin in Genesis, and the enemy was seeking to dominate Cain over offense at God's choice of his brother's offering.

The beast being called "sin" emphasizes the fact that there was something fundamental about the temptation to envy another who seems to have God's acceptance. God had already guaranteed Cain that he would be accepted if he did well, but He warned Cain that acceptance depended on his ability to resist a beast, really a monster, who wanted to dominate him through envy.

This beast wanted to dominate Cain through envy, but Cain had to rule over him. This implied that the destruction of sin required humans to settle the issue of election. We must see how fundamental this issue is. Envy over election longs to rule over you. It is the tool of the serpent. But you must rule over it. This is why, as we will see, the

Bible warns us the age will end in a massive conflict over Israel's election.[9]

Cain did not dominate the beast and, instead, was disfigured into the snake's image. This theme is so fundamental that it comes back up in the Exodus story. The Exodus was not simply an event. It is the foundational narrative of God's redemption. It is the story that establishes Israel as a people, and it is the story the prophets constantly referred to as a picture and foreshadowing of a future redemption.

The Exodus begins with Moses' encounter with God on Mount Sinai, where he was commissioned to lead the Exodus. Moses was given a number of powerful signs to confront Pharaoh with God's power, and the first one involved a snake. Moses threw down his rod, and it became a serpent. When that happened, Moses ran away from it,[10] indicating the snake was not a small little thing. It was big enough to frighten a grown man. It's obviously a link back to the ancient enemy in the garden that seduced Eve and dominated Cain.

God commanded Moses to pick up the snake by the tail. Moses did not grab the head because he was not to be bitten by the snake and infected by him. And when he picked the snake up, it became a staff again. The message was clear. Moses was shrinking back from the serpent, the image of the ancient enemy from the garden. But he had to rule over it. He had to dominate the serpent.

Deliverance begins with humans who dominate the serpent instead of submitting to him or fleeing from him.

The account of Cain and Abel occurs just a few verses after God warned the serpent there would be great conflict between the seed of the woman and the seed of the serpent, but He would eventually crush the serpent's head:

---

9. Psalm 98; Isaiah 13:8; 34; Jeremiah 30:7; Daniel 7:21-22; Daniel 12:1; Joel 3:1-16; Zechariah 12:2-3; 13:8-9; 14:1-4, 9, 11; Jeremiah 30:5-7; Matthew 24:15-30; Revelation 11:2; 12:13.
10. Exodus 4:3.

I will put enmity between you and the woman, and between your offspring and her offspring; he shall bruise your head, and you shall bruise his heel. (Genesis 3:15)

The Cain and Abel story was put just after this so that you would read it in context to this prophecy. The prophecy of Genesis 3:15 ultimately refers to a "seed of the woman," a human who is miraculously born and defeats the serpent, and an ultimate "seed of the serpent" commonly referred to as the "antichrist" or "the beast." However, the prophecy is also a warning that you can align with the seed of the woman and become like Him, *or* you can choose the way of the snake and become like the seed of the serpent.

If you align with the seed of the serpent, you will seek to "bruise" the chosen one (elect), but in the end, your head will be "bruised" with the serpent. (The word *bruised* can be translated *crushed*.)

This context adds another layer to God's command to Cain. *You must rule over the serpent who seeks to dominate you.* The warning is very serious. If you do not dominate the serpent, he will dominate you. Instead of crushing his head, you will become his "seed." And you will bruise the heel of the one God has chosen when you take on the likeness of the serpent. However, in time, you will be crushed like the serpent. When Cain did not dominate the serpent, he essentially became a (not "the") seed of the serpent. He attacked his brother and came under the influence of the serpent.

My Brother's Keeper

Cain did not rule over sin. Instead, he yielded to it, and sin took dominion over him. In the end, his envy produced murder.

Cain spoke to Abel his brother. And when they were in the field, Cain rose up against his brother Abel and killed him. Then the LORD said to Cain, "Where is Abel your brother?" He said, "I do not know; am I my brother's keeper?" (Genesis 4:8–9)

This horrible story of the first sin outside the garden warns us of the seriousness of tolerating the seed of envy.

Cain's envy produced murder which is a graphic representation of what envy really is. Envy is much more than an emotion. Offense and anger at someone else's position are expressions of murder. We want the other person gone and out of the way. We do not agree that they should be chosen, privileged, or exalted. We do not want them in their place. We do not want them to exist—at least not in their proper place. And to not want someone to exist is the essence of murder. Social norms, consequences, and other things may restrain us from physical murder, but the reality of the spirit of murder remains. Any envy and offense you harbor against the one chosen are expressions of murder. Jesus addressed this directly in the well-known "Sermon on the Mount":

> *You have heard that it was said to those of old, "You shall not murder; and whoever murders will be liable to judgment." But I say to you that everyone who is angry with his brother will be liable to judgment; whoever insults his brother will be liable to the council; and whoever says, "You fool!" will be liable to the hell of fire. (Matthew 5:21–22)*

It is not an accident that the first sin outside the garden is to murder one you are envious of. It's exactly what the serpent did in Genesis 3.

Sin inside the garden began with envy, and sinful life outside the garden began with murder over envy, which means there is something about the root of envy when another is chosen or does well that is foundational to evil in this age. There are many sins Cain could have succumbed to, but it was not just any sin. It was this one called envy. And the one "crouching" wanted to dominate Cain with this sin. Cain was told to rule over it, but he did not.

When he succumbed to sin and followed the crouching one, it was more than just a failure. It set something very dark into motion. The Bible teaches very clearly that humans are designed as an "image" of God[11] in a special way. The idea of being an image means you reflect something else. It is very close to the idea of an idol. An idol is not the "god" worshipped, but it represents that god. Humans are not God, and yet we are called to represent Him and be shaped into visible manifestations of His likeness and character so He can be known in the earth. We humans cannot decide whether to "image" something or not. We will be images of whatever we follow because this is how we are made.

The Bible teaches us plainly that you become what you worship, which is why God repeatedly commands us to worship Him.[12] *This also means when we follow the path of the envious, crouching beast, we become like him.*

People always become what they worship. This is plainly observable. Whatever people give their worship to determines their time, money, lifestyle, etc. God repeatedly rebuked the Israelites for becoming like the gods that they worshipped, and many of God's judgments on Israel were based on Israel becoming like her gods. The most gruesome example may be when Jeremiah predicted mothers would eat their children when Jerusalem was destroyed.[13] The reason for this biblically is very simple. The people had sacrificed their children to false gods. Because their "gods" ate children, they would becaome like them and do the same thing.

If we understand that humans become what they worship, envy becomes even more significant. In the garden, Eve was seduced by a creature who came to her and appeared wise and trustworthy. Cain was also threatened with some kind of beast. The nature of sin was much more obvious outside the garden. And it wanted to dominate him. And the first act of domination was to inflame envy that led to murder. So if we "worship" or agree with this beast, we will become like him just as Cain became like him.

"Sin" wanted Cain to become like him. He wanted to rule over

---

11. Genesis 1:26-27; 5:1–2; James 3:9.
12. Greg Beale's book *We Become What We Worship: A Biblical Theology of Idolatry* is an excellent work on this topic.
13. Jeremiah 19:9.

him, which means he wants to infect Cain, and humanity, with his envy and a spirit of murder. Humans were made to be immortals because of the life of God, but through sin, we now bear the penalty of death. While humans were responsible for their rebellion, the serpent came to Eve with the intent to commit murder. He knew the penalty of sin was death, and he wanted to murder a creature that bore the glory of God.

Genesis 3 contains a devious and seductive form of violence, but it also contains the first act of murder. The serpent knew the penalty was death, and he sought to murder an entire species.

When God confronted Cain over his sin, Cain gave Him a simple answer: *"Am I my brother's keeper?"* Cain's question was very revealing. Sin had taken dominion over him, and he had taken on the image and likeness of the serpent by murdering his brother out of envy.

Cain's question should stop us in our reading to consider his question. Should Cain, as a brother, be responsible for his brother? "Out of the heart the mouth speaks,"[14] and Cain's question exposed his envy. He basically said, "Why should I care for my brother? What concern is he of mine?" When we hear this question, we instantly know something is off.

This question is in Genesis to force us to address it. Are we our "brother's keeper"? Are we, in some way, responsible for others? Are we somehow responsible for the success of those who are chosen when we are not? Are we responsible to guard the calling of Israel (and others)? The obvious answer is *yes,* which means that those who are not "chosen" for a certain thing are in fact called as a "brother's keeper" to support, strengthen, encourage, and work for the success of those called.

It is not enough to say "I am not envious. Let them have the special place they were given." We are to go a step further and do what we can to ensure their success in that special place that we ourselves were not given. *The way of the serpent is to murder the one who is given a special place. The way of God is to actively fight for the*

---

14. Proverbs 4:23; Matthew 12:34-35; Luke 6:45.

chosen one(s) to fully function and succeed in the special place they were given. Remember that is what the serpent was called to do, but he chose the path of envy and became a murderer instead.

How do you know you are free from the root of envy over election? The answer is simple: Are you your brother's keeper? Will you give your strength to serve the success of the elect in their election? The implication of Cain's question was obvious. He was called to help his brother succeed, and the same is true for us.

Cain was challenged by the question of his brother because he did not choose his brother. It is one thing to "keep" the calling of a friend you choose but another thing to contend for a person you did not choose, a person you may also have conflict with. The Lord's question to Cain confronts us all: Do we "keep" the calling of those the Lord chose but we did not choose?

You may ask, "But what about the elect? Are we simply servants of their calling?" While we are called to be more than servants of the elect, we also must remember that giving our lives serving another's calling is part of the imitation of Jesus who emptied Himself out, became a human, and suffered a gruesome death to serve our calling.[15] Jesus' exaltation is inseparably tied to His decision to serve our calling, which means the same is true for us.[16] If we live as servants of another's calling, we are imitating God who serves creation day after day and upholds it with His life and strength. He even bears affliction and suffers with it.[17] Jesus said, if we want true greatness, we will become the "servant of all:"

"The greatest among you shall be your servant." (Matthew 23:11)

And he sat down and called the twelve. And he said to them, "If anyone would be first, he must be last of all and servant of all." (Mark 9:35)

---

15. Philippians 2:5–8.
16. Philippians 2:5–10.
17. Psalm 104:27-28; Isaiah 63:9; Acts 9:4–5; 17:24-25; Colossians 1:16–17; Hebrews 1:3.

Second of all, the Bible makes it very clear that God knows how to deal with the elect so that their calling becomes the blessing it is meant to be. Israel, for example, has suffered more than any other people over millennia because of her calling. We often view election through the lens of privileges because we crave honor. But election comes with great responsibility to produce blessing for others. And God knows exactly how to deal with the elect.

Are You Your Brother's Keeper?

In the story of Cain, we discover the enemy seeks to dominate us through the sin of envy because that is the sin that dominates him. We also discover that the battleground over envy is the key to destroying sin. Because of envy, we try to "kill" the chosen one to secure our own future because we simply cannot trust the God who elects has designed a process that is ultimately for our benefit and blessing.

Murder is the fruit of envy. It may stay under the surface for years, perhaps centuries. But in a moment, it can suddenly erupt in the most graphic forms of violence by people who thought they were "okay."

Sometimes, envy is obvious as it was in the case of Cain. At other times, it is more veiled or sophisticated. Some of the most horrifying examples are disguised in ideas that are "theological." For example, many Christian theologians over the centuries honestly wrestled to understand God's promises to Israel in the centuries after the Diaspora and the destruction of Jerusalem. The New Testament and the apostle Paul's writings made it very clear that Israel remained elect,[18] but the Church did not hold to the apostles' teaching. And in the struggle over Israel, theologies emerged which erased Israel's identity, purpose, and ongoing calling, and those theologies became fruitful ground for a sophisticated envy. They erased Israel's unique election when Jesus, the apostles, and the New Testament clearly did not.

---

18. For example see Romans 11:29.

Do not be deceived. Envy that is not dealt with will produce murder when given time.

Rather than respect Israel's election regardless of Israel's failures, some theologians essentially "killed" Israel theologically, and that theological act ultimately resulted in physical harm, suffering, and murder for the Jewish people. While this is obviously *not* the path of Jesus, and the entire Church did not agree with the persecution of the Jewish people, it is demonstrably true that some in the institutional Church did. In the process, they committed horrific sins against the Jewish people.

Let's consider a few quotes by theologians who remain respected to some extent by most Christians. Martin Luther, who is still respected by most Christians for his role in the Protestant Reformation, wrote truly shocking things about the Jewish people:[19]

"First, to set fire to their synagogues or schools..."

"Second, I advise that their houses also be razed and destroyed."

"I had made up my mind to write no more about the Jews, but their lying and slandering has compelled me to do so."

"We are at fault in not slaying them."

"They are nothing but a devilish, venomous, and poisonous people."

As another example, one of the best known preachers in the early church, John Chrysostum, wrote:[20]

Are they not inveterate murderers, destroyers, men possessed by the devil? Jews are impure and impious, and their synagogue is a house of prostitution, a lair of beasts, a place of shame and ridicule, the domicile of the devil,

---

19. Excerpts from Martin Luther's 1543 treatise *On the Jews and Their Lies.*
20. Homily 4:1

as is the soul of the Jew... As a matter of fact, Jews worship the devil; their rites are criminal and unchaste; their religion a disease; their synagogue an assembly of crooks, a den of thieves, a cavern of devils, an abyss of perdition!

The vast majority of Christians are shocked to read works like these, and they should be. But there have been many more quotes like throughout history, and we must also recognize that, if we do not stand with divine election, we can end up saying and doing things we would never imagine.[21]

Rather than stare into the mystery of God's election, the failure of the election, and the promise of God to bring the elect to a glorious future, theologians painted a distorted version of Israel's failures. Instead of being a "brother's keeper" when it came to Israel, the institutional Church "murdered" Israel's calling and set themselves in the chosen place that Israel had occupied. Over the centuries, the institutional Church failed in that calling and proved no better than Israel had ever been in her calling.

The vast majority of Christian scholars did not intend to set a context for the persecution of the Jews, but a theology that does not respect election is dangerous in ways we simply do not understand, and the Holocaust is the most gruesome demonstration of that. Nazi propaganda tried to utilize statements and teachings that, while horrific, were never intended to support that kind of genocide. Regardless of the theologians' intent, the Holocaust gave us a severe warning: A theology that does not ensure people act as their brother's keeper when it comes to election inevitably creates a vacuum where unimaginable things can suddenly become acceptable when pressure comes.

We cannot be passive about this. We must learn the lesson of the Holocaust because the prophets warned that the age will end with a

---

21. This has been a serious issue throughout church history, and readers are encouraged to educate themselves on the very serious sin of anti-semitism throughout church history. One book to start with is *Our Hands Are Stained With Blood: The Tragic Story of the "Church" and the Jewish People* by Dr. Michael Brown.

severe moment in which the nations will express their envy over Jerusalem and the people of Israel in an unprecedented way. God has given us these verses so we will actively root envy out of our hearts instead of letting it fester or remain undisturbed. The good news is that the Bible predicts God will produce a mature people who have won this battle. They will not only agree with God's election, but they will be willing to suffer for it. They will even use their strength to contend for the elect (especially Israel) to come into the fullness of their blessing and their promises.[22]

Much more is at stake in election and envy than we realize. When you seek to disqualify the elect and take their place, whether you realize it or not, or intend it or not, it contains the seed of murder.

Envy over election is the viral sin that we fail to notice. We are tested by it constantly, though. God tests the nations by Israel, but He also tests us with this issue in our churches, our families, and our neighborhoods. Nearly every area of our lives is touched by the test of envy over election or blessing. The serpent "killed" an entire species out of his envy, and all too often humans unknowingly and knowingly follow the same path.

And, as we have seen, the issues of the last 2,000 years are not new issues. When we read the first and second sin in Genesis in context with the subsequent stories of election, envy, and conflict we can begin to see what the book of Genesis is trying to tell us about sin, the satan, and ourselves. The most we read and meditate, the clearer it becomes.

---

22. For example, this is implied by Matthew 25:31–46 and Revelation 12:13–17, and we will examine this in another chapter.

13

THE ENVIOUS ONE

WE ARE TOLD VERY little about the serpent's fall, but there are times when God breaks out into lament over him.

For example, Isaiah 14 is widely considered a lament over the satan:

> "How you are fallen from heaven, O Day Star, son of the Dawn! How you are cut down to the ground, you who laid the nations low! You said in your heart, 'I will ascend to heaven; above the stars of God I will set my throne on high; I will sit on the mount of assembly in the far reaches of the north; I will ascend above the heights of the clouds; I will make myself like the Most High.' But you are brought down to Sheol, to the far reaches of the pit." (Isaiah 14:12–15)

In this oracle against the "King of Babylon," God suddenly addressed the arrogant one behind the arrogance of Babylon. He was a "Day Star" or a "son of the Dawn." Commentators debate about the origin of this phrase, but it is clearly a reference to a heavenly being.

In fact, "stars" are frequently used to refer to heavenly powers in the Hebrew Bible.[1]

The Messiah is also described as a glorious star:[2]

"I see him, but not now; I behold him, but not near: a star shall come out of Jacob, and a scepter shall rise out of Israel...." (Numbers 24:17)

Daniel was told the saints would shine like the stars:[3]

"At that time shall arise Michael, the great prince who has charge of your people. And there shall be a time of trouble, such as never has been since there was a nation till that time. But at that time your people shall be delivered, everyone whose name shall be found written in the book. And many of those who sleep in the dust of the earth shall awake, some to everlasting life, and some to shame and everlasting contempt. And those who are wise shall shine like the brightness of the sky above; and those who turn many to righteousness, like the stars forever and ever." (Daniel 12:1–3)

The satan understood God's intention to elevate humans to be like the "stars," which were symbols of heavenly beings in the ancient world, and he was enraged at the idea of a lower creature being given an exaltation he wanted. When you read Daniel 12 with Isaiah 14 in

---

1. The messianic deliverer is referred to as a star in Numbers 24:17, so there are multiple themes here of glory and exaltation. And in light of Job 38:7, it is also a reference to this creature's status as an exalted spiritual power, "Where were you when I laid the foundation of the earth?...when the morning stars sang together and all the sons of God shouted for joy?" (Job 38:4, 7). While it's possible "morning stars" refer to creation in general, it is more likely Job used the poetic language of "morning stars" to describe the spiritual powers that rejoiced at creation. For one, they are singing. For another, the stars are not made until day four in Genesis after the foundation of the earth is laid. In addition, morning stars here are poetically parallel to angels as if they are two kinds of spiritual beings. As a result, commentators see this is a reference to spiritual powers. See John E. Hartley, *The Book of Job*, The New International Commentary on the Old Testament (Grand Rapids, MI: Wm. B. Eerdmans Publishing Co., 1988), 495.

2. Jesus is also described as the "morning star" in Revelation 22:16.

3. Jesus made a similar promise in Revelation 2:28, promising to give the morning star to those who overcome.

mind, the root of the conflict is clear. In context, Daniel 12 declares the greatest conflict in history described as a "conflict that is unlike any other conflict." We will look at that conflict in another chapter, but the point here is clear. The end of the great conflict is the exaltation of the saints to become like stars, which means the conflict is an attempt by the satan to *prevent* humans from being exalted like the spiritual powers.

The creature of Isaiah 14 was beautiful and "heavenly" and created with great glory, but he nurtured an offense. He was not satisfied with his glory; he wanted to become like His Creator. Furthermore, both the Messiah and the saints are compared to stars. And the satan wanted to be exalted *above all the other stars,* which is a poetic statement he was not satisfied with his own election as a beautiful creature. The Messiah is a star, and the saints will be exalted like stars, but the satan wanted to ascend to a higher place far above the other spiritual powers, Messiah, and the saints. It's very clear the issue here is envy. The satan wanted exaltation above the place given to others. He did not want them to be exalted above him.

There is a poetry to his judgment. He chose to *ascend* to a place not given to him, so instead he will *descend.* As a result of his rebellion, he has fallen from the heavens and been cast down to the ground and down to *Sheol,* which is the Hebrew word for the place of the dead. This language is an intentional reference to God's judgment in Genesis. In Genesis 3, the serpent came into the garden to "ascend" by destroying humanity, but the human and the serpent were condemned to go down to dust as a result of their rebellion. The serpent led humans into death, so he too will go to the place of the dead. The serpent who seduced the humans will share in the human's judgment.

Ezekiel 28 is another lamentation that is also widely considered to describe the satan's fall:[4]

---

4. There are some who believe this passage is a poetic description of Adam's fall. But the language centers on a heavenly being who corrupts himself over his own beauty and for the sake of his own splendor, a being who deviates from his divine purpose and will come to a dreadful end.

Thus says the Lord GOD: "You were the signet of perfection, full of wisdom and perfect in beauty. You were in Eden, the garden of God; every precious stone was your covering, sardius, topaz, and diamond, beryl, onyx, and jasper, sapphire, emerald, and carbuncle; and crafted in gold were your settings and your engravings. On the day that you were created they were prepared. You were an anointed guardian cherub. I placed you; you were on the holy mountain of God; in the midst of the stones of fire you walked. You were blameless in your ways from the day you were created, till unrighteousness was found in you. In the abundance of your trade you were filled with violence in your midst, and you sinned; so I cast you as a profane thing from the mountain of God, and I destroyed you, O guardian cherub, from the midst of the stones of fire. Your heart was proud because of your beauty; you corrupted your wisdom for the sake of your splendor.... All who know you among the peoples are appalled at you; you have come to a dreadful end and shall be no more forever." (Ezekiel 28:12–17, 19)

Again, we get a similar picture of a beautiful, glorious being who was created in perfection until sin grew in his heart. And that sin was for the sake of his own splendor, meaning he wanted to exalt himself and be the most glorious creature. He clearly did not want his glory to be eclipsed by any other creature. His sin included violence, which describes the murder of all humanity that flowed out of his envious seduction of Eve. He had wisdom or intelligence, but he corrupted both and used them for the sake of his own splendor and humanity's death instead of using them to partner with God in stewarding creation.

Paul reminded Timothy that the satan fell because of arrogance:

He must not be a recent convert, or he may become puffed up with conceit and fall into the condemnation of the devil. (1 Timothy 3:6)

Arrogance (conceit) is the fruit of envy. You cannot be conceited when there is no one to compare yourself to. The satan's condemnation was that he became "puffed up with conceit," thinking himself to be superior to the human creature that God had destined for a unique election and glory. And that led to him challenging God, which is the true root of envy. Envy is not ultimately a challenge of another person. It is a challenge of God Himself who has given different measures to different humans.

James summarized what we have seen in the first few chapters of Genesis, Isaiah, and Ezekiel:

> *But if you have bitter jealousy and selfish ambition in your hearts, do not boast and be false to the truth. This is not the wisdom that comes down from above, but is earthly, unspiritual, demonic. For where jealousy and selfish ambition exist, there will be disorder and every vile practice. (James 3:14–16)*

James sternly warned the Church not to take on the way of the satan. "Bitter jealousy [envy] and selfish ambition" perfectly describe the satan's conflict with God and humanity. James reminded the Church this is not divine wisdom but *demonic* wisdom. And where selfish ambition and jealousy exist, there is disorder and every vile practice. Disorder is the conflict that comes when we reject God's order, which includes God's election. When you reject or ignore election, you reject God's order. And "every vile practice" is self-explanatory. James's warning emphasizes the fundamental nature of these sins because they are the basis of the serpent's rebellion.

Paul linked Jesus to Adam by referring to Jesus as the "last Adam."[5] We have already seen that the first Adam was killed by the serpent's envy, and Matthew tells us that Pilate knew that Jesus was handed over for death out of envy:

> *For he knew that it was out of envy that they had delivered him up. (Matthew 27:18)*

Over and over throughout Scripture we are warned about the

---

5. 1 Corinthians 15:45, 47.

fundamental nature of envy[6] because it is the serpent's sin and he longs to infect each one of us with it. And when we tolerate it, we begin to take on his image, and we can end up doing unspeakable things. We would never anticipate.

Finally, Revelation 12 also describes the satan's envy and desire for murder in apocalyptic terms:

> And a great sign appeared in heaven: a woman clothed with the sun, with the moon under her feet, and on her head a crown of twelve stars. She was pregnant and was crying out in birth pains and the agony of giving birth. And another sign appeared in heaven: behold, a great red dragon, with seven heads and ten horns, and on his heads seven diadems. His tail swept down a third of the stars of heaven and cast them to the earth. And the dragon stood before the woman who was about to give birth, so that when she bore her child he might devour it.... And the great dragon was thrown down, that ancient serpent, who is called the devil and Satan, the deceiver of the whole world—he was thrown down to the earth, and his angels were thrown down with him.... And when the dragon saw that he had been thrown down to the earth, he pursued the woman who had given birth to the male child. But the woman was given the two wings of the great eagle so that she might fly from the serpent into the wilderness, to the place where she is to be nourished for a time, and times, and half a time. The serpent poured water like a river out of his mouth after the woman, to sweep her away with a flood. But the earth came to the help of the woman, and the earth opened its mouth and swallowed the river that the dragon had poured from his mouth. Then the dragon became furious with the woman and went off to make war on the rest of her offspring, on those who keep the commandments of God and hold to the testimony of Jesus. And he stood on the sand of the sea. (Revelation 12:1–4, 9, 13–17)

Revelation 12 is an incredibly important text that summarizes the conflict of this age, the intensity of the end-time conflict, and the resolution to it. For our purposes, there are a few things immediately

---

6. For example, Proverbs 14:30; Romans 1:28; 1 Peter 2:1.

apparent in the text. The "dragon" and "ancient serpent" in this text is the satan, and we are told that his envy caused him to infect and "cast down" a third of the powers in the heavens.

The "woman" in this vision with a crown of twelve stars represents Israel, and the dragon is eager to devour her child. This is the "seed of the woman" that Genesis 3:15 predicted would destroy the "seed of the serpent." While Israel was chosen by God as a corporate people, this one seed or child is the ultimate elect one. He is the elect one produced by the elect woman. He is destined to rule and destroy the serpent. The serpent's desire to devour him is his desire to destroy the One God has chosen.

The satan in this vision is thrown down to the earth, which parallels his own deception of humanity. He deceived humanity so that humans now go down to the earth ("dust") in death. In this vision, the satan is judged by being cast down from his place as a spiritual power to the earth. And when he is cast down, he is in a rage. Immediately, he goes to destroy the elect people symbolized by the woman. And he is also in a rage with other people who are identified with the woman. In this passage, the other people are those who follow the commands of Jesus.

The passage is filled with meaning, but for our purposes, we can see a very clear conflict. The satan is obviously at war with God, but because he cannot challenge God directly, he makes war against God by seeking to devour and destroy those God has elected. He tries to devour the elect One, the "child" whom we now know as Jesus, but the child is taken away from the satan, so he seeks to devour the woman, God's elect people. He knows that God's plan flows through the ones God has chosen, and he cannot destroy the child, so he makes war on God's choice, the people of Israel, with all his strength. Note the text does not make any comment on the righteousness of the woman or describe her aggression toward the dragon. The issue is not that the woman is perfect, holy, or militant. The dragon's rage is against the woman simply because she is chosen.

An Ancient Witness to an Ancient Envy

Interestingly, one ancient text known as "The Life of Adam and Eve" contains a conversation between the satan and Adam, where the satan plainly states the reason for his fall:

11:1 *When Eve heard that it was the Devil who had deceived her, she fell down before him and Adam's distress for Eve increased twofold for he saw her lying on the earth like one dead. 2He was sad and called out with great groaning, "Woe to you who fight against us! What evil have we done to you? For it is because of your calumnies that we went out from the Garden. Is it because we have caused you to be expelled that you are angry against us? 3Or is it because of us that you were despoiled of your glory? Or is it, in some way, by our action that you are in such deficiency? Or are we the only creatures of God that you fight against us alone?*

12:1 *The Devil began to cry with forced tears and the Devil told Adam, "O Adam, all the greed and the anger and all the grief of my heart are directed against you because (it was) through you that I fell from my dwellings; (it was) by you that I was alienated from my own throne. My wings were more numerous than those of the cherubim, and I concealed myself under them. Because of you, now my feet walk on the earth, which I would never have believed." 2Adam replied to the Devil and told him, 3"What is my fault, by which I have done all that to you?"*

13:1 *The Devil replied to him and told him, "You did nothing to me, but it is because of you that I have fallen upon the earth. 2The very day when you were created, on that day I fell from before the face of God, because when God breathed a spirit onto your face, you had the image and likeness of Divinity. And Michael came; he presented you and made you bow down before God. And God told Michael, 'I have created Adam according to (my) image and my Divinity.'*

14:1 *Then Michael came; he summoned all the troops of angels and told them, 'Bow down before the likeness and the image of the Divinity.' 2And then, when Michael summoned them and all had bowed down to you, he summoned me also. 3And I told him, 'Go away from me, for I shall not bow down to him who is younger than I; indeed, I was master before him and it is proper for him to bow down to me.'"*

16:1Then God became angry with us and ordered us, them and me, to be cast down from our dwellings to the earth. As for you, he ordered you to dwell in the Garden. 2When I had realized that I had fallen by your power, that I was in distress and you were in rest, 3then I aimed at hunting you so that I might alienate you from the garden of delights, just as I had been alienated because of you."[7]

The origin of the stories in this account cannot be verified though they likely have their origin in second temple era Jewish sources. The text is definitely not Scripture and should not be treated as such, but what it does show is that ancient readers understood from Scripture that the satan fell from envy.

Do we realize that, when we also make war on those God has chosen, we are aligned with the serpent?

---

7.   Gary A. Anderson, "Life of Adam and Eve," in *Outside the Bible: Ancient Jewish Writings Related to Scripture: Translation, ed.* Louis H. Feldman, James L. Kugel, and Lawrence H. Schiffman, vol. 2 (Philadelphia: The Jewish Publication Society, 2013), 1339–1340.

14

THE BEGINNING OF EVIL IN THIS AGE

ALL OUR HUMAN conflict and envy flows out of the serpent's offense at God's redemptive plan. That offense began with his envy over the calling of humans. When God picked one specific people to be the instruments of His blessing, the serpent's envy focused in on that one people. This is the biblical basis for the conflict between Jew and Gentile. Ethnic conflict, which begins with Jew and Gentile and then extends across all people groups, is the foundation of hostility in the earth[1] because envy is the foundational sin of the age.

Envy is a symptom of those infected by the snake.

The serpent's envy manifests itself in gruesome ways over Israel's election, but it is not limited to the issue of Israel. Once we understand the serpent's poison and the way it has infected our own hearts, we can see innumerable expressions of it. We are envious of the blessings or opportunities others receive. We are envious of those "chosen" for a role in churches or our businesses. We long to have what others have. We cannot be content with what we are given. We are always thinking about what others may have.

In our time, there is more envy than at any other moment in

---

1. Matthew 24:7; Ephesians 2:14-16.

history because we are immersed in advertisements and social media constantly. Night and day, we are shown what other people have, and corporations spend billions of dollars deviously cultivating desire for what we do not yet have. Our social media, online shopping, physical shopping, and constant advertising fuel a steady diet of envy. It has become so second nature to us that we do not realize just how much of our money is spent, not on things we need, but on things that we want because we saw someone else with them. Models wear clothes and use objects to stir envy. Our friend's latest purchase stirs desire to obtain the same. A friend's video on social media makes us wish we could "do that" or "go there." It is an unprecedented escalation of envy if we have eyes to see it. And in time, it is going to produce grotesque fruit that we can barely imagine right now.

Envy is a deep root that has infected us. It is so deep in our hearts, and we are so accustomed to it, that we find ways to justify and legitimize it. This is one reason why God confronts us so directly about the issue of election and why He presses the question of Israel's election on the nations. He wants to confront the root of self-righteousness, pride, and envy that is in our hearts. We have become so deceived that we often defend our envy in the name of "justice" or "righteousness." We can and should confront sin and injustice, but if we listen carefully, we often arrogantly accuse others by defending our moral superiority, and that is a deception creating space for the deadly sin of envy.

None of us think we really harbor pride and envy in our hearts, so God confronts us daily with it to expose what is in our hearts:

- God confronts us with the people of Israel. Do we agree with His election?
- We at times endure injustice. When we address injustice, do we assume those suffering are superior in character or righteousness to those perpetuating injustice?
- Others succeed or are blessed in ways we are not. Can we rejoice with them?

- Others are given talents, gifts, and opportunities we are not given. Are we able to truly long to see them succeed, even if we do not have the same gifts?
- We have the chance to use our gifts to help others succeed instead of ourselves. Do we delight in someone else coming into their fullness if it comes at the expense of our own prosperity or exaltation?

The serpent still crouches like a monster trying to dominate us. And because we have all been infected by sin, if we do not allow God to confront this issue and heal our offense, in time, we may be shocked by the evil that can suddenly spring from our own hearts. The serpent's venom is like a deadly cancer. We may be unaware of how sick we are because we feel okay. And then one day, suddenly, like a cancer that has reached the tipping point, we find that venom has corrupted our hearts, and it can take us places we never imaged we would go.

When we are confronted by the gruesome things others have done in their envy, we tend to tell ourselves, *I would never do that,* but we are deceiving ourselves. We are often seduced by our own self-righteousness and believe we are superior to other humans while, in reality, we simply have not faced a crucible that exposes the envy that we tolerate in our own hearts. Many of us have not yet faced the full offense of God's election.

If you doubt this, simply review Jewish history, and you will find that people who lived "happily" with their Jewish neighbors often "suddenly" gave in to antisemitism when the environment was right. When pressure came and their own comfort was threatened, they chose their comfort over God's election. They were unprepared for the crisis, and they did not realize that standing with God's election put them in a war with the serpent. God's approval means the serpent's hostility. If, however, you have the serpent's approval, you will face God's hostility. You cannot have the approval of both. You must be approved by one and resisted by the other. Election is one of the areas of conflict because it was the crucible that led to the serpent's rebellion.

Because the serpent is the "god of this age," if you choose to stand with God's election, you will face the hostility of the serpent. You will be blessed by God, but you must be prepared for trouble in this age.

Agreeing with God's election puts you in direct conflict with the serpent who uses envy as a primary tactic to destroy God's purposes in this age. If you commit to God's ways and allow Him to cleanse you from envy, you will become the serpent's adversary, and you must expect him to strike. Yes, you will be blessed by God in the long run. And there is no comparison between living free of offense and in agreement with God *and* living bound by envy. Living free of offense is a blessed life. But it is not a trouble-free life in this age. This is why it's deceptive to ask people to agree with God's election simply so they can be blessed. People assume God's blessing means comfort and peace in this age, which the Bible warns us that the opposite is often true.[2]

When we teach people to agree with election primarily for blessing, we are setting them up for failure. They will not be equipped to stand with God's purposes at the cost of their own lives.

Because the serpent's objective is the murder of the elect, and he is at war with the God who elects, we must be prepared to agree with God's election at the cost of our own lives. Anything less indicates we have not rooted the serpent's venom out of our hearts. This is why God confronts us on the issue of election and demands we respect His election on the basis of His choice, not on the basis of the righteousness of the elect or on the basis of whatever blessing we may receive.

This is why we *must* learn the lesson of the Holocaust. The failure to deal with the Holocaust theologically is one of the greatest theological failures of the twentieth century. The God of Israel was present in Israel's greatest crisis, and He expects us to study it carefully and to allow it to shape our understanding and our discipleship.

---

2. Matthew 5:10-12; John 15:18-20; Romans 8:17-18; 2 Timothy 3:12; 1 Peter 4:12-14.

Standing with God's election of Israel in the Holocaust did not lead to blessing. It led to suffering, intense suffering. The great shock of the Holocaust is that Europe was a "Christian" culture with access to the Bible, and yet the evil root of envy had been left undisturbed. If we bless Israel to be blessed, then we turn God's election into some sort of good luck charm, leaving the root of envy undisturbed. And when that root is undisturbed, unthinkable things like the Holocaust can happen suddenly.

Jesus' response to the hostility of those who participated in His execution was so different from the Church's historical response. While many in the institutional Church condemned the Jews because of Jesus' execution, Jesus took a very different approach. First, "the Jews" as a corporate people did not participate in Jesus' death. Only a few Jewish leaders did out of jealousy and in cooperation with Rome. Second, when Jesus was dying, He asked the Father to have mercy on those who called for His execution because they did not understand their actions. The difference between Jesus' response to hostility and the institutional Church's response is striking. We must recover Jesus' gracious, merciful response to those who participated in His death– both Jew and Gentile.

Most of us would say in response to what I just said, "I would never turn on my neighbor whether Jewish or of another ethnicity." *But how do you know?* It is likely you have simply never been tested on the issue. Pressure and suffering expose what we truly believe. We all love our neighbors when it does not cost us anything. But what do you do when your love of your neighbor costs you something? You may be convinced you would always stand with the Jewish people or any other people different from you, but you have probably never been tested on this. A few comments on social media or liking a post is not a test. The test is your own physical suffering.

It is a fantasy to assume we are better than our ancestors and will always stand with God's election when we are tolerating envy in other areas of our lives and have not been tested on this issue.

Whose Image Will You Reflect?

If you tolerate the root of envy toward Israel or anyone else God has elected, it causes you to reflect the image of the serpent to some extent.

Whether we realize it or not, our rage against those chosen is an expression of our rage against God. Our offense is really an offense against God that is expressed through hostility to those *He* has chosen. The chosen did not choose themselves, so our real conflict is with the One who chose them, not the ones chosen themselves. In our rage, we assume our wisdom is superior to His, and so we challenge what He has decided by every means possible. It's an attempt to challenge God's right to be God and to put our wisdom against His. Attempts to exalt ourselves to a place He did not give us is an attempt to exalt ourselves to His place. And as we do, we reflect the image of the serpent. We follow the path of self-exaltation that the serpent took.[3]

The irony of our offense against God is that He is actually a servant. He upholds creation through His power.[4] He is ultimately good and self-sacrificing.[5] He takes great pleasure in exalting the lowly and showing favor to those we would not. Throughout the biblical story, God constantly takes pleasure in exalting the lowly and choosing those we would not. He is long-suffering, patient, and merciful with nearly every significant biblical figure. The stories of the Bible are given to us for one reason: so we will know who God is. Therefore, the message of these stores is clear: If God is consistently merciful, long-suffering, and patient, and if He is the One who chooses the unqualified, the one we would not choose, then this tells us who God is.

God's goodness reaches a crescendo in the Person of Jesus, who fully displays the self-sacrificing nature of God. Jesus became a servant, just as Isaiah prophesied,[6] and told us that the greatest

---

3. Isaiah 14:12-15; Ezekiel 28:12-17.
4. Psalm 145:16; Colossians 1:16-17; Acts 17:24-25; Hebrews 1:3.
5. Isaiah 53:5; John 3:16; Romans 5:8; Philippians 2:6–8; 1 John 4:9-10.
6. Isaiah 42; 49; 50; 52; 53.

would become a servant. Jesus repeatedly confronted His followers with the concept that greatness is tied to servanthood.[7] The reason for this is very simple: *God is a servant.*

> *A dispute also arose among them, as to which of them was to be regarded as the greatest. And he said to them, "The kings of the Gentiles exercise lordship over them, and those in authority over them are called benefactors. But not so with you. Rather, let the greatest among you become as the youngest, and the leader as one who serves. For who is the greater, one who reclines at table or one who serves? Is it not the one who reclines at table? But I am among you as the one who serves. (Luke 22:24–27)*

Jesus gave this command as He was serving the disciples to make a point: If you want to be great, you must become a servant because that's who God is. The God against whom we rage is actually serving His creation. From the Hebrew Bible to the New Testament, God is described as a servant. He is graciously giving every creature a place they do not deserve. He upholds creation at the cost of His own life and power. While God is eternal, it still costs something of Him to uphold creation. He is self-sacrificing and gives His life. And when He died, He asked God to have mercy on His opponents who did not understand their sin:

> *And Jesus said, "Father, forgive them, for they know not what they do." And they cast lots to divide his garments. (Luke 23:34)*

God has proven Himself from Genesis to Revelation to be self-sacrificing and good—the ultimate Servant. God does not simply choose and elect. He *serves* the calling of those He has chosen. When we do the same, we take on the image of God. And when we do not, we reflect the image of the serpent.

Resisting the election of God when He serves our election is completely absurd.

---

7. Isaiah 53:11; Matthew 20:26-28; Mark 10:43-45; John 13:12-15; Philippians 2:5-7.

Jesus was a servant because He was God in human form, and that's who God is. When you read the Bible with this in mind, you can see it clearly. God's greatness is demonstrated in His identity as a servant. The satan could have become great by God's definition, but he chose another path.

What path are you choosing? Do you have more confidence in Jesus' definition of greatness than the satan's?

15

THE WEAPON OF ACCUSATION

NAMES in the Bible are very significant because they often describe a person's character, and as we have discussed, one of the primary names given to the satan is "the accuser":

And I heard a loud voice in heaven, saying, "Now the salvation and the power and the kingdom of our God and the authority of his Christ have come, for the accuser of our brothers has been thrown down, who accuses them day and night before our God." (Revelation 12:10)

Not only is the satan called the accuser, we are told that he accuses "day and night." As one of the satan's primary weapons, accusation is also one of the most common manifestations of envy. Accusation is an evil strategy to disqualify anyone God has chosen. Accusation is not simply a matter of information. It may be based on facts that are true or even partially true. The issue is not whether the data shared is true or not; the issue is what this information is being used to do. Advance a person's calling? Or destroy it?

Accusation is the manipulative use of information to disqualify someone so they cannot fulfill their calling.

Zechariah 3 gives one of the best summaries of accusation in this age:

> Then he showed me Joshua the high priest standing before the angel of the LORD, and Satan standing at his right hand to accuse him. And the LORD said to Satan, "The LORD rebuke you, O Satan! The LORD who has chosen Jerusalem rebuke you! Is not this a brand plucked from the fire?" Now Joshua was standing before the angel, clothed with filthy garments. And the angel said to those who were standing before him, "Remove the filthy garments from him." And to him he said, "Behold, I have taken your iniquity away from you, and I will clothe you with pure vestments." And I said, "Let them put a clean turban on his head." So they put a clean turban on his head and clothed him with garments. And the angel of the LORD was standing by. (Zechariah 3:1–5)

This encounter addresses the core issues of election and accusation.

- The satan boldly accused Joshua in order to disqualify him.
- The Lord rebuked the satan, not on the basis of what Joshua had done, but on the basis of the Lord's choosing. The core issue was the Lord had chosen Jerusalem and Joshua. As we have repeatedly seen, election is based entirely on the Lord's choosing, not a people's performance. Israel and the priests have been repeatedly guilty of deep compromise. But they remain chosen, just as humanity has committed horrific sins and yet remains chosen for a divine purpose.
- The Lord's honor is at stake in His ability to transform those He has chosen, and they are *not* chosen on the basis of their qualifications. Election is divine choosing before

those chosen have even had a chance to do right or wrong.[1]

- The Lord's rebuke brings the central issue into focus. The Lord had chosen Joshua, but the satan wanted to disqualify him. The Lord did not address Joshua's condition with the satan because Joshua's condition was not the real issue. The satan wants to disqualify the chosen simply because they are chosen. The Lord's choosing triggers the satan's envy, and he does not want the redemptive blessing the Lord will bring through choosing.

- Joshua was in filthy garments, which means the satan's accusations were based on legitimate facts. Joshua was not "clean" and was unable to walk in the fullness of his calling. But Joshua's condition was not the primary issue. The satan was envious of Joshua's election and the Lord's purpose for Jerusalem.

Because election is based on God's choice and not the qualifications of the one chosen, accusation is a direct attack against God's choice, His desire, and His ability to use the disqualified. When we join in accusation, we are not ultimately in conflict with the individual we accuse. We are in conflict with God Himself who made the choice.

Accusation is an evolution of the serpent's strategy in the garden. In the garden, the serpent accused God in an attempt to destroy Eve and her offspring through the curse of death. To his shock, the consequences of human sin were painful and severe, but man's calling was not destroyed. Instead, God predicted that He would resolve the crisis and fulfill man's election and His redemptive purpose. Once the serpent realized that the penalty of death would not eliminate man, he adapted his strategy and continued to use accusation as one of his key weapons.

---

1. Romans 9:11.

First, he accuses God before humans because he knows that humans cannot fulfill their election apart from God. *When we take in the serpent's accusations against God, we cut ourselves off from the only One who can bring us into the fulfillment of our calling as humans.* The serpent obviously cannot eliminate God, but if we believe his accusations, we will cut ourselves off from God, which serves the serpent's purposes of preventing humans from walking in their election.

Second, the serpent also accuses humans before God "day and night."[2] His accusations are a direct challenge to God's ability to accomplish His purposes through the ones He has chosen. The serpent mocks God before the spiritual powers and charges that God cannot stay true to His own holiness and exalt disqualified and sinful humans. The serpent is so envious that he tries to manipulate God's own nature to prevent God from doing what God has plainly stated He will do. This tactic is ridiculous because God created the satan. The satan is not wiser than God, and God knows well how to accomplish what He has determined. But the serpent is so envious and bitter that he mocks God.

All accusations are direct challenges to God. This is why you must know the God of Jacob—the God who calls the unqualified and fulfills their calling by His own strength.

The Image of God or the Image of the Serpent

The enemy's strategy is to accuse God before humans and accuse humans before God. This is the exact opposite of our divine assignment.

Humans were created as priestly creatures who represent God in creation. We will be priests and intercessors *forever.*[3] (Tragically, most people put more emphasis on their temporary assignment in this age than their priestly assignment which will last forever.[4]) Our priestly intercessory calling is demonstrated throughout Scripture in the lives

---

2. Zechariah 3:1–2; Job 1:6–11; Revelation 12:10.
3. 1 Peter 2:9; Revelation 1:5–6; 5:9–10.
4. For more on humans as priests and intercessors, see *Mercy Before Judgment.*

of prophets and leaders[5] and ultimately in the Person of Jesus. This calling can be summarized in two ways:

- Stand before God on behalf of people. Advocate for people on the basis of what God has said (Scripture) and what God has done and will do (His redemptive work through Jesus).
- Stand before people on behalf of God. Represent God in creation declaring what God has said about Himself in His Word.

This calling was demonstrated in Exodus 32 when Israel sinned with the golden calf. When God told Moses about the people's rebellion, Moses understood God was giving him an invitation to stand before Him and intercede on behalf of the people. He interceded on the basis of what God had said about Israel, and in the process, he secured mercy for the nation. Israel clearly deserved God's judgment, but Moses understood that God's honor was at stake in His election of Israel for a glorious purpose. (And that purpose is not yet complete.) Moses did not know how God was going to redeem a rebellious people, but He challenged God to do everything He had promised to Abraham:

> But Moses implored the LORD his God and said, "O LORD, why does your wrath burn hot against your people, whom you have brought out of the land of Egypt with great power and with a mighty hand? Why should the Egyptians say, 'With evil intent did he bring them out, to kill them in the mountains and to consume them from the face of the earth'?... Remember Abraham, Isaac, and Israel, your servants, to whom you swore by your own self, and said to them, 'I will multiply your offspring as the stars of heaven, and all this land that I have promised I will give to your offspring, and they shall inherit it forever.'" (Exodus 32:11–13)

---

5. Genesis 18:22-33; Exodus 32:11-14; Numbers 14:13-19; 1 Samuel 7:5-9; 12:23; 2 Samuel 24:17; 1 Kings 8:22-53; Daniel 9:3-19.

Moses challenged God that His honor was at stake in accomplishing the impossible through a people who were not qualified for their own election. And we are called to do the same. Moses then descended to the people and stood before the people on behalf of God. Moses called the people to repentance and addressed their sin:

> And as soon as he came near the camp and saw the calf and the dancing, Moses' anger burned hot, and he threw the tablets out of his hands and broke them at the foot of the mountain.... And Moses said to Aaron, "What did this people do to you that you have brought such a great sin upon them?"... The next day Moses said to the people, "You have sinned a great sin. And now I will go up to the LORD; perhaps I can make atonement for your sin." (Exodus 32:19, 21, 30)

When Moses stood before God, he understood Israel was in a serious state, but he interceded on the basis of God's character and what God had said. And when he stood before the people, he was also very serious in calling the people to repentance. He confronted their sin directly. In both interactions, Moses demonstrated the heart of God. His words were strong and direct, but his goal was reconciliation and restoration. We were created to be priests where the goal is restoration, recovery, and the fulfillment of human destiny. Accusation is the exact opposite. Accusation may "confront" sin, but the focus is on disqualification and not redemption.

Priests are people who have been given the special privilege of access before God so they can lead people to approach God and draw close, not simply expose their faults.

Do you function more like a priest or more like the serpent?

We live in a time when accusations are justified in an unprecedented way. We must recognize this as the venom of the serpent who always seeks to normalize accusation because it is his way. And as we accept his poison, we are slowly being prepared to agree with him in ways we would never anticipate.

Accusation is not simply a matter of facts. The facts may be true. But what are the facts being used to do? Advance or destroy a calling?

Christians sometimes spread information when they should cover sin.[6] Certain sharing may appear religious when it is really accusation because of what it produces. Even "prayer requests" can be used as ways to share accusations. When you share information, is it done with genuine concern for the success of the one who has "failed" in mind? If not, accusation has infected your words.

Our enemy is devious, and we have to constantly guard ourselves because we have been infected by sin, and this naturally produces accusation. This is one of the reasons why James said that the tongue is evil and produces great harm and that, if anyone can control their tongue, they can do anything:

For we all stumble in many ways. And if anyone does not stumble in what he says, he is a perfect man, able also to bridle his whole body. (James 3:2)

Accusation angers God for multiple reasons:

- The nature of God is to give His own life to secure the calling of the disqualified. This is plain throughout the Bible and displayed ultimately in the Person of Jesus and His death on the cross. God was not forced to give His life. He designed a story that He knew would require His life and His suffering because this is His nature. God's nature is self-sacrifice to secure the exaltation of the disqualified, and accusation runs contrary to His nature because accusation seeks self-exaltation through the destruction of others.
- Humanity is destined for exaltation, not because humans are superior in any way to the rest of creation, but simply because God chose to exalt a humble creature over other more outwardly impressive creatures. When we seek to destroy others, it plainly demonstrates we do not realize that our intelligence, gifts, and life are a generous and

---

6. Proverbs 10:12; Colossians 3:13; 1 Peter 4:8; James 5:20.

undeserved gift from God. If we understood the mercy and generosity we have received from God, we should give that same mercy and generosity to others.

- God's election is God's right to be God. When we accuse others, we challenge God's right to choose who He will and accomplish His purposes the way He desires. This is the envy of the serpent. The serpent was offended at God's decision to lead creation the way He wants to. When we accuse, we are not ultimately attacking a person; we are attacking God's right to be God and lead creation as He wishes.

- God suffered more than anyone else[7] to *remove* every accusation against those who have sinned, are disqualified, and are His enemies. God's entire plan of redemption from the beginning of Genesis is plainly designed to choose the disqualified and bring about a glorious and undeserved purpose through His work in them. When we accuse, we are challenging the God of Jacob who does not accuse, but instead intentionally chooses the obviously disqualified.

Accusation based on envy has become so normalized that we must assume it is rooted in our heart and actively remove it.

Enthroned by Accusation

When we accuse anyone, including Israel, we are engaging in the serpent's war against God's choosing.

While the Bible refers to the satan as the "god of this age,"[8] he has no intrinsic authority. He only has the "authority" given by "this age" by humans who empower him. We do this by agreeing with him in our thoughts and deeds. Tragically, the vast majority of people do not

---

7. Isaiah 53:3-5.
8. 2 Corinthians 4:4.

realize that they empower and enthrone the serpent when they follow his path of envy and accusation.

Revelation 12 focuses on the satan's identity as an accuser and the Lord's plan to bring his accusation to an end:

And the great dragon was thrown down, that ancient serpent, who is called the devil and Satan, the deceiver of the whole world—he was thrown down to the earth, and his angels were thrown down with him. And I heard a loud voice in heaven, saying, "Now the salvation and the power and the kingdom of our God and the authority of his Christ have come, for the accuser of our brothers has been thrown down, who accuses them day and night before our God. And they have conquered him by the blood of the Lamb and by the word of their testimony, for they loved not their lives even unto death." (Revelation 12:9–11)

- The serpent "accuses" day and night.
- The serpent will be conquered and thrown down.
- The serpent is conquered and thrown down *by the saints.* He currently has a place of influence only because humans have not yet conquered him. The satan is enthroned by human agreement with him.
- The salvation, power, authority of Jesus, and Kingdom of God come when *people* conquer the accuser.
- Revelation 12 is a prophecy, which means a time will come when a people face what is in their hearts, they conquer the accuser, and he loses the place he now holds.

Revelation gives us a brief description for the people who will conquer the accuser, and it lists three key ways they conquer him:[9]

- The blood of the Lamb—The people who conquer the satan will put all their confidence in what Jesus has done for them, not in their own goodness. Their confidence in

---

9. Revelation 12:11.

the blood will allow them to face the evil in their own soul, receive God's forgiveness, and be transformed by what God has done for them. It is very significant that they will not be transformed by their own perfection. This requires a profound humility which will be transformative because God responds to humility, and He resists humanistic pride. Humanistic pride includes the idea that we in our own strength can ride ourselves of the sinful root of envy. And this is not a "New Testament" idea. From the very beginning, the Hebrew Bible exhorts us to put our faith and confidence in God's ability to cover our sin.[10]

- The word of their testimony—What you speak has incredible power. Do you speak words that agree with God or perpetuate accusation? The people who conquer the serpent will speak words that agree with God. They will speak Scripture instead of envious words and words polluted by the god of this age. The word *testimony* carries the idea of a legal witness. It refers to the kind of witness who could testify in a court of law to identify the truth. So these words are words backed up by a life transformed by these words. They are the words *of their witness*—the spoken declaration of who they are and what they have become. And if their words can dethrone the ultimate accuser, they have obviously overcome the issue of accusation.

- They do not love their lives to the death—They have abandoned self-centered living. They are no longer dominated by envy, so instead of being murderers, they are the exact opposite. They are self-sacrificing. They do not exalt themselves at the cost of someone else's life; they willingly lay down their own lives and choose death over sin. They give the ultimate demonstration of love.[11]

---

10. Psalm 103:10-12; Isaiah 1:18; Micah 7:18-19; Romans 5:8; Ephesians 1:7; 1 John 1:9.
11. John 15:13.

Satan holds the place he currently has because humans keep him there. And to the extent that you engage in or even tolerate accusation, you enthrone the accuser.

Because the serpent is enthroned by accusation, he uses it to manipulate humans into agreeing with him and giving him great influence. And then he uses accusation to prevent humans from taking their God-ordained place. This encompasses every expression of accusation, including accusation against the people of Israel. Entertaining accusations is at the core of all sin. It is expressed in the way we relate to God and the way we relate to each other.

Evil acts like stealing, murder, or immorality are not the core of sin. The core of sin is very simple: choosing *our* evaluation of what is best over God's. Eve chose what she saw over what God had said. This is the root of all sin: Do you choose your evaluation of what is good or God's? But why would anyone choose their own evaluation over God's? We know that God is deeply good to the point of His own self-sacrifice. The answer is simple: *because we choose to believe accusations against God.*

The only reason we do not obey God is that we believe accusations that say He is not truly good and that what He asks us to do is either too difficult, unreasonable, or unenjoyable. God calls us to:

- Avoid things that may appear pleasurable but are not good.[12]
- Follow His example, and embrace obedience that leads to suffering.[13]

We choose to disobey God because we harbor accusation against Him. We are not convinced He is who He says He is. We are not convinced He truly has our good in mind. We think we know "better" and our ways are superior to His. We do not think He has our best interest in mind. This is what disobedience is. In reality, it is very

---

12. Genesis 3:2–6; Proverbs 14:12; Hebrews 11:24-25; James 1:14-15.
13. Matthew 16:24-26; Mark 8:34-36; Luke 9:23-25.

simple. It's not merely that we don't want to obey. We do not want to obey because deep down we are tolerating an accusation: God's ways are not really the best ways for us. We have a better way to be human.

When we believe accusations against God, we will not fully obey God. We may partially obey, but we will not obey everything. However, if we conquer accusation, we will do whatever God asks us to, even if it is costly. All accusation is really sin against God. Even when we accuse others, we are really accusing God and refusing to relate to others the way He does. We think the serpent, that ancient mass murderer, has a better way.

All sin flows from accusation, and the satan remains in his place of influence because we entertain accusation. When we abandon our accusations, he will lose his place.

16

THE NATURE OF & SOLUTION TO ACCUSATION

ACCUSATION IS a distortion that has no redemptive purpose. But we can have conflict without a spirit of accusation. If we think all criticism is rooted in accusation, we create another kind of distorted reality where people cannot mature in the grace of God. Accusation is not:

- Criticism or difficult conversations—There are times when things need to be addressed. Biblical criticism is a gift[1] and must not be rejected as "accusation." Rejecting criticism when true repentance or change is needed is also a form of distorting reality. A culture that is free of accusation does not remove difficult conversations; it creates a context for them to be had in a biblical way. We can, and should, have honest, difficult conversations without a spirit of accusation.
- Anything negative—In Scripture, we find quite a few "negative" warnings and rebukes. A negative statement is

---

1. Proverbs 15:31-32; 19:20; 27:5–6.

not automatically an accusation. If we avoid everything negative, we also live in a distorted reality.

- Disagreement—People can have biblical disagreements without falling into accusation.

Accusation Distorts Reality

Genesis 3 tells us that the serpent was *"more crafty than any other beast of the field that the LORD God had made"* (Genesis 3:1). There is a word-play going on in the original Hebrew because the word for *serpent* (נָחָשׁ) is the same root word for *divination*. The serpent's accusation against God is being compared to divination, and this wordplay gives us a tremendous insight into just how dangerous accusation is.

Accusation is like operating in the realm of divination because you manipulate and distort reality to accomplish something that is ungodly. Any time you operate in the realm of accusation you are acting like the satan.

Divination and witchcraft are control, distortion, and manipulation that seek to harm people and destroy their future, which is precisely what accusation does. Conviction and accusation are very different. Conviction is based on the truth of your reality, and it leads to a hope-filled future if you respond to it in repentance. Accusation is a distortion of your reality, and it predicts a negative future with no hope.

When you live in accusation, you inevitably distort the reality of your life and deprive God from what He wants. Many people give in to accusation, assuming they are being godly or "repentant" when in reality they are disfiguring who they are as an image of God. And when you accuse others, you manipulate their reality and distort their future because your accusations leave them unable to live in the reality God has designed for them.

Accusation is just like the sin of divination, and you can destroy yourself and others by accepting and propagating it.

Accusation leads to pride or shame, depending on whether you receive it or engage in it. When you operate in accusation, you become arrogant like the serpent, and you are transformed into his image. When you receive accusation, shame puts you under the dominion of the serpent with the belief that you are far from God. And when you withdraw from God, you struggle to reflect His image the way you are intended to, which allows the serpent to distort and disfigure who you are called to be.

The serpent's accusation in Genesis 3 shows us that the goal of accusation is death.

Two Profound Realms of Accusation

Accusation primarily operates in two realms. It operates in the human realm, which includes our internal accusations against ourselves *and* our accusations against each other. Deep down, we know that something is wrong, and the awareness of our situation produces a deep insecurity. We accept accusation and accuse others because we do not have a biblical grasp of how God relates to us.

The second realm of accusation is our accusation against God. This is the sin that seduced Eve.

You cannot resolve your own sense of accusation or your propensity to accuse others until you deal with your accusations against God because it is the root issue.

All sin flows from accusation against God. We sin because we believe we know better than God what is in our best interests and that is a bold accusation against His character. Anytime you sin, you are basically telling God He does not want what is best for you and His commands are in His self-interest, but not in your best interest. You are accusing Him of manipulating us or keeping us from pleasure or prosperity.

We accuse God by filtering all His commands through our own wisdom. But what we call wisdom, God calls doubt fueled by accusation against Him. And these accusations take on a number of forms. One is open rebellion against God, which is a bold declaration that His ways are restrictive and cruel and that He does not want what is best for us. This is exactly what the serpent declared in the garden.

The truth is we only struggle with obedience because we do not believe that what God calls us to do is in our best interest.

Another way we accuse God is when we lack confidence in the grace of God after we have genuinely repented. People frequently distance themselves from God until they have "done better" or try to express repentance by living in guilt and shame. But this is really just another accusation against what God says about the free gift of mercy available through Jesus. It is a statement that Jesus' blood is not enough, so we need our own actions to restore full relationship with God.

Another subtle form of accusation is when we do not seek to live like Jesus. Jesus is not a better human; He is God in human form, which means the way Jesus lives is the way God lives as a human. When we excuse ourselves from following the path of Jesus, we are essentially disagreeing with what God says because Jesus' life is not a "superior" way of living. It is the way we are called to live. When we excuse ourselves by saying, "Well that was Jesus," or "Jesus was perfect," it is really just an excuse. The truth is we do not agree with God, and the evidence is our failure to follow the path of Jesus. If we consider Him especially holy rather than the example we should imitate, it shows we do not agree with God's definition of how we should live.

The fact that we are comfortable not imitating Jesus indicates we disagree with God. We do not truly believe in His definition of humanity. We think our definition, which does not seek to live like Jesus, is more comfortable and more appropriate for our lives.

Any area where you do not seek to imitate Jesus is an area of accusation in your life.

The Solution to Accusation

This age will not end until the saints deal with the issue of accusation because our accusations against God empower the satan. The saints must conquer the accuser to bring an end to this age:

...the accuser of our brothers has been thrown down, who accuses them day and night before our God. And they have conquered him by the blood of the Lamb and by the word of their testimony, for they loved not their lives even unto death. (Revelation 12:10–11)

Furthermore, God does not want to transition the age with a people who have not dealt with the issue of accusation. The next age will be radically different in part because the people of God will have overcome the issue of accusation.

God has a powerful solution for accusation that is radical *and* simple: **the grace of God.** The grace of God is not the mercy of God, nor is it specifically the forgiveness of God. The grace of God is the *favor* of God that shatters accusation. It means God's posture toward us is positive. His grace is secure because it comes from who He is, not who we are. It is secured by what He has done and not what we have done or are doing.

God's grace is given to us through the Person of Jesus, so it is absolutely settled and secure. If we are in Jesus, we are loved *as Jesus is loved.*[2] And this is the biblical solution to accusation because accusation can only flourish when our knowledge of God is distorted and we behave accordingly.

We are saved *by grace,* and it is going to take ages for God to reveal the full glory of the grace we have in the Person of Jesus:

*But God, being rich in mercy, because of the great love with which he loved us, even when we were dead in our trespasses, made us alive together with Christ—**by grace you have been saved**—and raised us up with him and seated us with him in the heavenly places in Christ Jesus, so that **in the coming ages he might show the immeasurable riches of his grace in kindness toward us in Christ Jesus. For by grace you have been saved through faith.** And this is not your own doing; it is the gift of God. (Ephesians 2:4–8)*

Notice that we are saved by grace *through faith.* You have to believe

---

2. John 17:23.

the grace of God instead of accusation. When you believe the grace of God, you realize that God has your best interest in mind and that you have relationship with Him entirely based on what He has done. And that is what shatters the power and effects of accusation if we put our faith in it.

We are saved by "His grace":

> *Therefore do not be ashamed of the testimony about our Lord, nor of me his prisoner, but share in suffering for the gospel by the power of God, **who saved us and called us to a holy calling, not because of our works but because of his own purpose and grace, which he gave us in Christ Jesus before the ages began,** and which now has been manifested through the appearing of our Savior Christ Jesus, who abolished death and brought life and immortality to light through the gospel ... which is why I suffer as I do. But I am not ashamed, for I know whom I have believed, and I am convinced that he is able to guard until that day what has been entrusted to me. (2 Timothy 1:8–10, 12)*

When the early church operated in power, signs, wonders, and loving community, Luke told us that "great grace was upon them all." The glory and power of this community was an expression of the grace of God:

> *"... while you stretch out your hand to heal, and signs and wonders are performed through the name of your holy servant Jesus." And when they had prayed, the place in which they were gathered together was shaken, and they were all filled with the Holy Spirit and continued to speak the word of God with boldness. Now the full number of those who believed were of one heart and soul, and no one said that any of the things that belonged to him was his own, but they had everything in common. And with great power the apostles were giving their testimony to the resurrection of the Lord Jesus, **and great grace was upon them all.** There was not a needy person among them, for as many as were owners of lands or houses sold them and brought the proceeds of what was sold and laid it at the apostles' feet, and it was distributed to each as any had need. (Acts 4:30–35)*

Stephen did signs and wonders among the people because he was "full of grace":

*And the word of God continued to increase, and the number of the disciples multiplied greatly in Jerusalem, and a great many of the priests became obedient to the faith. And Stephen, **full of grace and power**, was doing great wonders and signs among the people. (Acts 6:7–8)*

The power of the grace of God allows us to break the power of accusation and live as humans were intended to live. The grace of God allows the power of God to flow through us whether that is in the form of miracles or selfless living with each other.

Every Pauline Epistle begins with "grace to you" from Jesus. This is how powerful and foundational the power of God's grace is.

God's grace is not blindness. The grace of God does not deny the facts, and that is precisely why it is so powerful. We have the grace of God because of what He has done and not because of what we have done. The grace of God joyfully and gladly operates through us even when we are still growing through immaturity. Because God's grace is secured by Him, we can confidently live in the grace of God even when we are immature. The grace of God does not obscure issues in our lives, but it gives us the power to address them. God's grace does not overlook sin, but His favor gives us power to abandon sin. Accordingly, we can, and must, address our sin and the sin of others. Our experience of God's grace gives us the ability to face the truth and allow God to transform us.

The grace of God does not wait for you to become mature. It provides the necessary missing maturity to enable you to function on a level you cannot function.

The grace of God removes accusation, but it does not overlook sin. Instead, the power of the grace of God gives us the strength to face the rebuke of God without the distortion field of accusation. When we know we have His favor and grace, we can endure His corrections. A biblical understanding of the grace of God does not give a license to live in sin.

If you cannot handle conviction and rebuke, you do not know the grace of God because His grace does not remove correction; it enables us to receive it. A person who rejects all correction because it is "accusation" and they are under "grace" does not know the biblical grace of God.

Accusation depends on shame, and it causes us to live in shame and others to live in shame as well. The power of the grace of God breaks the power of shame, which enables us in turn to break the power of accusation. And once that power is broken, we can experience the conviction of God and walk rightly with Him. And we can also address the sin of others in a clean way. We must address each others' sin, and the power of the grace of God enables us to do that without the poison of accusation. Accusation destroys a person, but conviction and correction equips them to walk in their calling. When we truly know the grace of God, we can correct others and assure them the power of the grace of God is able to overcome the weaknesses in their lives and bring them to maturity.

Conquering Accusation

Revelation 12:10–11 tells us what happens when the saints conquer and dethrone the accuser, and it's what happens when we deal with accusation: *The power, Kingdom, and authority of God come.*

When the saints conquer the accuser, all sorts of things follow:

- A people from every tribe and tongue emerge as one people. There is no division or envy among the people.[3]
- The followers of Jesus love and fully support the election of Israel.[4]
- The saints willingly embrace the cross and follow what the Father asks because they no longer accuse God and avoid His clear commands.

---

3. Revelation 5:9; 7:9.
4. This is the clear implication of Revelation 12:14–17.

Overcoming the accuser produces a global open heaven, something we can barely imagine. The satan will lose his place, and the heavens will be cleansed. We will then live with each other free of accusation. We are accustomed to living in an internal and external world of accusation day and night. After this moment, we will begin to live in an entirely new world, which is why we are told the power, Kingdom, and authority of God come when the accuser is removed.

The mature people of God at the end of the age will provide an undeniable witness of Jesus.[5] And this witness will include suffering and betrayal, just like Jesus experienced. Betrayal is based on accusation, and Jesus was able to endure betrayal because He refused accusation and was confident in the love of His Father. When you are confident in the grace of God, you can endure accusation and not be offended by betrayal.

Loving when betrayed is part of becoming like God who loves us deeply even though we have accused and betrayed Him.

The Church is meant to be a place that demonstrates the victory of God, so it must be an accusation-free zone. This age is saturated with the influence of the accuser, but the Church is meant to preview the age to come when the accuser is cast down and judged. The atmosphere among the people of God should be radically different from the culture. At first, this atmosphere will feel very strange. And it will feel almost alien to people who don't live according to the grace of God but according to their shortcomings, prejudices, or accusations.

The Church should be a community where people can begin to taste what it would be like to live in an accusation free world.

Does your life and ministry in the Church tolerate, encourage, or destroy accusation? It will not be destroyed passively because the god of this age perpetuates it day and night. If you are not actively making war on accusation, you are tolerating it and passively propagating it. It is such a deep part of sin that it will require intentional, ongoing, aggressive action to remove it.

---

5. John 17:21, 23. For more on this subject, see *What Does God Want?*

Accusation Can Masquerade as False Justice

The serpent loves *subtle* deception. His goal is to deceive us, not shock us. His goal is our destruction, and he is incredibly intelligent and patient. He does not care how overtly evil you become. He simply cares that you allow the root of envy to be undisturbed in your heart so that you do not challenge his influence. Half-truths and "nearly true" ideas are fertile ground for him. He loves things that sound true but are not, or prodding people to do the "right" thing the wrong way.

One of the ways the serpent loves to seduce us into accusation is through a false, unbiblical concept of justice.

Justice is very important to God. The Hebrew prophets repeatedly rebuked Israel and the nations over the issue of justice, and injustice was a basis for God's severe judgments against Israel.[6] God declared He will judge the nations because of their injustice:[7]

> *Woe to those who decree iniquitous decrees, and the writers who keep writing oppression, to turn aside the needy from justice and to rob the poor of my people of their right, that widows may be their spoil, and that they may make the fatherless their prey! (Isaiah 10:1–2)*

> *Thus says the LORD: Do justice and righteousness, and deliver from the hand of the oppressor him who has been robbed. And do no wrong or violence to the resident alien, the fatherless, and the widow, nor shed innocent blood in this place. (Jeremiah 22:3)*

> *...oppresses the poor and needy, commits robbery, does not restore the pledge, lifts up his eyes to the idols, commits abomination, 13 lends at interest, and takes profit; shall he then live? He shall not live. He has done all these abominations; he shall surely die; his blood shall be upon himself. (Ezekiel 18:12–13)*

---

6. Isaiah 1:16-17; Jeremiah 22:3; Ezekiel 18:30; Micah 6:8; Amos 5:21-24; Zechariah 7:9-10.
7. See also Ezekiel 16:49-50; Nahum 3:1; Revelation 17–18.

Therefore because you trample on the poor and you exact taxes of grain from him, you have built houses of hewn stone, but you shall not dwell in them; you have planted pleasant vineyards, but you shall not drink their wine. For I know how many are your transgressions and how great are your sins— you who afflict the righteous, who take a bribe, and turn aside the needy in the gate. (Amos 5:11–12)

Come now, you rich, weep and howl for the miseries that are coming upon you. Your riches have rotted and your garments are moth-eaten. Your gold and silver have corroded, and their corrosion will be evidence against you and will eat your flesh like fire. You have laid up treasure in the last days. Behold, the wages of the laborers who mowed your fields, which you kept back by fraud, are crying out against you, and the cries of the harvesters have reached the ears of the Lord of hosts. (James 5:1–4)

THE NEW TESTAMENT is also strongly focused on a people who demonstrate a different way of living and a justice society in the way they live together and interact with the culture.[8] This is such a major theme, you do not find any exhortations to evangelism in the New Testament (though we should share the good news of the gospel); instead, you find repeated commands to live as a corporate people who are a just community. When the Church does not live as a community of justice whose way of life challenges the injustice of the culture, it is not the demonstration of the Church described in the New Testament.

God has put His longing for justice in our hearts, and the serpent loves to manipulate our longing for justice. He empowers accusation by promoting and celebrating a false justice that is saturated with self-right-eousness.[9]

---

8. For example Acts 2:42-47; 1 Corinthians 6:9–10; 12:12-14; Ephesians 4:1-3; 29–32; Galatians 5:19–21; Hebrews 13:5; 1 Peter 1:15-16; 2:13-14; James 1:27; 5:1–13.

9. The book *False Justice* by Stuart Greaves is an excellent resource on the subject of justice.

The subject of justice is one of the most fertile grounds for deception because parts of the Church have practically ignored the subject, and any time you ignore the biblical answer to a subject, you create a vacuum that is fertile ground for deception. Because so many suffer from injustice, it is easy to perpetuate and glorify accusation in the name of justice. And if the mistreated secure power on the basis of accusation, they can easily become perpetrators of injustice *themselves* committing horrible acts out of their own expressions of envy and rage.

For example, false justice presumes that those who have endured injustice are intrinsically more righteous than those who have perpetuated injustice. This is a denial of the Bible's plain message that *all* have sinned,[10] and this assumption is extremely common and deeply embedded in society and even in the Church. We assume the poor and those who have suffered are naturally "better" than those who have had power or wealth and taken advantage of people. However, when the poor are given power, they do the same things the rich do because both are fallen. We must confront the injustice perpetuated by the powerful, but we do not attribute unbiblical righteousness to those who suffer more. Again, *all* have sinned.

The spirit of accusation often exaggerates the oppressor's sins because envy does not want the oppressor to walk in their God-given calling, it wants to be exalted over the oppressor. This particular sin is rampant, and in many cases, we expect a perfection from others who are more prominent that we do not demonstrate in our own lives. We constantly expect to receive mercy and grace from God but do not always extend that same mercy or grace to others. Most people live by a double standard, expecting to receive mercy because we assume our intentions are "good" while demanding judgment for others because their deeds are bad. This double standard as an example of the spirit of accusation. We expect mercy even as we condemn others.

Injustice is real, and the Church should confront it as the prophets did. However, the Church cannot ascribe unbiblical righteousness to those who

---

10. Ecclesiastes 7:20; Psalm 14:2-3; Isaiah 53:6; Romans 3:23; 5:12; 1 John 1:8.

suffer injustice nor irrevocably condemn the unjust in an unbiblical way. It is a denial of our true condition and fertile ground for accusation.

When those who are chosen sin and use their calling or position to oppress others or treat others as disposable, it is wrong and sinful. And the Bible is very clear that God will judge people for that. But when those not called to the same position are willing to destroy those whom God has called, this is also sinful.

If we do not love mercy, we cannot produce true justice. Biblical justice does not come through accusation as it is full of mercy. A just community can only exist when mercy is loved, celebrated, and treasured. God severely judged Israel for injustice, but He *loves* mercy, and His judgments are part of a process to bring Israel into her promises, not disqualify her from them:

> Yet for all that, when they are in the land of their enemies, I will not spurn them, neither will I abhor them so as to destroy them utterly and break my covenant with them, for I am the LORD their God. But I will for their sake remember the covenant with their forefathers, whom I brought out of the land of Egypt in the sight of the nations, that I might be their God: I am the LORD." (Leviticus 26:44–45)

> For a brief moment I deserted you, but with great compassion I will gather you. In overflowing anger for a moment I hid my face from you, but with everlasting love I will have compassion on you," says the LORD, your Redeemer. (Isaiah 54:7–8)

> "For thus says the LORD: When seventy years are completed for Babylon, I will visit you, and I will fulfill to you my promise and bring you back to this place. For I know the plans I have for you, declares the LORD, plans for welfare and not for evil, to give you a future and a hope. Then you will call upon me and come and pray to me, and I will hear you. (Jeremiah 29:10–12)

> "Therefore say to the house of Israel, Thus says the Lord GOD: It is not for your sake, O house of Israel, that I am about to act, but for the sake of my

holy name, which you have profaned among the nations to which you came. And I will vindicate the holiness of my great name, which has been profaned among the nations, and which you have profaned among them. And the nations will know that I am the LORD, declares the Lord GOD, when through you I vindicate my holiness before their eyes. I will take you from the nations and gather you from all the countries and bring you into your own land. I will sprinkle clean water on you, and you shall be clean from all your uncleannesses, and from all your idols I will cleanse you. And I will give you a new heart, and a new spirit I will put within you. And I will remove the heart of stone from your flesh and give you a heart of flesh. And I will put my Spirit within you, and cause you to walk in my statutes and be careful to obey my rules. 28 You shall dwell in the land that I gave to your fathers, and you shall be my people, and I will be your God. And I will deliver you from all your uncleannesses. And I will summon the grain and make it abundant and lay no famine upon you. I will make the fruit of the tree and the increase of the field abundant, that you may never again suffer the disgrace of famine among the nations. (Ezekiel 36:22–30)

Therefore I will hedge up her way with thorns, and I will build a wall against her, so that she cannot find her paths. She shall pursue her lovers but not overtake them, and she shall seek them but shall not find them. Then she shall say, 'I will go and return to my first husband, for it was better for me then than now.' (Hosea 2:6–7)

"Come, let us return to the LORD; for he has torn us, that he may heal us; he has struck us down, and he will bind us up. After two days he will revive us; on the third day he will raise us up, that we may live before him. (Hosea 6:1–2)

When we recognize the sin of the elect, such as the sin of Jacob, what gives us more joy? Do we fight to see Jacob receive mercy for his sin and be transformed into the fullness of his calling? Or are we more energized by the discipline of his sin and the consequences he suffers for it? In summary, do we *love mercy* or *love accusation*?

There are times when those given great responsibility in the

Church, for example, use their authority in sinful ways that truly harm other people. When this happens, those sins must be addressed. There are times that people need to be restrained or removed from the place God has called and equipped them for because they are not stewarding their assignment well. So, in our communities, we need careful and wise leadership that does not protect the powerful when they are truly destructive. Avoiding accusation does not mean neglecting biblical government and discipline in the community. And it certainly does not mean those elect are exempt from living accountable lives in the community. This is clear in the long history of Israel who has repeatedly suffered for her sin. And not only has Israel suffered, individuals within Israel were cut off because of their sin, and they lost their inheritance.[11] However, this was never the end of Israel's story. Even when God cut individuals off from Israel, God declared a future purpose for Israel secured by His mercy.[12]

This perspective of Israel's story did not change in the New Testament. When Paul dealt with the complexity of Israel's story, he quoted Hosea's prediction that Israel's story was not yet finished and in the same passage predicts that, despite Israel's failures, God will finish His plan and has a glorious future for them:[13]

"And in the very place where it was said to them, 'You are not my people,' there they will be called 'sons of the living God.'" (Romans 9:26)

Paul did not quote this verse out of context. When he wrote this, he assumed his readers would know the original context and understand this as an affirmation that Israel's story is not yet finished.

---

11. For example, see Hosea 1:9.
12. For example, see Hosea 1:10–2:23.
13. See also Romans 11:2, 12, 15.

17

THE GLORY OF ONE NEW MAN

AS WE HAVE SEEN REPEATEDLY, God has revealed something about Himself in His choosing of Jacob and His ongoing commitment to that choice. Accordingly, that choice is not ultimately about Jacob; it is about *God*. It is critical that we do not dismiss the application to the Jewish people, but it is also important that we recognize our offense with Jacob is a core offense with God's election; something God confronts us with on a daily basis.

While there are Jewish communities across the earth, there are many people who do not live among the Jewish people, so when we speak about the election of Jacob, it is mostly a concept to them; it is not a part of their daily lives. It is easy to agree with the election of "Jacob" if you don't live with "Jacob." The simple truth is that it is easy to love a people or agree with their calling when you do not have to actually live with that people. The evidence of this is that there are people who "love Israel" but cannot love their neighbor.

The election of Israel is a divinely ordained stumbling block for the nations, but if we "agree" with God's election of Jacob yet are offended by His election of a person in our family, business, city, or church, it exposes the fact that we do not really agree with God's election.

If we "love Israel" but are offended with the people who live in our neighborhood, it is evidence we have not really resolved the issue of election. We are simply "undisturbed."

The Revelation of the Mystery of Jesus

If you ask Christians what the "revelation of the mystery of Jesus" is, they would give you all sorts of answers. Many would probably be accurate descriptions of Jesus. But Paul focused in on one specific thing: The revelation of the mystery of Jesus is the redemptive power of the gospel that so transforms human hearts that Jew and Gentile can walk together through Jesus as *one new human*. This "one new human" is a unified humanity that walks in mutual love and sacrifice yet maintains their respective distinction. Consider Paul's words in context:

> *Therefore remember that at one time you Gentiles in the flesh, called "the uncircumcision" by what is called the circumcision, which is made in the flesh by hands—remember that you were at that time separated from Christ, alienated from the commonwealth of Israel and strangers to the covenants of promise, having no hope and without God in the world. But now in Christ Jesus you who once were far off have been brought near by the blood of Christ. For he himself is our peace, who has made us both one and has broken down in his flesh the dividing wall of hostility by abolishing the law of commandments expressed in ordinances, that he might create in himself one new man in place of the two, so making peace, and might reconcile us both to God in one body through the cross, thereby killing the hostility. And he came and preached peace to you who were far off and peace to those who were near. For through him we both have access in one Spirit to the Father. So then you are no longer strangers and aliens, but you are fellow citizens with the saints and members of the household of God.... When you read this, you can perceive my insight into the mystery of Christ, which was not made known to the sons of men in other generations as it has now been revealed to his holy apostles and prophets by the Spirit. **This mystery is that the Gentiles are fellow heirs, members of the same***

body, and partakers of the promise in Christ Jesus through the gospel.
(Ephesians 2:11–19; 3:4–6)

According to Paul, the mystery of Jesus is revealed when Jew and Gentile are brought together into one body in peace, unity, and mutual blessing through the word of Jesus. If distinction between Jew and Gentile is lost, the glory of the gospel is lost because there is nothing glorious about humans who are identical, moving in unity.

It is important to remember that Paul lived in a very different period of time and culture than our own. In Paul's time, his great challenge was demonstrating that the Gentiles could be accepted and join the people of God through Jesus. The unique calling of the Jewish people was still recognized at the time because most of the early leaders in the Church were all Jewish. Furthermore, the early followers of "the way" who were later referred to as Christians were nearly all Jewish. In Paul's time, then, the challenge was whether the Gentiles could become part of the people of God, but in our time and in most places, we face an opposite challenge. In our time, Gentiles seem to dominate the religious landscape and either overlook or oppose the idea that the Jewish people carry a unique, distinct, and ongoing calling.

Paul's words focus on gentile inclusion and participation with the Jewish people, but we must not overlook the fact that he believed in a distinct calling for the Jewish people and a significance to their ongoing election. Instead of dismissing Israel's calling, he explained the beautiful reconciliation that is possible in Jesus as Jew and Gentile are brought together with the assumption that Israel's unique election remains.

When Paul's words are considered in light of the larger biblical conflict that we have been tracing, they are truly stunning.

When we read Paul's words in context, we should be truly horrified by many of the theological conclusions that have been accepted as biblical over the last 2,000 years. On one hand, we can be gracious toward theologians who assumed Israel's story was finished based on what they observed. For example, when Babylon destroyed

Jerusalem, just seventy years later, a Jewish remnant began to rebuild the city and the temple. However, after the Roman destruction of the temple, centuries began to pass with no visible, significant restoration of the Jewish people to Jerusalem. One can see how it seemed plausible that perhaps God was finished with the story of Israel despite the fact that the Bible clearly says otherwise.

However, the ongoing preservation of the Jewish people over 2,000 years and the events of 1948 were a shockwave throughout history that settled the issue: God is obviously not finished with the story of the people of Israel.

We should be gracious with people who lived without the witness of 1948, but we also have to acknowledge the theologies that ignored the biblical witness about Israel because the consequences of ignoring that witness were severe. Gentiles persecuted the Jewish people based on ideas that were completely unbiblical and the complete antithesis of the God of Israel, the Person of Jesus, and the teaching of the New Testament apostles. These persecutors attempted to justify themselves, in part, based on distorted theological conclusions.

In Ephesians, Paul directly tied the revelation of the mystery of Jesus to recognition between Jew and Gentile. There are a number of reasons for this, but we have to recognize that the glory of the gospel Paul proclaimed was that the transformation that comes through Jesus is capable of resolving the long-running animosity between Jew and Gentile.

The glory of the gospel is that it resolves the envy and anger between the election of Israel and the nations.

Many people assume Paul's description of "one new man" is a prediction that the gospel creates a new kind of humanity where there is no ongoing distinction in this age. They assume "one new man" is a kind of uniform, generic, "vanilla" people. Yet if the work of Jesus creates a homogenous people, then it is not a miraculous work at all. Humans have always sought unity on the basis of some kind of uniformity, and people who are the same can easily be brought together. In our time, social media networks are used for this very purpose. People seek out people like them for friendship, partnership, and collaboration. Social media-driven groups may have a sense of unity, but it is not biblical unity, and it is not the gospel.

The power of the gospel is demonstrated when people who are not alike can be brought tougher in deep unity and mutual love, which exist in the context of their ongoing distinction.

Paul's words do not make any sense if Jewish distinction has ended. And if that were the case, Paul would have said, "Jewish identity has ended, and gentile identity has ended, so now we can get along." But he did not say that. He said the mystery of Jesus is revealed when Jew and Gentile, as Jew and Gentile, come together in mutual unity, love, humility, and service. That is the true power of what Jesus did. His work of redemption carries the power to resolve the ancient envy and rage over election. Gentiles can honor, celebrate, enjoy, and serve the unique election of the Jewish people. And the Jewish people can serve God's purposes for the nations and be a profound blessing to the Gentiles.

Some people may note Paul also wrote there was no longer a separation between Jew, Gentile, male, female, slave, or free.[1] We do not have space to fully examine all of these verses, but these passages must be read in the full context of Paul's teaching. Paul's point was not that distinction no longer exists or matters, but rather that the conflict between our distinctions can be resolved in Jesus so that we become part of a large family with deep love and respect for each other, leading to self-sacrificing service for others not like us. That is the equality of the gospel. *The equality of the gospel is not based on sameness. It is demonstrated in diversity.*

Paul affirmed the value of being Jewish,[2] agreed with the ongoing practice of maintaining Jewish identity,[3] and very clearly held to an

---

1. Galatians 3:28; Colossians 3:11.
2. Romans 3:1–2; 9:4–5; 11:1, 29.
3. While Paul confronted the issue of Jewish believers who were trying to "convert" Gentiles into Jews, Paul was always positive about Jewish identity and never taught Jews should abandon their identity. The concept of the glory of one new man Paul taught in Ephesians 2–3 requires "Jews" and "Gentiles" to be present in the church.

ongoing and future purpose for the Jewish people.[4] He articulated the glory of Jesus' comprehensive work of redemption and ministered primarily among the Gentiles, but he would be horrified by the idea that people took his words to mean that Jewish distinction no longer exists. If there is no distinction, then the glory of reconciliation is not glorious at all because there cannot be reconciliation if there is not distinction and ongoing conflict. If the New Testament eliminates the value of Jewish distinction, much of Paul's teaching loses all its meaning.

If you asked Paul, "Do men and women still exist? Or do slave and master still exist?" he would be very confused. Those distinctions obviously remain. And the same is true of Jew and Gentile. Distinctions in this age obviously remain, and those distinctions, and the conflicts that exist because of those distinctions, provide the context for the glory of the gospel to be demonstrated. In fact, Paul's entire letter to the Ephesians deals with the glory of unity and love amid distinction. He began with Jew and Gentile[5] because that was a fundamental conflict in that age. He then moved on to the different gifts God gives people and how people are very different and yet made to function in unity.[6] And then Paul continued to describe God's purpose in male and female and parents and children.[7] In each context, distinctions exist that are ongoing in this age and create a context for the beauty of the gospel to be demonstrated.

If your gospel does not value, pursue, and demonstrate the glory of love, unity, and reconciliation between Jew and Gentile as Jew and Gentile, then it is not Paul's gospel.

Throughout history in the Church, there have been attempts to resolve the tension between peoples by removing the distinction

---

Paul's admonitions in his other letters also clearly assume that Jewish believers maintain a Jewish identity or at minimum are identifiably Jewish. Paul is flexible on the expression of Jewish identity, but he clearly assumes it can and must continue in the church. See also Acts 21:17-26; Romans 3:1–2; 11:1; 1 Corinthians 7:18.

4. Romans 11:1, 2, 11–12, 15, 23–24, 29.
5. Ephesians 2–3.
6. Ephesians 3:7, 11–13.
7. Ephesians 5–6.

between Jew and Gentile, but this is the opposite of the glory of "one new man." The mystery of Jesus is not revealed by stripping everyone of their distinction. It is revealed in the context of deep love between those who are distinct and naturally hostile to each other. To put it in context to our subject, Jesus is only revealed when Gentiles enjoy, love, celebrate, and serve the unique election of "Jacob" (and when the people of Israel come into their calling to serve the Gentiles with the knowledge of God). When we rage against that election and tolerate envy, we are harboring the root of sin in this age. We may cover it up with complex theology, and many of our Christian "heroes" have harbored these ideas, but they are not biblical.

Glory, Unity, and Distinction

It is common for Christians to say the purpose of Israel's election has been "fulfilled," and now God loves everyone the same. However, this is like reading the Jacob and Esau story and saying the resolution came when Jacob failed and was no longer called, and then he and his brother were reconciled by being given the same identity and assignment. Or like saying the tension between Isaac and Ishmael was removed by eliminating Isaac's calling. Or bringing peace among Jacob's sons by eliminating Joseph's prophetic promise. The arc of Genesis was very different. In each case, God brought brothers to unity while maintaining their distinct callings.

To say that everything is "the same" sounds good, but it is a humanistic concept that ignores the offense of God's election and does not display the glory of God. God's solution is much more glorious. His solution is to bring reconciliation so that groups of people who were in opposition displaying the envy of the serpent instead wholeheartedly contend for the success of the ones chosen. This is the true glory of reconciliation. *Reconciliation is not destroying the election of another and making them "like me." It is celebrating God-given election, fighting for it, and rooting out the envy of the snake.*

If we do not honor God-given distinction, we superficially cover up the root of envy in our hearts because, if everyone is the same, then envy can just "go away" when, in reality, envy is only resolved when we value and honor the election of another——*especially when the chosen demonstrate they are not qualified.* This is where the real test of our respect for election comes.

All humans are worthy of equal value, treatment, and opportunity because they are made in the image of God. But to say that everyone is the same is obviously false. The differences are innumerable and go for beyond the distinction of Jew and Gentile. Some are smarter. Some are more athletic. Some can lead. Others cannot. Some are artistic or musical. We know we are not the same, and to deny our differences may sound enlightened, but it is obviously false. Everyone should have the same opportunity, but a person cannot be whatever they want to be. Some have gifts others do not. We are given different abilities when we are born, and those abilities, and the lack of abilities, give us limitations, create distinctions, and are fertile ground for offense.

The serpent's poison came over offense at God's election, and God requires we face that offense. And Jesus came to resolve that offense, not overlook it.

In the next chapter, we will see that this is exactly why the end of the age tests our response to God's election. The issue is not whether or not Israel is a righteous people at the end of the age. The issue is whether we will honor God's election of Israel *because we fear God.* We can, and must, speak to Israel about her calling and address her sins just as the prophets did. But it will not be out of a spirit of accusation. It will be out of a genuine heart desire to see Israel succeed *with complete confidence* that God will bring out the fullness of Israel's calling according to His own power.

The rebellion began with the serpent's rejection of divine election, which means the restoration the gospel means must include the honoring and celebrating of divine election.

Because God's glory and His redemptive plan are based on His ability to fulfill the plan He declared to Abraham and began with Israel, the conflict between Jew and Gentile is a fundamental conflict. The serpent hates election and rages against Jewish election because God's redemptive plan depends on it. If that fails, everything fails.

The rage over election begins with Jew and Gentile, but it is multiplied to every facet of our lives. Ethnic groups rage against ethnic groups. Rich and poor, male and female, "powerful" and "weak" are all in conflict. Every expression of election in this age creates conflict, envy, and jealousy because we have all been infected by the serpent's venom. And any gospel that does not deal with the offense of election and form a people who are delivered from envy and celebrate God's divine election is an incomplete gospel which lacks a full demonstration of the power of God. If election is not honored and celebrated in a context of mutual love and unity, then we lack the revelation of the mystery of Jesus, even if we give a message of individual salvation. That message may bring some measure of blessing, but it's not the full gospel.

The fruit of the gospel creates an environment where those who are elect can walk in their election in such a way that their election brings a blessing. And they can see their election primarily through the lens of serving others and not their own exaltation. And they can be free of fear and suspicion toward others and free of their insecurity that causes them to cling to their exaltation and despise and distrust others. Those "not chosen" in a certain way can celebrate the election of those chosen and advocate for the elect with genuine love and affection, no longer envious of the elect or living with a murderous spirit toward the "chosen." This includes all manner of election or choosing, but it must include Jew and Gentile. *This is the gospel.*

Humans are called to reflect the image of God, and the Bible presents a glorious, unified, and yet diverse description of God. Christians call this the "Trinity" to describe the idea that God is One and yet consists of a Father, Son, and Spirit. This concept is found in the Hebrew Bible through the various descriptions of God. God is described in the heavens on His glorious throne, but then His Spirit is described as both Him and distinct. And then we have descriptions of God in a somewhat human form typically as the "Angel of the

Lord," "Word of the Lord," or what Daniel called "one [who looked] like a Son of Man [human]."[8] Through these mysterious descriptions of God, we get a picture of God as One and unified and yet appearing in distinct Persons. This divine glory is meant to be reflected by humans. We are meant to be a single, unified people, reflecting God's image with God-given distinctions of Jew, Gentile, male, female, etc.

The implications are clear: As long as gentile believers do not honor, celebrate, and advocate for the distinct calling of the Jewish people, they are not demonstrating the power of the gospel.

The sins of antisemitism, ethnic conflict, or prejudice are not a small thing. It's the serpent's venom, and if we tolerate it, we are not demonstrating the gospel. The sins of the historical Church against the Jewish people are not simply "mistakes." They are part of a devious plan by the serpent to destroy Jew and Gentile, pervert the gospel message, and hinder God's redemptive plan by destroying Gentiles and Jews. The biblical message of the gospel is not the elimination of Israel in favor of "the Church." The biblical message of the gospel is the power of God through Jesus to bring about the calling of Jew *and* Gentile by including Gentiles in His vast redemptive plan that is still deeply tied to the story of Israel. Obviously, not every theologian that minimizes Israel was antisemitic, so we can be gracious toward others, but we have to recognize we are in conflict with a devious and deceptive spiritual power.[9] He deceives through outright lies, twisting things, and distorting what God has said.

We can be gracious toward people who may be on a journey to understand God's ongoing purpose for Israel while also recognizing that the serpent perpetuates the rejection of Israel's election. And he is crafty, so he is able to influence people in subtle ways. The conflict over election, including Israel's election, is not a conflict with humans. It is ultimately a conflict with a crafty serpent.

There is a whole spectrum when it comes to rejecting Israel's

---

8. Daniel 7:13.

9. Genesis 3:1; John 8:44; 2 Corinthians 4:4; 11:3, 14; Ephesians 6:10-12; 1 Peter 5:8-9; 1 John 5:19; Revelation 12:9.

election. It can be antisemitism and persecution, which the Church has been guilty of. It can be the simple rejection of Israel's election by people who genuinely have no hostility toward the people of Israel. Even in the horrors of the Nazi Holocaust and the failure of the institutional Church, there were believers who suffered with Israel. And many of them probably held theological positions that did not recognize the fullness of God's ongoing purpose for Israel. But they recognized the evil of the Nazi agenda. We cannot paint everyone with a broad brush, but we must recognize that the rejection of election is not a small thing. Its origins and its outcomes are very dark, and we must root out every expression of it. Until we do, we are not walking in the full gospel.

The enemy loves to obscure this part of the gospel because everything is at stake. But now that his deception has been exposed, you cannot claim ignorance. So how will you deal with the controversy of Israel's election? And every other "election" of God that affects your life?

PART IV

THE FINAL CONFLICT OF THE AGE

18

AN UNPRECEDENTED CONFLICT OVER ENVY

WHILE MANY PEOPLE want to avoid the subject of the "end times" because of the many ways the subject is sensationalized or approached in unbiblical ways, the Bible gives is important important about how the age ends so we can in turn understand the time we are living in. While we cannot know every detail about the end, and it is difficult to know in advance exactly how some prophecies will unfold, the Bible gives us key themes and expects that we understand them.[1] When you take a long journey to a new place you do not know everything about the destination, but understanding the destination is necessary in order to travel. In the same way understanding end time themes is important. We can cooperate better with God's purposes when we know where the story is going. And, as we will see, end time themes are the ultimately culmination of themes throughout history and nations repeatedly pass through events that are foreshadows of the final crisis of the age. We need to first consider how the age ends, and then we will see that the nations have, and will, face intense crises that are not the end but revolve around the same essential issues.

---

1. I Chronicles 12:32; Matthew 16:2-3; Luke 12:56; I Thessalonians 5:1–6.

The Bible is very clear on the way this age ends, but unfortunately, many people are unaware of what the Bible plainly predicts. The subject of eschatology or the "end times" can be complex, and it is not within the scope of this book to discuss the end times in detail. However, it is critical that we recognize how central the theme of Israel is in end-time predictions. These predictions make it crystal clear that God's purpose for Israel is not yet finished. God is so committed to His purpose for Israel that a global controversy will erupt over His purposes for Israel, and the nations will rage against God by resisting the people of Israel. It is common to ignore these verses or reinterpret them, but they are frighteningly real. And there are multiple events in history that give us a preview of the end of the age. There are even current events that demonstrate the coming reality of what Scripture says will happen, and it all has to do with an unprecedented conflict over envy.

The biblical prophets frequently used historical events to "illustrate" their predictions of the final conflict, so historical previews give us sober pictures of what the Bible says.

It is completely irresponsible not to take what the Bible says about the end of the age seriously. The Hebrew Bible and the New Testament both clearly warn us that this age will end in an unprecedented conflict over election. And this conflict will be expressed in rage against the election of Jerusalem and the Jewish people. The nations' response to the election of Israel will be a key litmus test in God's judgment of the nations.

Let's begin with a few passages that describe the final conflict. Perhaps you have never read these passages or never seen them, seeing them as they're meant to be—literal events at the end of the age. Read these passages slowly and carefully. Virtually all these passages are direct statements by God, which means every word matters. Many people are quick to skip these verses, but the language is strong, and the predictions are sobering.

Wail, for the day of the LORD is near; as destruction from the Almighty it will come! Therefore all hands will be feeble, and every human heart will melt. They will be dismayed: pangs and agony will seize them; they will be in anguish like a woman in labor. They will look aghast at one another; their faces will be aflame. (Isaiah 13:6–8)

Draw near, O nations, to hear, and give attention, O peoples! Let the earth hear, and all that fills it; the world, and all that comes from it. For the LORD is enraged against all the nations, and furious against all their host; he has devoted them to destruction, has given them over for slaughter. Their slain shall be cast out, and the stench of their corpses shall rise; the mountains shall flow with their blood. All the host of heaven shall rot away, and the skies roll up like a scroll. All their host shall fall, as leaves fall from the vine, like leaves falling from the fig tree. For my sword has drunk its fill in the heavens; behold, it descends for judgment.... For the LORD has a day of vengeance, a year of recompense for the cause of Zion. (Isaiah 34:1–5, 8)

Why is your apparel red, and your garments like his who treads in the winepress? I have trodden the winepress alone, and from the peoples no one was with me; I trod them in my anger and trampled them in my wrath; their lifeblood spattered on my garments, and stained all my apparel. For the day of vengeance was in my heart, and my year of redemption had come.... I trampled down the peoples in my anger; I made them drunk in my wrath, and I poured out their lifeblood on the earth." I will recount the steadfast love of the LORD, the praises of the LORD, according to all that the LORD has granted us, and the great goodness to the house of Israel that he has granted them according to his compassion, according to the abundance of his steadfast love. (Isaiah 63:2–4, 6–7)

Ask now, and see, can a man bear a child? Why then do I see every man with his hands on his stomach like a woman in labor? Why has every face turned pale? Alas! That day is so great there is none like it; it is a time of distress for Jacob; yet he shall be saved out of it. (Jeremiah 30:6–7)

At that time shall arise Michael, the great prince who has charge of your people. And there shall be a time of trouble, such as never has been since there was a nation till that time. But at that time your people shall be delivered, everyone whose name shall be found written in the book. (Daniel 12:1)

And I will show wonders in the heavens and on the earth, blood and fire and columns of smoke. The sun shall be turned to darkness, and the moon to blood, before the great and awesome day of the LORD comes. And it shall come to pass that everyone who calls on the name of the LORD shall be saved. For in Mount Zion and in Jerusalem there shall be those who escape, as the LORD has said, and among the survivors shall be those whom the LORD calls. For behold, in those days and at that time, when I restore the fortunes of Judah and Jerusalem, I will gather all the nations and bring them down to the Valley of Jehoshaphat. And I will enter into judgment with them there, on behalf of my people and my heritage Israel.... So you shall know that I am the LORD your God, who dwells in Zion, my holy mountain. And Jerusalem shall be holy, and strangers shall never again pass through it. (Joel 2:30–32; 3:1–2, 17)

Behold, I am about to make Jerusalem a cup of staggering to all the surrounding peoples. The siege of Jerusalem will also be against Judah. On that day I will make Jerusalem a heavy stone for all the peoples. All who lift it will surely hurt themselves. And all the nations of the earth will gather against it. (Zechariah 12:2–3)

In the whole land, declares the LORD, two thirds shall be cut off and perish, and one third shall be left alive. And I will put this third into the fire, and refine them as one refines silver, and test them as gold is tested. They will call upon my name, and I will answer them. I will say, "They are my people"; and they will say, "The LORD is my God." ... For I will gather all the nations against Jerusalem to battle, and the city shall be taken and the houses plundered and the women raped. Half of the city shall go out into exile, but the rest of the people shall not be cut off from the city. Then the LORD will go out and fight against those nations as when he fights on a day of battle. On that day his feet shall stand on the Mount of Olives that lies before Jerusalem on the east, and the Mount of Olives shall be split in two from east to west by a very wide valley, so that one half of the Mount shall move northward, and the other half southward.... And the LORD will be king over all the earth. On that day the LORD will be one and his name one.... And this shall be the plague with which the LORD will strike all the peoples that wage war against Jerusalem: their flesh will rot while they are still standing on their feet, their eyes will rot in their sockets, and their tongues will rot in their mouths. And on that day a great panic from the LORD shall fall on them, so that each will seize the hand of another, and the hand of the one will be raised against the hand of the other. (Zechariah 13:8–9; 14:2–4, 9, 12–13)

The oracles of the prophets can be difficult to understand because many people read them quickly, metaphorically, or simply do not read them at all. But the prophets spoke words directly from God, words that built on the foundations Moses laid in the Torah. When you read the prophets this way, their predictions become much clearer. When these passage are read as literal predictions, several themes begin to emerge:

- The prophets predicted a day when *all nations* become caught up in a conflict over Jerusalem and the people of Israel.
- This day will be a day of unprecedented trouble, affecting the entire earth. But the epicenter of that trouble will be Jerusalem and the people of Israel.
- The prophets' predictions that the final trouble will center on Israel is a bold and clear statement that the calling of Israel is not finished. If there was no longer an ongoing call on Jerusalem or the people of Israel, the age would not end with a crisis over the very existence of the people and the city.
- Biblically, Israel is subject to crisis and harassment from the nations when she is not righteous. The fact that Israel is the center of a crisis indicates that Israel will not yet be completely righteous. But the fact the nations will center

in on Jerusalem indicates Israel and her people are *still* elect.

- This harassment from the nations is unprecedented. It is a "time like no other time," indicating that the conflict over election is not yet over. There will be one last final crisis over envy in this age.
- The prophets predicted this day will be similar to days of trouble in the past but will eclipse them all in the end because it is the final conflict of the age. After this conflict, the earth is transitioned into a new age and a new era.
- These events will trigger the judgment or vengeance of God on the nations on behalf of Israel: *"For the Lord has a day of vengeance, a year of recompense for the cause of Zion."*
- The final test over election in this age ends with God's judgment on the nations. He will display His vengeance in a way He never has. The Bible's descriptions of this day are terrifying.

These predictions are not exclusive to the Hebrew Bible. They are repeated in the New Testament. For example, Jesus repeated the prophets' predictions:[2]

So when you see the abomination of desolation spoken of by the prophet Daniel, standing in the holy place (let the reader understand), then let those who are in Judea flee to the mountains. Let the one who is on the housetop not go down to take what is in his house, and let the one who is in the field not turn back to take his cloak. And alas for women who are pregnant and for those who are nursing infants in those days! Pray that your flight may not be in winter or on a Sabbath. For then there will be great tribulation, such as has not been from the beginning of the world until now, no, and never will be. And if those days had not been cut short, no human being would be saved. But for the sake of the elect those days will be cut short. (Matthew 24:15–22)

---

2. See also Mark 13 and Luke 21.

The message is clear: *This age will end with an unprecedented conflict.* When you read everything the Bible says about these days, the entire earth is caught up in this conflict. It is not a conflict that is limited to Jerusalem or Israel. The entire world will experience the trouble of these days. But this conflict is clearly focused on Jerusalem and Israel.

The prophets predicted a day of unequalled trouble, but they also gave strong words of comfort and encouragement for Israel. The great trouble at the end of the age concludes with something never seen before: God's cataclysmic judgment of the nations for their treatment of the people of Israel and a new era in which Israel is a saved, righteous people celebrated by the nations and defended by God:

"For the LORD will vindicate his people and have compassion on his servants, when he sees that their power is gone and there is none remaining, bond or free ... if I sharpen my flashing sword and my hand takes hold on judgment, I will take vengeance on my adversaries and will repay those who hate me. I will make my arrows drunk with blood, and my sword shall devour flesh—with the blood of the slain and the captives, from the long-haired heads of the enemy. Rejoice with him, O heavens; bow down to him, all gods, for he avenges the blood of his children and takes vengeance on his adversaries. He repays those who hate him and cleanses his people's land." (Deuteronomy 32:36, 41–43)

Say to those who have an anxious heart, "Be strong; fear not! Behold, your God will come with vengeance, with the recompense of God. He will come and save you." (Isaiah 35:4)

Your people shall all be righteous; they shall possess the land forever, the branch of my planting, the work of my hands, that I might be glorified. (Isaiah 60:21)

"Behold, the days are coming, declares the LORD, when I will make a new covenant with the house of Israel and the house of Judah, not like the covenant that I made with their fathers on the day when I took them by

the hand to bring them out of the land of Egypt, my covenant that they broke, though I was their husband, declares the LORD. For this is the covenant that I will make with the house of Israel after those days, declares the LORD: I will put my law within them, and I will write it on their hearts. And I will be their God, and they shall be my people. And no longer shall each one teach his neighbor and each his brother, saying, 'Know the LORD,' for they shall all know me, from the least of them to the greatest, declares the LORD. For I will forgive their iniquity, and I will remember their sin no more." Thus says the LORD, who gives the sun for light by day and the fixed order of the moon and the stars for light by night, who stirs up the sea so that its waves roar—the LORD of hosts is his name: "If this fixed order departs from before me, declares the LORD, then shall the offspring of Israel cease from being a nation before me forever." Thus says the LORD: "If the heavens above can be measured, and the foundations of the earth below can be explored, then I will cast off all the offspring of Israel for all that they have done, declares the LORD." (Jeremiah 31:31–37)

"Behold, the days are coming, declares the LORD, when I will fulfill the promise I made to the house of Israel and the house of Judah. In those days and at that time I will cause a righteous Branch to spring up for David, and he shall execute justice and righteousness in the land. In those days Judah will be saved, and Jerusalem will dwell securely. And this is the name by which it will be called: 'The LORD is our righteousness.'... Thus says the LORD: If I have not established my covenant with day and night and the fixed order of heaven and earth, then I will reject the offspring of Jacob and David my servant and will not choose one of his offspring to rule over the offspring of Abraham, Isaac, and Jacob. For I will restore their fortunes and will have mercy on them." (Jeremiah 33:14–16, 25–26)

I will cleanse them from all the guilt of their sin against me, and I will forgive all the guilt of their sin and rebellion against me. And this city shall be to me a name of joy, a praise and a glory before all the nations of the earth who shall hear of all the good that I do for them. They shall fear and tremble because of all the good and all the prosperity I provide for it. (Jeremiah 33:8–9)

So the angel who talked with me said to me, "Cry out, Thus says the LORD of hosts: I am exceedingly jealous for Jerusalem and for Zion. And I am exceedingly angry with the nations that are at ease; for while I was angry but a little, they furthered the disaster." (Zechariah 1:14–15)

On that day the LORD will protect the inhabitants of Jerusalem, so that the feeblest among them on that day shall be like David, and the house of David shall be like God, like the angel of the LORD, going before them. And on that day I will seek to destroy all the nations that come against Jerusalem. (Zechariah 12:8–9)

And the LORD will be king over all the earth. On that day the LORD will be one and his name one.... And it shall be inhabited, for there shall never again be a decree of utter destruction. Jerusalem shall dwell in security. And this shall be the plague with which the LORD will strike all the peoples that wage war against Jerusalem: their flesh will rot while they are still standing on their feet, their eyes will rot in their sockets, and their tongues will rot in their mouths. And on that day a great panic from the LORD shall fall on them, so that each will seize the hand of another, and the hand of the one will be raised against the hand of the other. (Zechariah 14:9, 11–13)

These prophecies give us even more of the picture:

- God has staked His honor on His ability to preserve Israel in a distinct way. He stated that, if He cannot preserve Israel in a distinct way, He cannot uphold creation. God's commitment to preserve Israel's unique identity means there is an ongoing purpose for the unique election of the Jewish people that justifies the Lord's unique preservation of Israel.
- God staked His honor on His ability to preserve Israel when the nation was idolatrous, just before the nation endured the destruction of Babylon, indicating God's commitment remains regardless of Israel's condition.

- God is going to answer the great conflict over Israel with unprecedented judgments. He will save, transform, and defend Israel.
- God will execute terrifying judgments on the nations. The nations' rage against Israel is obviously part of a bigger conflict against God Himself. He is going to answer that rage in a way He has never done before, and the nations will understand that their rejection of Israel's election was, in reality, a rejection of God Himself.
- God is going to transform Israel into a holy people and a glorious Kingdom that becomes the leading nation on the earth in a new era. They will no longer suffer the rage of the nations.
- God's response to the nations indicates two things: 1) The rage of the nations is going to reach a climax that it has never reached in history. 2) God is fully committed to the future of Israel. Israel's story is clearly not over because it sets the context for God's judgment of the nations at the end of this age.

There is simply no way to reinterpret these verses. The things the prophets described have never happened in history. And they are frighteningly real. Yet we can see the events in our current day beginning to show us that the predictions actually will take place. We can see things setting the stage, as it were. The prophets used very strong language, and there is no reason to dismiss their language as metaphorical. To do so is to mishandle the Scriptures and disregard what they said. These predictions are the very words of God.

Furthermore, the New Testament also affirms a future day of restoration and salvation for Israel. The timing is not given, but the restoration is clearly affirmed:

So when they had come together, they asked him, "Lord, will you at this time restore the kingdom to Israel?" He said to them, "It is not for you to

know times or seasons that the Father has fixed by his own authority."
(Acts 1:6–8)

Repent therefore, and turn back, that your sins may be blotted out, that
times of refreshing may come from the presence of the Lord, and that he
may send the Christ appointed for you, Jesus, whom heaven must receive
until the time for restoring all the things about which God spoke by the
mouth of his holy prophets long ago. (Acts 3:19–21)

Now if their trespass means riches for the world, and if their failure means
riches for the Gentiles, how much more will their full inclusion mean! ...
what will their acceptance mean but life from the dead?... And in this way
all Israel will be saved, as it is written, "The Deliverer will come from Zion,
he will banish ungodliness from Jacob." (Romans 11:12, 15, 26)

The New Testament not only affirms the day of trouble and the
restoration of Israel, it also affirms God's judgment on the nations on
behalf of Israel. For example, when Jesus taught on the Mount of
Olives, looking over the Valley of Jehoshaphat, He predicted He
would judge the nations based on their response to Israel. Jesus'
message was a clear reference to the prophecy of Joel 3, which
predicts God will judge the nations in the Valley of Jehoshaphat
based on their response to the people of Israel:

"For behold, in those days and at that time, when I restore the fortunes of
Judah and Jerusalem, I will gather all the nations and bring them down to
the Valley of Jehoshaphat. And I will enter into judgment with them there,
on behalf of my people and my heritage Israel, because they have scattered
them among the nations and have divided up my land, and have cast lots
for my people, and have traded a boy for a prostitute, and have sold a girl
for wine and have drunk it.... Let the nations stir themselves up and come
up to the Valley of Jehoshaphat; for there I will sit to judge all the
surrounding nations.... Multitudes, multitudes, in the valley of decision! For
the day of the LORD is near in the valley of decision.... The LORD roars
from Zion, and utters his voice from Jerusalem, and the heavens and the

earth quake. But the LORD is a refuge to his people, a stronghold to the people of Israel. "So you shall know that I am the LORD your God, who dwells in Zion, my holy mountain. And Jerusalem shall be holy, and strangers shall never again pass through it." (Joel 3:1–3, 12, 14, 16–17)

"When the Son of Man comes in his glory, and all the angels with him, then he will sit on his glorious throne. Before him will be gathered all the nations, and he will separate people one from another as a shepherd separates the sheep from the goats. And he will place the sheep on his right, but the goats on the left. Then the King will say to those on his right, 'Come, you who are blessed by my Father, inherit the kingdom prepared for you from the foundation of the world. For I was hungry and you gave me food, I was thirsty and you gave me drink, I was a stranger and you welcomed me, I was naked and you clothed me, I was sick and you visited me, I was in prison and you came to me.' Then the righteous will answer him, saying, 'Lord, when did we see you hungry and feed you, or thirsty and give you drink? And when did we see you a stranger and welcome you, or naked and clothe you? And when did we see you sick or in prison and visit you?' And the King will answer them, 'Truly, I say to you, as you did it to one of the least of these my brothers, you did it to me.' "Then he will say to those on his left, 'Depart from me, you cursed, into the eternal fire prepared for the devil and his angels. For I was hungry and you gave me no food, I was thirsty and you gave me no drink, I was a stranger and you did not welcome me, naked and you did not clothe me, sick and in prison and you did not visit me.' Then they also will answer, saying, 'Lord, when did we see you hungry or thirsty or a stranger or naked or sick or in prison, and did not minister to you?' Then he will answer them, saying, 'Truly, I say to you, as you did not do it to one of the least of these, you did not do it to me.' And these will go away into eternal punishment, but the righteous into eternal life." (Matthew 25:31–46)

Because Matthew 25 is a reference to Joel 3, the "brethren" in

Matthew 25 are clearly the people of Israel.[3] Jesus finished His longest teaching on the end times with this prophecy so that we would take it seriously. This is a direct warning, not simply a bit of information we can afford to learn but not respond to. Jesus did not predict He would give a theology test on what you think about Israel. He predicted He would judge based on *actions* which are the true indicator of real theology. It is not what you "say" but what you "do" that indicates what you truly believe. Correct theology will produce the right response. And as we have repeatedly said, bad theology eventually produces evil actions.

There is so much that could be said about these passages, and if they are new to you, you will likely need to give extended time to study these passages and read them in context to feel the full weight of them. But a few things become immediately apparent:

- These predictions are not metaphorical. They are completely real, and these judgments will be terrifying. People ignore these passages because of their intensity, but we should do the opposite. The intensity should cause us to pay even closer attention. Many people dismiss passages like these because they seem too dramatic, exaggerated, or impossible, but the Bible is full of dramatic events that seem "impossible." The creation of everything from nothing, the Exodus, the Incarnation, and even the existence of God Himself—all of these things are far beyond what we can comprehend, and yet they are plainly true. This should give us courage to believe what the prophets predicted.
- The prophets predicted things that have never happened: 1) a conflict beyond every conflict in history; 2) a conflict that includes "all nations" (not "a nation") involved in a battle over Jerusalem and the people of Israel; 3) God's

---

3. There are also a number of other reasons why the "brethren" are the people of Israel, but it is outside the scope of this book.

unprecedented and terrifying judgment and vengeance on the nations because of their hostility toward Jerusalem and Israel; and 4) Israel's full deliverance, salvation, and transformation into a glorious people.

When considering the weight of these various passages of Scripture regarding end-time prophecy, it is important for you to understand that you and I live in the first generation in all of human history when Israel has become a global conversation. This was not true in the days of Moses, David, Jesus, or Paul. Now, *for the first time,* God is forcing all the nations to deal with the question of Israel. We see this in our 24-hour news cycles. And we must face that question and answer this question: *Why does the age end with a distinct conflict over Jerusalem and the people of Israel?*

Some Christians do take these passages seriously, but they quickly become "end-time details" rather than actual people. They reduce the significance of Israel and its people to an end-time sign or a part of an end-time sequence of events. They see the significance of Israel's regathering simply as part of a sequence of events necessary to see Jesus' return. However, Israel is not simply a piece in an end-time puzzle, a thing that is required so that other things will happen. The significance of Israel in God's end-time story is a much bigger subject. We are supposed to meditate on Israel's prominent role in the end-time story and reflect on *why Israel is so significant in prophecy. Why does it seem like the final conflict plays out, in part, as a conflict over Israel?*

We should not see Israel as a chess piece on some cosmic chessboard. Instead, we should meditate on Scripture and ponder God's commitment, not to Israel as an abstract entity, but to Israel as a people. "Israel" is people. A real people. A people with hope, fears, pressures, and joys like anyone else. We are so numbed by media and information that we can forget the biblical narrative is a story about real people. And when we speak of trouble or salvation, we are speaking of events that will affect real people.

Furthermore, God's commitment to Israel and Jacob tells us

something about God, and that is the main point we have been addressing in this book. If we simply look for end-time information or details, we can miss the main point. The main point is the revelation of God through a people. The God of Jacob wants to reveal Himself on a global stage, and He is committed to doing this through Jacob's people.

19

IT BEGINS AND ENDS WITH ENVY

Sin in this age began with a great conflict over election, and sin in this age concludes with an unprecedented conflict over election. This is why the prophets boldly predicted the age ends with a crisis over the city of Jerusalem and the election of Israel.

The end-times storyline revolves around Jerusalem for one simple reason: God has elected Jerusalem. Jerusalem may even be an unrighteous city at the end of the age, but that does not change God's election. In the same way, the people of Israel were chosen to play a significant role in God's redemptive plan, and that role is not yet finished.[1] Perhaps most of Israel will be sinful at the end of the age, and only a remnant will be righteous. Again, this does not affect God's election or His commitment to accomplish His work through Israel. Israel was not chosen on the basis of her righteousness, and she will not be rejected on the basis of her unrighteousness.[2] As we know, election is on the basis of God's *desire,* not human *performance.*[3]

The idea that the age ends in a conflict around Jerusalem is strange to

---

1. Jeremiah 31:35-37; Ezekiel 36:24-26; Acts 1:6–7; Romans 11:1–2, 11–12, 15, 25–29.
2. Deuteronomy 7:7-8; 9:4–6; Ezekiel 36:22-23.
3. Deuteronomy 7:7-8; 10:15; Isaiah 43:4; Jeremiah 31:3; Malachi 1:2; Romans 9:11.

us if we do not grasp God's commitment to election. Many people see the final conflict over Israel as a secondary issue, a detail not worthy of their attention, because they do not grasp the seriousness of election and envy.

God's commitment to His election is so strong that, in the case of Israel, His honor is at stake in the story of Israel. He is the *God of Jacob,* which means God has chosen to reveal who He is through His story with Jacob and Jacob's family. He has forever tied our understanding of who He is to His story with Jacob. And God is so committed to election that His redemptive plan depends on His relationship to Jacob. There is no "plan B." That very idea of a "plan B" violates the whole purpose of election. As Paul said, the calling of God is "irrevocable,"[4] because it is based on God's choosing, not the performance of the one chosen.[5]

The enemy understands God's commitment to election, which is why the city of Jerusalem and the people of Jacob become the area of conflict at the end of the age. God has repeatedly promised that Israel will become an entirely holy and righteous people who dwell at peace in their land. These promises have clearly never been fulfilled, and the prophets looked forward to a time when these promises would be fulfilled.[6] The New Testament also looked forward to a future day when God's promises to Israel would be fulfilled.[7]

The enemy knows that God's plan for the age cannot end without the fulfillment of His promises to Israel. And he knows that, as long as those promises remain unfulfilled, he has a measure of influence on the nations as the "god of this age."[8]

---

4. Romans 11:29.
5. Romans 9:11.
6. Genesis 12:1-3, 7; 13:15; 15; 17:7-8, 19; 25:5-6; 26:3; 28:3-4; 35:9-15; Leviticus 25:18-19; 26:5-6, 42; Deuteronomy 12:10; 32:43; 33:27-19; 2 Samuel 7:10; 1 Chronicles 16:17-18; Psalm 105:10-11; Isaiah 14:30; 32:17-18; 54:14; 60:21; 61:8-9; Jeremiah 23:6; 24:6; 30:10; 32:37, 33:16; 40-41; 46:27; Ezekiel 11:17; 28:25-26; 34:25, 27-28; 36:26-28; 38:8, 11, 14; 39:25-28; Hosea 2:18; Amos 9:15; Micah 4:4; Zephaniah 3:13; Zechariah 14:11.
7. Acts 1:6–8; 3:19-21; Romans 11:1–2, 11–12, 15, 25–26; Hebrews 8:8–12.
8. 2 Corinthians 4:4.

But he knows that, when God fulfills His promises and transitions the age, it will also bring about his judgment.[9]

In the biblical narrative, there is a direct connection between the end of the satan's influence and the fulfillment of the promises made to Israel.

God has designed a redemptive plan that is dependent on His plan of election, which includes the election of Israel. And that plan is dependent on everyone, not just Israel, agreeing with His election. The satan knows this, so he rages against election because he knows that God's plan depends on God's election *and* that God's plan depends on God's people honoring that election. History is building toward a shocking moment when God's people agree completely with His election, and that agreement will remove the place the satan has to infect us with his envy. Israel will then come into the fullness of her election. There is a deep connection between the satan's influence and the nations' rage against Israel.

We are now in the first generation in history when God is forcing all the nations to consider His ongoing election of the Jewish people and the city of Jerusalem. That means we are in a new season of history. God has not forgotten His promises, and He is clearly setting the stage for their fulfillment. The fulfillment of the promises means the judgment of the evil powers of this age. The enemy knows this well, and he is going to oppose the fulfillment of these promises in ways we cannot fully imagine right now.

God's election is certainly not limited to His choice of Jacob. As we have seen, it is a fundamental part of the creation story, and we encounter God's election in every area of our lives. But the election of Israel will become a global controversy, a way the nations will challenge God's right to lead the way He wants to lead. And this controversy will not really be about Jacob. It will be about the God of Jacob. *The conflict over Israel is really a conflict over the God of Israel who has tied Himself to her destiny.*

The satan's fall began with envy over God's election, and that envy will be expressed in an ultimate way at the end of the age. The satan

---

9. Matthew 8:29; 1 John 3:8; Revelation 12:12; 20:2–3, 10.

has been consumed with envy since humans were first created. And envy produces murder when it is ripe. The enemy knows that God is absolutely committed to election, which means the only way to destroy God's redemptive plan is to destroy the elect. That is what the serpent did in the garden when he brought about the death of every human ever born, and that root of envy will also spark the greatest conflict in human history. The goal will remain the same—the destruction of humanity—but the prophets warned the rage will be focused on Jacob because, if you can destroy Jacob, you can destroy the plan of the God of Jacob.

Jesus or Israel?

God continues to challenge the earth with His election of Israel, but there is another election that is even more controversial: the election of Jesus. And we need to see that the two are deeply connected. The ultimate offense in election is, of course, our natural offense at God's election of Jesus because He is not the kind of deliverer or messiah that we would have chosen. Centuries before He came, the prophet Isaiah predicted He is not the kind of deliver we would choose:

> Behold, my servant shall act wisely; he shall be high and lifted up, and shall be exalted. As many were astonished at you—his appearance was so marred, beyond human semblance, and his form beyond that of the children of mankind—so shall he sprinkle many nations. Kings shall shut their mouths because of him, for that which has not been told them they see, and that which they have not heard they understand. Who has believed what he has heard from us? And to whom has the arm of the LORD been revealed? For he grew up before him like a young plant, and like a root out of dry ground; he had no form or majesty that we should look at him, and no beauty that we should desire him. He was despised and rejected by men, a man of sorrows and acquainted with grief; and as one from whom men hide their faces he was despised, and we esteemed him not. Surely he has borne our griefs and carried our sorrows; yet we esteemed him stricken, smitten by God, and afflicted. But he was pierced

for our transgressions; he was crushed for our iniquities; upon him was the chastisement that brought us peace, and with his wounds we are healed. All we like sheep have gone astray; we have turned—every one—to his own way; and the LORD has laid on him the iniquity of us all. He was oppressed, and he was afflicted, yet he opened not his mouth; like a lamb that is led to the slaughter, and like a sheep that before its shearers is silent, so he opened not his mouth. By oppression and judgment he was taken away; and as for his generation, who considered that he was cut off out of the land of the living, stricken for the transgression of my people? And they made his grave with the wicked and with a rich man in his death, although he had done no violence, and there was no deceit in his mouth. (Isaiah 52:13-53:9)

Isaiah's description of God's chosen "servant" plainly warns us that He will not be the kind of deliverer we would choose. He will be "despised and rejected." The truth is there are probably many followers of Jesus who have not fully grappled with who Jesus is. They have an image of Jesus based on their own ideas that do not fully represent who Jesus is. If you doubt that, look at any image of Jesus. The image always reflects the culture of the artist. Jesus is rarely depicted as a Jewish man from the Middle East. Furthermore, most Christians never consider the fact that Jesus is a Jewish man. His native culture is very different from our native cultures.

Isaiah's message is clear: If the election of Jacob is shocking, God's choice of Jesus is even more shocking.

For 2,000 years, many people have been convinced that God's election of Jesus was the end of His election of Israel. However, this is not what the Bible says. The New Testament plainly states that God's election of Jesus is the way God will secure His promises to Israel and the nations. Christians assume that the coming of Jesus fulfilled all the promises of God, but this is not what the Bible teaches. The Bible teaches that the coming of Jesus *secured* all God's promises. Those promises must still be fulfilled. The apostles plainly believed the promises made to Israel would be fulfilled in the future. This is easily proven by a few passages that have already been quoted:

So when they had come together, they asked him, "Lord, will you at this time restore the kingdom to Israel?" He said to them, "It is not for you to know times or seasons that the Father has fixed by his own authority. (Acts 1:6–7)

...that he may send the Christ appointed for you, Jesus, whom heaven must receive until the time for restoring all the things about which God spoke by the mouth of his holy prophets long ago. (Acts 3:20–21)

God has not rejected his people whom he foreknew.... What will their acceptance mean but life from the dead? (Romans 11:2, 15)

With a few references, we can easily see the authors of the New Testament believed Israel's promises had not been fulfilled, but they would be fulfilled in the future. In order words, the work of Jesus was part of the process of fulfilling Israel's story and election. It did not replace them. And there is clearly a future moment of fulfillment. Now that the people of Israel and the Modern State of Israel have suddenly became a global conversation 2,000 years after most people assumed Israel's story was finished, we must ask if we are in the beginning of the days the prophets and the apostles predicted.

Some Christians have noticed these verses but reduced the people of Israel to a chess piece on an end-times chessboard. They see Israel only as a requirement that must be fulfilled so Jesus can return and the next age can begin—almost like an obligation, something that must happen so we can continue with the bigger story. This is not the perspective of the New Testament, however. The New Testament brings us into a much bigger story. The authors of the New Testament all assumed that the Hebrew Bible was "The Bible" and that their readers would be very familiar with it.

When the New Testament is read correctly, it does not present Israel as a mere chess piece that must believe so Jesus can come to end everything.[10] Instead, the New Testament described God's

---

10. In fact, if you read the New Testament carefully, it does predict Israel will be recon-

ongoing commitment to Israel. The emphasis on Israel in end-time passages is an emphasis on God's covenantal commitment to Israel's election and His promises. He is going to do everything He said He is going to do. He is committed to His election of Israel to the end. There is a knowledge of Him as the God of Jacob that He wants us to discover when He predicts the age cannot end without the fulfillment of His promises to Israel. God's election of Jesus is His ultimate election, but what we need to notice is that it is an integrated part of God's story with Israel. A biblical view shows that Jesus is part of God's commitment to Israel, not His replacement of Israel.

When you read passages carefully, you discover something that is truly astonishing in light of the last 2,000 years: *The New Testament presented rage against the people of Israel as rage against Jesus.* This is truly shocking to many people because of the centuries of hostility against the people of Israel in the name of Jesus, but nevertheless, it is true.

Let's consider two passages we have already referenced. The first is Revelation 12. Revelation 12 is an apocalyptic passage that summarizes the great spiritual conflict of the age, but the characters in the passage are interpreted, and it is relatively easy to understand. The passage begins by describing a great conflict:

> And a great sign appeared in heaven: a woman clothed with the sun, with the moon under her feet, and on her head a crown of twelve stars. She was pregnant and was crying out in birth pains and the agony of giving birth. And another sign appeared in heaven: behold, a great red dragon.... And the dragon stood before the woman who was about to give birth, so that when she bore her child he might devour it. She gave birth to a male child, one who is to rule all the nations with a rod of iron, but her child was caught up to God and to his throne. (Revelation 12:1–5)

The imagery is relatively straightforward. There is a "woman"

---

ciled to Jesus, but it does not predict Israel must believe in Jesus before Jesus will return.

who has a crown of twelve stars and will give birth to the deliverer (messiah) destined the rule. The woman is obviously Israel. Israel is often described as a woman,[11] has twelve tribes, and is the one through whom the Messiah comes. And later in the passage, we are told that the dragon is the satan. So we have the rage of the satan against the deliverer being expressed in a conflict with the woman.

The passage continues to summarize the end-time conflict, and it predicts the satan's rage will be expressed against the *woman:*

> And the great dragon was thrown down, that ancient serpent, who is called the devil and Satan, the deceiver of the whole world—he was thrown down to the earth.... Woe to you, O earth and sea, for the devil has come down to you in great wrath, because he knows that his time is short!" And when the dragon saw that he had been thrown down to the earth, he pursued the woman who had given birth to the male child.... The serpent poured water like a river out of his mouth after the woman, to sweep her away with a flood. But the earth came to the help of the woman, and the earth opened its mouth and swallowed the river that the dragon had poured from his mouth. Then the dragon became furious with the woman and went off to make war on the rest of her offspring, on those who keep the commandments of God and hold to the testimony of Jesus. And he stood on the sand of the sea. (Revelation 12:9, 12–13, 15–17)

There is a lot contained in these few verses, but let's summarize the main points:

- The satan will be thrown down to the earth, and when this happens, he will be in a great rage because he knows that his time is short.
- When he is thrown down, he will vent his rage by pursuing *the woman* who gives birth to the Messiah.
- He will focus his rage against the woman and release a "flood" against her.

---

11. Isaiah 54:5; 66:7–8; Jeremiah 2:2; 3:6–8; Ezekiel 16:8; Hosea 2:19–20; Revelation 12:1.

- The satan will be furious because the woman is preserved and he cannot destroy her.
- The satan will also make war against the "rest of the offspring" of the woman. These other "children" are identified as those who follow Jesus.

The passage says that Satan's rage against God and against the Messiah will be expressed against the *woman*. In this passage, Israel is the primary object of the satan's rage in his conflict against God. However, she will be preserved, and he will be unable to destroy her. When the satan is unable to destroy the woman, he will pursue the *rest* of her children, those who follow Jesus. This passage has profound implications for the way most Christians understand the end of the age. Most Christians think the age ends with persecutions against Christians. However, Revelation 12 gives us a more nuanced answer. And that answer matches up perfectly with what the prophets predicted.

We need to carefully consider the implications of Revelation 12 because the implications are profound and disruptive to many Christian assumptions about Israel and the end of the age.

Revelation 12 predicts that, first of all, the satan releases his rage against Israel and seeks to destroy Israel. This has a number of implications, and it means that Israel still matters. The fact that he can target Israel means the people of Israel are still a distinct people. From the beginning, the serpent targeted what was most dear to God, so the fact that he targets the Jewish people indicates how special and precious they are to God. This is the satan's last great rebellion, so he vents all his rage against a people who are quite precious to God.

The fact that the satan vents his rage *primarily* against the people of Israel means there is something incomplete in God's redemptive plan regarding Israel. If God were finished with Israel, the satan would not target her because his objective is to destroy God's redemptive plan. So his focused assault means God is still committed to Israel and His redemptive plan depends on what He will do with her in the *future,* not only what He has done with her in the past.

The satan knows that God's purposes cannot be fulfilled if the Jewish people cease to exist. God not only staked His honor on His ability to preserve them,[12] but their purpose is obviously not fulfilled. Furthermore, God still has deep affection for them,[13] and the satan's rage is intended to cause God deep pain.

The implications of Revelation 12 are obvious, but they must be clearly stated because they have been ignored by so many throughout most of church history. We could say it this way: The satan's actions reveal his understanding of God's redemptive purpose concerning Israel. If he could break God's purposes by first of all targeting followers of Jesus, he would. But instead, first of all, he targets the people of Israel. Why? Because he understands God's covenantal commitments. If the satan could eliminate every follower of Jesus, nothing in God's covenantal promises would be jeopardized. If, on the other hand, he can eliminate the people of Israel, God's covenantal promises and redemptive purposes all break down. To say it in a more graphic way: If the satan could eliminate 1.5–2 billion Christians, nothing in the redemptive plan would break down. But eliminating approximately 16 million Jewish people[14] destroys God's redemptive plan because the God of Jacob is unable to keep His promises. We have to understand this because it is the enemy's logic.

The rage of satan in Revelation 12 shatters any notion of the so-called replacement theology or any notion that God's unique purpose for the Jewish people is finished.

Revelation 12 is one of the most concise descriptions of the satan's rage, but the warning of Revelation 12 is not unique in the New Testament. Jesus taught the same thing in Matthew 25. We have already quoted the passage, but it is important to see just how similar it is to Revelation 12:

---

12. For example see Jeremiah 31:35–37; 33:14–26.
13. Deuteronomy 7:7-8; Isaiah 43:4; Jeremiah 31:3; Zephaniah 3:17.
14. The world's Jewish population is generally estimated at 15–16 million people. For example, see https://www.jewishvirtuallibrary.org/jewish-population-of-the-world/.

"When the Son of Man comes in his glory, and all the angels with him, then he will sit on his glorious throne. Before him will be gathered all the nations, and he will separate people one from another as a shepherd separates the sheep from the goats. And he will place the sheep on his right, but the goats on the left. Then the King will say to those on his right, 'Come, you who are blessed by my Father, inherit the kingdom prepared for you from the foundation of the world. For I was hungry and you gave me food, I was thirsty and you gave me drink, I was a stranger and you welcomed me, I was naked and you clothed me, I was sick and you visited me, I was in prison and you came to me.' Then the righteous will answer him, saying, 'Lord, when did we see you hungry and feed you, or thirsty and give you drink? And when did we see you a stranger and welcome you, or naked and clothe you? And when did we see you sick or in prison and visit you?' And the King will answer them, 'Truly, I say to you, as you did it to one of the least of these my brothers, you did it to me.' Then he will say to those on his left, 'Depart from me, you cursed, into the eternal fire prepared for the devil and his angels. For I was hungry and you gave me no food, I was thirsty and you gave me no drink, I was a stranger and you did not welcome me, naked and you did not clothe me, sick and in prison and you did not visit me.' Then they also will answer, saying, 'Lord, when did we see you hungry or thirsty or a stranger or naked or sick or in prison, and did not minister to you?' Then he will answer them, saying, 'Truly, I say to you, as you did not do it to one of the least of these, you did not do it to me.' And these will go away into eternal punishment, but the righteous into eternal life." (Matthew 25:31–46)

As we saw in the last chapter, Jesus' brethren are clearly His Jewish brothers, and the message is the same as Revelation 12. Jesus predicted that, when He returns, He will judge nations on how they treated the Jewish people. If people can be judged on this basis, it clearly indicates that there is a great conflict over their destiny that will test the hearts of the nations. If Jesus can judge based on how people treat the Jewish people, it means He considers the persecution of the Jewish people a way of *resisting Him*. And both Revelation 12 and Matthew 25 predict that rage against God's purposes and His people will be expressed as rage against Israel.

When you read passages like Matthew 25 and Revelation 12 in context, the message is profound: Persecution against the Jewish people is one of the primary ways the satan vents his rage against the God of Israel *and* Jesus. This may sound quite shocking considering that fact that the institutional Church has been so deeply involved in the persecution of the Jewish people over the last 2,000 years. Yet the Scripture here is quite clear. By Jesus' own words and the New Testament's predictions, persecution against the Jewish people is a form of rage against the Jewish people, the God of Israel, *and* the Person of Jesus.

When we compare the history of the last 2,000 years to the plain words of Scripture, we can see the depth of the satan's deception. He has so seduced the nations that people who identify as Christians became instruments of persecution when in reality they were called to stand with the Jewish people to the point of suffering as an expression of loyalty to Jesus. But people have been deceived to use the name of Jesus and do the exact opposite. We must expose the reality of this sin, but also the fact that it is the exact opposite of what the New Testament teaches.

The New Testament tells us the the satan's rage against God's purposes is expressed through rage against the Jewish people. This is plainly stated in the Bible, and yet this idea has been foreign to much of Christianity.

We have only looked at two passages and already things have become very clear. Jesus is the only, unique Son of God, and He is the preeminent One.[15] And yet the Scripture plainly predicts that rage against Israel is considered rage against Jesus. So when we say that the issue of Israel, more specifically envy and rage against Israel's election, will become a defining issue in the earth, we are not dismissing the Person of Jesus. To the contrary, Jesus plainly predicted that people will resist Him in an ultimate way through hostility to His brethren according to the flesh.

---

15. John 1:1–3; Colossians 1:15-18; Philippians 2:9-11; Hebrews 1:1-3; Revelation 1:8.

Has the Christian world considered the full weight of the fact that the New Testament predicts rage against Jesus and the God of Israel will be expressed in rage against the people of Israel? Rage against Israel is actually rage about the Person of Jesus and the God of Israel.

When we look at the last several thousand years of history, we can see the failure of all peoples. Israel's story with God in the Hebrew Bible covers nearly 2,000 years of history and includes repeated examples of failure in idolatry. Though God revealed Himself to Israel in a unique way, most of Israel repeatedly chose false gods. In the same way over the last 2,000 years, the Gentiles have had the plain truth in the Scriptures but have also been deceived into following ideas that were not in the Scripture at all. Jews and Gentiles have both failed. We are both humbled by our disobedience. And the Jews have suffered from the disobedience of the Gentiles.

It is understandable that this may seem shocking, but it is plainly stated. It is not hidden or secret, but so much has happened in the last 2,000 years that the clear message of the Bible can seem surprising. However, there is another "surprise" in Revelation 12 that we need to notice before we continue.

A Surprising Prediction

Before we move on, we need to consider the final words of Revelation 12:

> But the earth came to the help of the woman, and the earth opened its mouth and swallowed the river that the dragon had poured from his mouth. Then the dragon became furious with the woman and went off to make war on the rest of her offspring, on those who keep the commandments of God and hold to the testimony of Jesus. And he stood on the sand of the sea. (Revelation 12:16–17)

We have already seen that Revelation 12 predicts the satan will rage against God *and* Jesus primarily by trying to destroy the Jewish people and their redemptive calling, and this is yet another very surprising prediction.

Most Christians assume that the satan and the "antichrist" will primarily persecute Christians, but Revelation 12 gives a very nuanced prediction. In Revelation 12, persecution comes against the Jewish people first, and then the followers of Jesus are persecuted only *after* the Jewish people are miraculously preserved. The dragon's rage against those who "hold to the testimony of Jesus" is an expression of his rage against the "woman" (Israel).

Revelation 12 does predict the satan will release rage against followers of Jesus, but this rage is released because of their connection to the people of Israel.

The implications of this are profound. Followers of Jesus are described as "offspring" of the people of Israel. In other words, they are part of the story of Israel and dynamically, and inseparably, tied to it. For centuries, many Christian theologians have presented "the Church" as separate from Israel, but Revelation 12 plainly states followers of Jesus are so tied to Israel that the satan's end-time persecution of Christians is based on their connection to Israel. Many are accustomed to thinking of the satan as the persecutor of Christians, but in this passage, he is the enemy of Israel who persecutes Christians because they are connected to Israel.

This indicates that, by the end of the age, true followers of Jesus will be so identified with the people of Israel that they will share in the persecution that comes at the very end. This is obviously a radical shift in the way Christians view themselves related to Israel now, but Revelation predicts that shift must happen. And Matthew 25 predicts the same thing. If Jesus can evaluate nations on how they respond to Israel's crisis, and if Jesus' followers are going to survive His own judgment, it means they must also be willing to identify with the people of Israel in the greatest crisis of human history.

Furthermore, Revelation 12 predicts the satan vents his rage against the followers of Jesus after he is unable to destroy the people of Israel. If his rage against Christians is tied to his inability to destroy

Israel, it indicates that the Christians must have something to do with the preservation of the people of Israel. This means, by the end of the age, Christians identify with the people of Israel to the point of persecution. This means they will play a God-ordained role in the preservation of Israel, engaged in speaking boldly about God's purposes for Israel, praying for those purposes, and engaged in those purposes to the point that they arouse the rage of the satan. And they will be willing to endure suffering and even death in their commitment to God's election of Israel.

This is a radical shift in the way Christians have responded to the Jewish people. For nearly 2,000 years, Christians have mostly presented themselves as the conclusion of Israel's story and the "new" people of God. But Revelation 12 predicts that, by the time the age is over, Christians will recognize Israel's unique calling and be so tied to that calling they will endure persecution *with* Israel and *because* of their commitment to God's promises for Israel.

When we consider what Revelation 12 says in light of the last 2,000 years, it seems impossible. But this is what the Bible predicts. So the question is will we respond and work to see this prediction come to pass? Prophecies aren't simply fulfilled. People must read them, agree with them, and do the hard work implied by those prophecies.

The story that God has predicted in Scripture is beautiful, mysterious, and at times shocking. When we read His story in context, we find that a day will come, perhaps soon, when the satan's rage against Israel will be an expression of his rage against:

- The Jewish people.
- The God of Israel.
- The Person of Jesus.
- The followers of Jesus.

God has designed a story where the whole world is going to watch Him fully accomplish His redemptive purposes through Israel, and He will be able to evaluate people on whether they cooperate with those purposes or resist them. This may seem like a strange idea, so next we need to turn our attention to one of the most alarming events in history.

20

A LITMUS TEST OF OBEDIENCE

WHILE GOD'S election of Jesus is the ultimate issue, the Bible is very clear God's election of Israel will be a litmus test He will use to evaluate the nations. Some are going to fail that test spectacularly, and God is going to respond with unprecedented judgments. But others will pass that test, even at the cost of their own lives. The question is not whether everyone fails or everyone passes. *The question is will you and those you influence pass or fail?*

Though it is plain in Scripture, the idea that God could use Israel as a litmus test for obedience to Jesus may be a relatively strange idea to many Christians, but after the events of the last eighty years there is no excuse to not understand this. We live in the shadow of two unimaginable events that confronted the earth with the election of Israel: the Holocaust and October 7th.

First we need to consider the Holocaust. The Holocaust has been processed many ways, but it is rarely processed theologically by Christians. It's possible the failure to process the Holocaust theologically may be one of the biggest theological failures of the twentieth century. And the failure of the Church during the Holocaust as a culmination of many failures over the preceding centuries may in fact be the greatest failure of the Church in history. In the midst of cries of "never again," there has been a rush to move on past the horrors of that event. And as a result, we have not let the Holocaust have its full effect on our thinking, our theology, our knowledge of God, and our own discipleship.

For two millennia, the Church ignored the plain reading of many passages we have already quoted. As a result, the idea that our response to the people of Israel could be a litmus test of our faithfulness to Jesus was an idea most Christians did not seriously consider —*until the Holocaust.*

A Gruesome Warning

We do not know everything that drove Hitler, but the Bible plainly says that God's honor is at stake in His ability to preserve Israel and bring about His promises, and this provides the gruesome logic for the Holocaust.[1] When Hitler rose to power, he declared he would build a thousand-year empire, which was a clear counterfeit of the thousand-year Kingdom commonly known as the "Millennium" that the Bible predicts will bring blessing to the earth. This thousand-year Kingdom is centered in Jerusalem, and blessing will flow to the entire earth from Jerusalem as the Messiah reigns.[2] Hitler's empire, which was clearly an attempt to subvert and replace the biblical hope and meant he had to break the God of Israel, set into motion what we now call the Holocaust.

The Nazi genocide was not logical or rational in any way. Typically, a genocide is the result of a violent conflict between two peoples, but there was no such conflict in Europe before World War II. The Jewish community was not in conflict with Germany or any other European people. The German Jews had fought and died alongside other Germans in World War I. Furthermore, the Jews were embedded in the society and culture to the extent that many

---

1. For example see Jeremiah 31:35–37; 33:14–26.
2. Isaiah 2:2–4; 11:6–9; 24:23; Zechariah 14:9; Revelation 20:1–6 (Note the thousand-year duration of the kingdom and the name "Millennium" typically are derived from from Revelation 19:6.)

lamented that German Jews were "more German than the Germans."[3]

If Hitler had simply declared a vision of a glorious, rebuilt Germany, the German Jews would have gladly made great contributions to that vision and been an incredible asset to Hitler's vision. Any reasonable person would have included the Jewish community in their dream to rebuild a glorious country. But instead, Hitler boldly proclaimed that his vision of a thousand-year empire depended on one thing: They had to eliminate the Jewish people. Instead of the biblical thousand-year kingdom centered in Jerusalem, Hitler would build an alternative empire, the success of which would depend on the elimination of the people God chose.

The Holocaust was a gruesome and graphic picture of the serpent's envy. That envy was systematically expressed in the attempted elimination of a people whom God had called to lead the nations in order to build a substitute kingdom. And because many who were culturally Christian did not understand the root of envy, they became caught up in something they never imagined.

On one hand, the Nazi Holocaust was the climax of long-running antisemitism. On the other hand, it was a shocking event that no one fully saw coming. There are a number of reasons why the Holocaust happened where it did, but there is one lesson that must be learned. Germany was one of the most sophisticated cultures. Germany had education, art, philosophy, science, technology, and even theology. It was a pinnacle of humanism. The "best" human culture, in a moment, perpetuated one of the most systematic and gruesome expressions of evil and perhaps the greatest calamity of Israel's history. All this means is if the Holocaust could happen in Germany, it can happen anywhere. In fact, the Nazis even drew from philosophies imported from places like America.[4] It was not simply a "German" crisis.

---

3. Marvin Perry; Frederick M. Schweitzer (2002). *Anti-Semitism: Myth and Hate from Antiquity to the Present.* Palgrave Macmillan. p. 90.
4. There is evidence that Hitler was influenced by studying the American treatment

Education, philosophy, science, and even sophisticated theology cannot save you from the evil impulses of the human heart. If you do not deal with the root of sin, it can emerge suddenly in ways that you would never anticipate. Sin is a crouching beast,[5] and you cannot control how it expresses its rage. When the environment is just right, it emerges in surprising ways. Children raised in Sunday schools can end up as guards in concentration camps.

When the horror of the Nazi Holocaust emerged, we suddenly saw a graphic example of why the Bible, and Jesus Himself, predicted that our practical response to the people of Israel under pressure can be used as a litmus test for obedience to Jesus.

The story of Christians and the Holocaust is a complex and disturbing story. It is no secret that Hitler tried to present his rhetoric through a Christian lens. It is also well known that theologians like Martin Luther were quoted to justify antisemitism. The failure of institutional Christianity in the Holocaust is well known and must be very soberly examined. The vast majority of Christians are convinced they would never be silent in the face of something like the Holocaust, but history warns us that unusual pressure can expose things hidden deep in the human heart.

Though the story of Christianity in the Holocaust is a painful topic that we should not quickly dismiss, there are also beautiful stories amid the horror. Yad Vashem (the Holocaust Museum in Israel) refers to these as the "Righteous Among the Nations." These are individuals who risked their lives in an attempt to preserve Jewish lives and resist the Nazi rage. The painful truth is that they were the

---

of native Americans when he began conceiving of what became the Holocaust. In addition, Nazi Germany was influenced by American racism and eugenics. For more on this see James Q. Whitman's book *Hitler's American Model: The United States and the Making of Nazi Race Law*; Alex Ross' article, "How American Racism Influenced Hitler" in The New Yorker (https://www.newyorker.com/magazine/2018/04/30/how-american-racism-influenced-hitler); and or "How the Nazis Were Inspired by Jim Crow" by Becky Little (https://www.history.com/articles/how-the-nazis-were-inspired-by-jim-crow).

5. Genesis 4:7.

minority, but the beautiful fact is that they did exist. Many took great risks. And the majority of them are Christians.[6]

Books have been written on the failures of many professing Christians during the Holocaust, and the long story of antisemitism in Europe must be told. We need to seriously consider this reality and the role it played in the Holocaust. But there is another aspect of Christianity in relation to the Holocaust that must also be considered.

If you describe the failures of the Church during the Holocaust to any committed Christian,[7] they will instinctively respond, "That is not real Christianity." This statement itself forces us to address the complex history of the Church, where people considered to be "real Christians" perpetuated antisemitism, but it is significant. And if you then describe one of the stories of Christians who risked their lives with the Jewish people—for example, the story of Corrie ten Boom is probably the best known—a committed Christian will immediately and instinctively say, *"That is real Christianity."* This immediate response demonstrates that a committed Christian instinctively understands that their response to the Jewish people is an indicator of whether or not they follow Jesus. Those who love the Jewish people at the threat of death are displaying the heart of genuine Christianity.

In other words, the Nazi Holocaust gives us a graphic illustration of how our response to the Jewish people can serve as a litmus test of our obedience to Jesus.

Those who stood by in the Holocaust, or did even worse, demonstrated that they were not loyal to Jesus. And those who risked their lives and chose to suffer for the sake of the Jewish people demonstrated their faith in Jesus was real. The crucible of pressure demon-

---

6. Based on the research available on the "Righteous Among the Nations" at the World Holocaust Remembrance Center" at Yad Vashem. For more information, see https://collections.yadvashem.org/en/righteous

7. By "committed," I mean a Bible-believing Christian whose faith is expressed in their lifestyle choices.

strated the reality of faith. Israel became a litmus test for true loyalty to Jesus.

Many Christians are shocked when they truly encounter the persecution of the Jews in the name of Jesus. Most Christians have no idea that popular theologians said things like:[8]

"I had made up my mind to write no more about the Jews, but their lying and slandering has compelled me to do so."

"We are at fault in not slaying them."

"They are nothing but a devilish, venomous, and poisonous people."

However, Christians instinctively know the way of Jesus is to identify with Israel to the point of losing their own lives. They instinctively know that the path of Corrie ten Boom, André Trocmé, Maximilian Kolbe, and Maria Skobtsova was the path of Jesus while the path of the Christians who were silent or even participants is not the true path. This is instinctive because it is true, but it also forces us to face some difficult issues. First, will we pay the price to show the true face of Jesus to the Jewish people? They have seen another face. Will we show the actual face of Jesus? Second, most Christians immediately declare they would never act like many did in the Holocaust. And yet they have never faced that kind of pressure.

Today, when a government leader visits Israel as part of an official state visit to Israel, they are required by Israel's Foreign Ministry to visit Yad Vashem. It is easy to see this through a political lens, but what if God is warning the kings and rulers of the earth to carefully consider the gruesome details of the Holocaust? As the rulers of the earth walk through Yad Vashem, they are warned of:

---

8. Excerpts from Martin Luther's 1543 treatise On the Jews and Their Lies. As recommended in a previous chapter, the reader should educate themselves on the long history of Christian anti-semitism and can start with resources like *Our Hands Are Stained With Blood: The Tragic Story of the "Church" and the Jewish People* by Dr. Michael Brown.

- The true nature of antisemitism.
- The sudden way envy can escalate into the unthinkable when the root of envy has not been exposed and dealt with.
- The irrational but deadly logic of envy at divine election.
- The way a seemingly insignificant man can suddenly and shrewdly seize power and use impressive rhetoric and deceptive claims to coalesce people in rage against Israel's election.
- The relative ease with which people can be pulled into evil acts they would never premeditate or simply be passive and dismissive of the deep evil around them.

The rulers of the earth are being warned through one of the darkest moments in Israel's history. But do we consider it a divine warning or simply a history lesson?

What does it mean that you live in the first generation in all of history when the Lord is warning the rulers of the earth about the devious and sudden way rage against His election can intensify into unthinkable acts?

Arrogant Assumptions

Nearly every Christian declares they would "never do" what many Christians did in the Holocaust, but this is an arrogant assumption when they have not been tested by a severe crisis. History tells us how people perform under extreme pressure can be very different from how they assume they will behave. This is why Jesus warned that He will judge on right *actions* toward Israel, not simply right thinking. What are your actions?

In our time, there is more and more teaching about "blessing Israel so you will be blessed":

I will bless those who bless you, and him who dishonors you I will curse....
(Genesis 12:3)

People are strongly encouraged to bless Israel (which is often not well defined) so that they will be blessed by God. While there is great truth in the fact that God blesses those who agree with Him, that blessing may come in ways we do not expect. The Bible and history clearly demonstrate that being willing to stand with God's election may cause you incredible suffering. If material blessings are the primary motivation for standing with God's election, you are very vulnerable when pressure and trouble come because, when temporary blessings are lost, you may decide standing with God's election is not worth it and, instead, collaborate with something else that you believe brings greater "blessing."

Are you willing to stand with God's election at the point of suffering, pain, and loss?

Throughout most of history, Christians have not demonstrated their willingness to stand with God's election to the point of suffering. For sure, many have, such as the "Righteous Among the Nations" during the Holocaust, but many have not. Yet Revelation 12 indicates that, by the time this age is done, there must be a people who will stand with divine election at the cost of their own lives.

Would you have endured with the Jewish people during the Roman invasion when they crucified so many people they ran out of crosses? Would you have endured like Jeremiah during the Babylonian invasion? Jeremiah did not prophesy and escape. Even though Judah was under divine judgment, he stayed with his people and prophesied the glorious promises to come.

Would you have stood with God's election in the Holocaust? Would you have been able to give your life and remind Israel of her previous, unfulfilled promises? Though we might answer "yes" to both of these questions, what makes us so sure of our answer? History challenges our quick yes.

The prophets warned us that the controversy over Israel's election is not yet over. In fact, they warned that the most intense days in history, days unlike any other, are coming.[9] Considering all the evil that has occurred throughout history, this is a chilling prediction.

---

9. Jeremiah 30:7; Daniel 12:1; Joel 2:2; Matthew 24:21.

Can we honestly say we have deeply pondered the Bible's prediction that the age ends with a brief, but unparalleled time of trouble and a great controversy over the Lord's election of Israel? Do we truly live in such a way that we will be prepared for unprecedented trouble? What do you do now in your daily life that makes you so confident you can stand in a crisis like that?

Israel is not the most important issue, but she will become a litmus test. She already is.

The clear warning of the Bible should be enough for you, but in addition, we live within a generation of two of most notorious and most gruesome preview of the end-time envy. While many are quick to say, "Never again," we would do well to face our own envy and the Bible's warning that the controversy over Israel's election is not yet over. The Holocaust is the most carefully studied genocide of all time. But do we treat it as history or as a warning? Do we quickly accuse those who failed the test of the Holocaust, or do we slowly and thoughtfully consider what we would do in the same situation at the cost of our own lives?

It is easy to love Israel for the blessings we may receive. But it is not as easy to love Israel when it comes at the cost of everything we have, and we must endure a suffering that appears to be Israel's suffering and not our own. This is genuine love. Love is not "affection" for a people in hopes of a blessing. That is simply a business deal. Even God did not choose Israel for His own benefit. He chose Israel even though it would cost Him suffering.[10] God expresses His love through His election of Israel, and He wants a people like Him who love what He loves and give their lives for it gladly, a people who express His love and His nature in flesh and blood. He is not looking for a people who relate to Israel, hoping they can get something from her. That kind of love will never endure a crisis.

The Bible predicts that this kind of people will emerge on the earth. The only question is will you be one of these people?

---

10. Exodus 3:7-8; Isaiah 63:9.

We Need to Ask Uncomfortable Questions

Everyone is quick to say, "Never again," and try to move on because they cannot face the full horror and the implications of the past. But we must face it. God is the God of Israel, and the Holocaust is the greatest crisis of Israel's history. It raises a lot of uncomfortable questions that ultimately confront our knowledge of God, our knowledge of ourselves, our knowledge of Israel, and our knowledge of sin.

Many people avoid painful questions about the Holocaust (and now October 7th) and in the process they avoid the knowledge of God. The reason is simple: We do not like to face pain. We do not like to face the unexplainable. We want a simple, cheap knowledge of God with easy answers. I am not suggesting that the biggest questions you can ask about the Holocaust have easy answers. Some of them do not have human answers that you can summarize in a book and move on. However, the questions themselves *must* be asked. If you do not ask them, your knowledge of God is lacking, and you are vulnerable to great deception.

"Never again" in the way it is generally used is an almost meaningless statement because the story of human history, and particularly Israel's story, is a painful story. Why should we expect that a sentimental, human response to the Holocaust would suddenly bring this long, painful history to an end?

We are quick to turn away from the true nature of our own sin because we do not want to face it. In our self-righteousness, we want to assume we may have "flaws" but we are not truly evil. We love to avoid just how sinful we are, but we must face it so we can be healed. We cover the roots of sin in our hearts with our "good behavior," but as the prophet Jeremiah said, it is a superficial healing of our wound.[11] And this is precisely why God wants to confront us and expose our sin—so He can heal us. Just as a person must hear a serious diagnosis before they will accept treatment, we must face our sin before we can be healed.

---

11. Jeremiah 6:14.

We assume we are "okay" until something like the Nazi Holocaust erupts and suddenly we find that people who have read a Jewish Bible are willing to participate in mass genocide against the Jewish people when the environment is right. One day, they were attending church on Sunday morning, and then in a short period of time, they were shuffling people into gas chambers. How could this be?

We have seen many genocides throughout history, and they are all revolting and horrifying. But how is it that, in the heart of a continent with access to the Bible, the most horrifying genocide was committed against the last people you would expect? You would expect that people who God used to give Europe its Bible, theology, Savior, and Christian culture would be the last people to endure hostility, and yet they endured the worse hostility. And why does it seem the hostility against the Jews never ends?

We have to face this question as Christians, not simply as a humans. The Nazi Holocaust exposes something that has largely gone unnoticed and been covered up by cries of "never again." "Never again" in the right context can be a useful phrase, but when it is declared without addressing the deep root that produced the horrors of the Holocaust itself, it is an unhelpful, deceptive, and superficial solution to a very deep issue.

The Holocaust, and every other genocide, shows you that, if you do not face the root of original of sin, you cannot predict what evil you will get swept up in. This root is deceptive and often hidden. But if you do not expose it and confront it, it is far more powerful than you can imagine. In an instant, people can transform from church attenders to perpetrators.

Of course, the vast majority of people do not recognize their offense with election, and they are horrified by events like the Holocaust or October 7th. The reason is simple: Our enemy is devious and intelligent. He knows how to deceive us so that we cannot see the roots of sin in our own hearts. And one of the ways he deceives us is by minimizing and obscuring the true nature of the evil that we accommodate in our own hearts. He loves it when we shrink back from overt and graphic evil because that shrinking back subconsciously convinces us that we are not capable of great evil and that only "evil" people like Antiochus, Hitler, Stalin, or the Khmer Rouge are "that evil." For sure we may make "mistakes," but we shudder when we hear about graphic examples of evil. In reality, however, that very shuddering can be deceptive. It can obscure the fact that we have tolerated the seeds of great evil even if we have not let those seeds fully blossom.

If people had been asked a decade before the Holocaust whether they would have been perpetrators of a systematic and chillingly efficient genocide, they would have recoiled at the thought and denied it wholeheartedly. Or if people were asked if they would march in the streets to support a terror organization that intentionally and systematically raped, dismembered, and butchered families resting in their homes on October 7th they would also denied it. However, in both causes, when the right context emerged, though, people found themselves doing things they would have never imagined only years before.

We think humans can be improved and even saved through education, philosophy, and technology. But the Holocaust screams, "No!" Men who were civilized and educated became monsters in a moment. You cannot seek safety in the things humans seek safety in. You can only find safety in having the courage to face your own sin no matter how subtle it may appear and letting God cut it out and transform you to love His election of people, especially when they are disqualified.

If you think you are incapable of such things, then you should open up your heart to deep examination. If you are unwilling to consider the fact that seeds of evil could rest in your own heart, then you are in a more dangerous place than you realize.

21

THE WORLD AFTER OCTOBER 7TH

WE LIVE in days when the world is changing at a breathtaking pace. Things people never imagined continue to happen very quickly. For example, the entire world shut down during the COVID pandemic within a few weeks. It was not triggered by a world war or a financial collapse or any of the things we would expect to trigger an event like that. Instead, the borders suddenly closed. Churches were closed on Easter, and synagogues were closed on Passover. And shortly thereafter, Israel suddenly came into a warm peace known as the "Abraham Accords" with several Muslims nations. And then a project to establish peace between Israel and Saudi Arabia emerged. Any of these events were unimaginable just months before each of them occurred, and yet they happened quickly in succession.

In seasons of massive historical change, life also continues and our "normal" rhythm of daily life can cause us to easily overlook the fact that we are in an unprecedented moment of change. While we should be careful not to obsess over the date of Jesus' return or engage in unbiblical end-time speculation, we also must be sober and realize we are in a historic moment when things are changing at a rate never before seen in history. And we must view that moment through a biblical lens.

The biblical narrative warns us that the age ends in a great crisis over Jacob's election, but that crisis is not limited to the very end of the age. Throughout history, there are shocking moments when the crisis over election erupts in a single moment and we get a glimpse of just how dark and evil envy is.

October 7th, 2023, was a moment that changed history. There is "before" and "after" October 7th. And you cannot understand October 7th correctly unless you view it through the biblical lens of the crisis over election.

On October 7th and the weeks that followed, we experienced events we could never have imagined. Things that were, and still are, unthinkable:

- For the first time in history, terrorists attempted genocide against the Jewish people and live streamed it on the internet for everyone to see. The Nazis tried to cover up their crimes. Hamas live streamed them. In fact, the events of October 7th were so shocking and disorientating that the best source of "news" on that day was the GoPros of Hamas.

- The terrorists' live streams were filled with images of the most gruesome acts. The visual evidence of things done that day is difficult to speak about.

- People were butchered and killed in grotesque and agonizing ways. Women were raped and then killed brutally. Corpses were dismembered and beheaded. Families were burned alive in their houses. Death, torture, and rape were celebrated. And the evidence of these acts was recorded and published by the perpetrators. The details and images of what was done are impossible to comprehend, and the truth is many people still have not heard the details of the worse of October 7th.

- The horror and terror of October 7th was publicly celebrated with joy and delight by the perpetrators. As they were killing, they were exuberant. Some could not wait to return to Gaza and called family members overcome with joy they had killed Jews.[1] After butchering people, they stole their phones and sent messages to their families with horrifying photos of their murdered loved ones. Parents were killed in front of children.

The events of that day were truly unthinkable. But it did not end on October 8th. For a brief moment, the nations were in shock about what they had observed. And then, very quickly, an unthinkable reaction erupted in the nations:

- A professor at Cornell University in the United States described the attack on October 7th as "exhilarating."[2]
- Within days of October 7th, masses of people marched in the streets of the world *supporting* the perpetrators of the genocide and threatening Jews worldwide, and that they did in "free" and Western nations.
- For the first time in history, global anti-semitism erupted in *response* to Jewish suffering.
- Jews living in "tolerant" and "free" societies worldwide suddenly found themselves in a world filled with anti-semitism, a terrifying world that evoked memories of the days before the Holocaust. *Only this time it was global.*

In thousands of years of history, there has never been a global controversy over the land and people of Israel until now. And never an event like October 7th where radical Islamists and Western secular humanists both openly celebrated in the streets such acts of terror and genocide against the Jewish people.

---

1. "IDF Publishes Audio of Hamas Terrorist Calling Family to Brag about Killing Jews." 2023. Timesofisrael.com. 2023. https://www.timesofisrael.com/idf-publishes-audio-of-hamas-terrorist-calling-family-to-brag-of-killing-jews/.
2. "Cornell Professor Who Praised Oct. 7 Massacre Allowed to Resume Teaching." 2023. Timesofisrael.com. 2023. https://www.timesofisrael.com/cornell-professor-who-praised-oct-7-massacre-allowed-to-resume-teaching/.

When I stood on the border of Gaza just outside an apartment where two young people were butchered in a gruesome way, a Jewish man who was also visiting the site began verbally processing what he had seen. He said, "What happened here was not conflict or even murder. It was an expression of true evil to do what was done to people here. It was something not even human." He was grasping at words to describe what he had observed and heard. And he was right. Though humans were the agents of deep evil on October 7th, there was something much deeper than normal human conflict. October 7th was an eruption of the spiritual controversy over election. And this is why it was gruesome, evil, and so very dark.

We must realize we are in a completely different moment of history. The controversy over Israel's election is now global. God leads history and the eruption of darkness on October 7th is a sign He has moved history into a new season. He is going to finish His purpose with Israel.

Biblical prophecy is a vast subject that includes mystery. Prophecy is multi-dimensional, and the details of its fulfillment are often not completely clear until it has happened. The prophetic is not necessarily only applicable to one fixed point in time. It is a realm of mystery in which the uncreated God who is eternal speaks and His words shape what we call history while also remaining eternal words from an uncreated Being.

October 7th is significant enough for the reasons we have already mentioned, but if you view it in light of details found in the biblical prophets it becomes even more significant because there are many things the prophets mention that have never happened in history that carry a shocking similarity to events that happened on October 7th and the days that followed. This does not mean the events of October 7th are a fulfillment of any of these prophecies, but we should notice details like this because they emphasize the significance of the season of history we are living through. Here are just a few examples:

- Israeli hostages (captives) have been kept in holes in the ground. Something Isaiah described (see Isaiah 42:7, 22).

- Ezekiel warned of a hostile attack on "unwalled villages" where people were at rest (Ezekiel 38:11). And there are other biblical warnings of sudden destruction coming when no one expects it (see Matthew 24:36-39; 1 Thessalonians 5:3; Ezekiel 38-39).
- Daniel warned the enemy would come in like a flood which is exactly what happened. The attack was called "Al-Aqsa Flood" in Arabic (see Daniel 9:26; 11:22).
- Several prophets warn of a moment when military strength will be completely absent and its power shattered, which is what seemed to happen (see Leviticus 26:19; Deuteronomy 32:36; Daniel 12:7).
- Jesus asked His followers to pray that a day of great trouble would not come on Shabbat, and October 7th was a special Shabbat (see Matthew 24:20).
- October 7th sparked a global controversy over Zion, something Zechariah predicted (see Zechariah 12:3).
- Daniel predicted a day when the "Ships from the West ('Chittim')" will be a significant factor in delaying a bigger conflict. And in the days after October 7th, multiple Western aircraft carriers were sent to contain the conflict (see Daniel 11:30).
- A "King of the North" (Turkey) has threatened Israel repeatedly throughout the conflict, something Daniel warned about (Daniel 11:28).
- People left the land in ships in the days after October 7th. Moses predicted something similar will happen one day (see Deuteronomy 28:68).

There are other verses that could be added to this list, but this short list should be alarming. I am not saying any of these verses are ultimately about October 7th, but these kinds of details have never quite converged this way in history. It means something profoundly significant occurred. Something that was more than a human conflict.

Israel's relationship with the Palestinians is complex and painful. And the State of Israel is not always righteous. And the war the followed October 7th is a complex and difficult war with no simple answer. Israelis recognize this and have passionate arguments about everything that occurred on October 7th and has occurred since. Political questions and questions of justice are legitimate and important questions, but if you view October 7th purely through a political lens, you will miss the core issue that was exposed by the raw horror of that day.

Many questions raised by the Holocaust have been left unanswered for nearly eighty years, but the events of October 7, 2023, are forcing the nations to confront those questions. All it took was a few hours on a quiet Saturday morning for the world to be confronted again with the issue of Jacob's election through an event that was unspeakably gruesome and yet celebrated all over the world.

One of the most critical questions that must be asked is: *Will Christians engage vocally and step into the conflict over election?* Time will tell. There have been notable examples of positive Christian engagement since October 7th. And there have been other examples of silence. And, sadly, there have been Christians who have fallen again into the trap of not recognizing the central issues that surround Jacob's election.

October 7th was a shockwave to the earth. The controversy over election is not over. It is intensifying. The question is do we realize the moment we are living in? And do our churches?

PART V

A BIBLICAL PARADIGM FOR A MODERN STATE

22

THE MODERN STATE OF JACOB

THE MODERN STATE of Israel is one of the most surprising, incredible, impossible, improbable, and yet perplexing events of the twentieth century. Because the State is now over seventy-five years old,[1] the vast majority of us humans have lived with the State of Israel all of our lives, and because we are accustomed to hearing about "Israel" regularly in the news, it is easy to overlook just how impossible it is that after 2,000 years:

- The Jewish people retained a corporate identity though they were scattered among other people as a vulnerable people often persecuted for their distinctive identity.
- An independent Jewish State suddenly reappeared and was established against all odds in the midst of great turmoil and opposition. To put this in historical perspective, since the beginning of Israel's history approximately 6,000 years ago, Israel has only had *two* united, independent kingdoms that ruled the entire land. And the combined length of their existence is only 141

1. As of 2023.

years.[2] For another united government to emerge after 2,000 years of exile is impossible, humanly speaking.

- The third "kingdom" or State of Israel has now existed for over seventy-five years.
- An evil man led an organized and efficient campaign to completely eliminate the Jewish people. It decimated the Jewish population, but the crisis was not the end of the story. The Jewish State appeared after the greatest crisis in Israel's history.
- The ancient language of Israel was preserved for centuries and then resurrected and adapted to become a modern language used as the language of daily life again for the first time in thousands of years.
- The relatively small State of Israel has risen to have global influence. Israeli technology, innovations, and ideas now affect the lives of nearly every single human on a daily basis.

The State of Israel has become such a part of our lives that it is easy to forget just how impossible its existence is. If you told someone who lived one hundred years ago that Israel would suddenly reemerge, nearly half of the world's Jewish population would live in the land again, Hebrew would become a language used in daily life, and Israel would become a global influence and a global controversy, they would not believe you. Things like that simply do not happen.

To say that the God of Israel is not involved in the reemergence of Israel and that Israel has no real significance is simply ludicrous. The State of Israel is one of the greatest and most visible pieces of evidence that the God of Israel is real and leading history, and His Scriptures are completely true.

And yet understanding the State of Israel is incredibly perplexing. It is both clearly related to biblical prophecy and yet not the

---

2. Israel has only had two united and independent kingdoms in history. The first was the reign of David and Solomon, and the second is the Hasmonean Kingdom. In general, the first lasted 75 years and the second 66 years.

fulfillment of everything the prophets spoke about a restored Israel. Ultra-Orthodox Jews struggle so much with the State of Israel that they believe it is completely invalid. The political concept of Zionism that undergirds the Modern State is complex and diverse. Many of those who support the State of Israel and declare themselves to be Zionists do not completely agree on what Zionism should look like.

One-dimensional views of Israel and Zionism distort the reality of Israel and cause people to become confused about Israel. Some are even so confused they become hostile. So how can we come to a biblical understanding of the complexity of the Modern State of Israel? How do we acknowledge the shortcomings of the State while honoring and respecting it biblically?

The answer is found in the person of Jacob. The story of Jacob enables us to understand the phenomenon that we call the "State of Israel." Once you view the State of Israel through the lens of the story of Jacob, you can come to a biblical view of the State that enables you to embrace the tension of the complexity of Israel, acknowledge the real sins of Israel, and stand with God's divine purpose as it is unfolding through Israel.

To say it one more time: *Israel is complex.* There are many tensions we have to bear to have a biblical view of Israel. As we examine Israel, it is important we bear everything in tension and do not exaggerate one thing or another, or ignore one thing over another. There are not easy answers or quick solutions to the complexity of Modern Israel, but we can come to a biblical perspective. And we can bear the pressure and tension of respect for divine election even when the elect have not come into the fullness of their calling.

A biblical perspective of Modern Israel includes many different factors, and you must bear the tension of all of these factors. You must not emphasize one of them in isolation. We are about to speak about many things, and if you emphasize just one aspect of Israel without putting it in context to the whole, you can end up with a picture that is not biblical.

To understand the State of Israel biblically, you must understand the person of Jacob.

The prophets repeatedly referred to Israel as Israel *and* as Jacob. That language was very intentional. God spoke through the prophets this way because the story of Jacob helps us understand the story of Israel and God's relationship to Israel. The biblical story predicts that God chose and loves Jacob *and* that He will transform Jacob into Israel. We have not yet seen the fullness of Israel, so the story of Israel continues to follow the arc of Jacob until it is fully resolved. Recognizing this part helps us relate to Israel in a biblical way, agree with God's election, and cooperate with His purposes.

Jacob must become Israel. And the modern state is a part of God's process of fulfilling His promises to Israel. It must be respected as such and also viewed through a biblical lens which acknowledges Jacob's sins and Jacob's God-ordained destiny.

When we look at the State of Israel through the story of Jacob, we see the story is complex, just like Jacob, but God's relationship with Jacob helps us understand His sovereign leadership of Israel's story. We cannot do the story of Israel justice in a few chapters. I strongly encouraged you to spend time reading about and understanding the fascinating story of the Modern State. My goal is a very narrow one: to address various Christian perspectives that are one-dimensional that can result either in an advocacy of Israel that is superficial and does not acknowledge the complexity of Israel's history, or can result in a negative view of Israel that does not recognize the way God leads history. To come into a biblical view, we must manage multiple tensions, and those tensions are not ultimately about Israel. They are about God's leadership of history.

As we have repeatedly seen, our real issue with Jacob is not with Jacob. It is with the God of Jacob and how He leads history. There is much, much more to the State of Israel than what we can describe in a few pages. But it is critical that we lay a biblical foundation for our relationship to the Modern State of Israel.

23

PROMISE, PAIN, AND PRESSURE

THE SIMILARITIES between the re-emergence of the Modern State and the story of Jacob's blessing by Isaac in Genesis 27 are very deep. Jacob deceived his father because he was motivated by pain over his promise. He knew he had been chosen to carry the family promise, but he had waited for years and not yet received his inheritance. What's more, his father appeared determined to give Esau the inheritance that God had given to Jacob.

The pressure and pain of a delayed promise caused Jacob to take his promise into his hands.

As we saw, Jacob's story confronts us with the mysterious sovereignty of God's leadership. On one hand, we can ask what would have God done for Jacob if Jacob had waited for God to accomplish His promise in a divine way? Should Jacob have followed the path of David who refused to seize his promise with his own ingenuity? The Bible never answers these difficult questions. Perhaps Jacob should have endured the crucible of waiting to receive his inheritance because Jacob did suffer as a result of his actions. Yet Jacob seized what was his and, in the process, accomplished what God had decreed. Jacob demonstrated a depth of desire for the promise that

Esau did not seem to have. Jacob even seemed to overcome his own father's resistance to giving him the blessing.

The mystery of God's sovereignty is that He will get what He wants and what He has determined. His will is also moved forward by righteous actions *and* unrighteous actions. And His will is moved forward by people when they agree with Him *and* when they oppose Him. God works His purposes in a complexing and perplexing environment, where some choose to obey Him, many choose to resist Him, and sometimes even His people disobey Him. Sin matters and causes unnecessary pain and suffering. But even sin does not disrupt His purposes. This does not excuse sinful actions because God judges sin. And when the right thing is done the wrong way, people suffer for their sin. For example, in Jacob's case, he suffered as a result of the way he sought his promise. And yet the mysterious thing is that Jacob pursued what was his and, in the process, accomplished the very thing God had decreed.

This is the nature of divine sovereignty, and it can be very offensive to our limited, human mindset. We have a very humanistic view that assumes God's will is only achieved through perfect people making righteous decisions. But this is not reality. The Bible is very open about the failures of many of its greatest heroes. Again and again, God works through flawed humans and accomplishes His purposes—even when they sin. If God only accomplished His will through perfectly righteous people, His will would never be accomplished.

This goes right to our knowledge of God. We have an idea of a God who only works with and through "perfect" people when these kinds of people do not actually exist. In reality, God is much more deeply engaged with humanity than we realize. He hates sin, but He deeply loves humanity, and He is intimately involved with us. God is much more intimately involved in your life than you realize. He is present in the failures, weaknesses, and shortcomings. He is not present only when you feel "holy." And He is much more involved in others than you realize. He works powerfully through people who may be immature or compromised in other ways. Sin does have consequences, so it is far better to follow God's path, but God is much more present in your reality, my reality, and that of others than we imagine. God even enjoys His people when He is angry with their sin.

If you do not learn this, you will run from God and push Him away as you become more and more aware of your own sinfulness when in reality God knows exactly who you are and He has come close to transform you. You must learn His way, or you will not enjoy an awareness of just how intimately He relates to us. If you are His, He is much closer to you than you imagine. When you become aware of this, it will transform your life. But if you push God away in your self-righteousness, imagining that He treats people the way you probably do, you will be robbed of the full glory of your salvation.

Also, if you do not learn this, you will relate to others in an ungodly way. You will not be able to receive from the gift of God flowing from a person who still has very real flaws. We assume, if a person is gifted or used by God, they must be perfect. And when we learn the reality of their humanity, we quickly dismiss their gift. This is why Jesus said a prophet has no honor in his hometown. We glory in the foreigner because we do not know them. And our lack of knowledge enables us to receive from their gift. When we know someone, however, we cannot receive from their gift because we know the reality of who they are. *This should not be.* This is not the God of Jacob.

The God of Jacob can work through people who are deeply flawed. He can even work through people trapped in sin. Sin matters, and God will judge it. There are times we need to actively discipline or remove gifted people for the sake of the Body. But we must learn to receive the gift of God as it comes through weak and flawed people because ideal people do not exist. There is only One who is perfect, and that is Jesus. Yet even Jesus was "too normal" for some people to receive.[1] Because we do not know how God relates with people, we lack so much that we could have received through others in the Body.

In many ways, God is more comfortable in our "mess" than we

---

1. Isaiah 53:2; Matthew 13:55-57; Mark 6:2-3.

are. And He also evaluates our stories *very* differently than we do. To give one example, consider Jeremiah 2:

> *"Go and proclaim in the hearing of Jerusalem, Thus says the LORD, 'I remember the devotion of your youth, your love as a bride, how you followed me in the wilderness, in a land not sown.'" (Jeremiah 2:2)*

When we read the Torah, it appears God was struggling with Israel's constant disobedience and rebellion. But when God thought over Israel's time in the wilderness, He remembered it very differently. God viewed His people through the lens of deep affection, and it caused Him to summarize the story very differently than we do. One reason for this is that God is confident in His own sovereignty. He knows where He is taking the story, so He can rejoice *now* in full confidence in the future. Even when Israel, or we, resist God, He still knows the outcome. He will get what He wants. And the certainty of His own sovereignty leads Him to interpret history differently than we do. God's great plan has *never been in doubt.* His certainty is a key factor in His leadership of history. He relates to Israel on the basis of His certainty, not her present condition. He is burdened over Israel's sin, but never in doubt of her final condition. His affection combined with His certainty causes Him to evaluate things differently than we do. And this is especially true in the story of Israel and in the story of all His people. We need to learn about His evaluation. God is evaluating you differently than you evaluate yourself because He knows His own power to bring you into the fullness of your salvation.

He is the God of Jacob. He is the God who leads history through those He has called, and this includes their wise decisions and their sin. Both accomplish His divine purposes.

A "Delayed" Promise

In many ways, the Modern State of Israel emerged from the same promise, pain, and pressure that compelled Jacob to take his promise. For centuries, the Jewish people lived with a painful sense of a delayed promise. Holiday celebrations and even weddings included a painful hope for God's promise:

Passover seders ended with, "Next year in Jerusalem."

Wedding vows included, "If I forget Jerusalem..."

As years turned to centuries, the Jewish people suffered among the nations, and the pain over the promise grew. This pain combined with the pressure of seemingly perpetual persecution ultimately sparked the political movement now referred to as *Zionism*. Over time, Zionism has become a complex word, but in this section, we will use the word to describe the political movement that led to the establishment of the State of Israel.

Zionism includes people with a wide spectrum of convictions regarding Israel. Some are religious while others are secular. Over time, Zionism became a diverse movement. Most supporters were Jewish, but others were not. For example, many of the key non-Jewish supporters and enablers of Zionism were Christians ("Christian Zionists") who saw the promise of Israel's regathering in the Bible and were convinced God was not finished with His purpose for Israel.

In our time, many Christians have distorted perspectives of Israel that are simplistic and do not acknowledge the complex history of Israel because they do not understand how God leads history. They assume God is only involved in "perfect" things. Therefore, if something is the work of God, it must be "perfect" and "holy" in every way. And some assume the inverse. If something is not completely righteous, God cannot be involved. But, as we have already stated, this is not true.

Distorted perspectives of God's leadership are far more dangerous than they may appear. First, and most importantly, because when we have a distorted view of God's leadership, we have a distorted view of God Himself. Second, because when we have a distorted view of reality, it means our conclusions rest on faulty assumptions of God's activity. And when we base our convictions on faulty assumptions, one of two things can happen. We either cling to faulty assumptions and refuse to accept what is plainly true. *Or* when those assumptions are exposed, we may overreact and adopt opposite perspectives that are also equally wrong in an attempt to overcorrect our previous error.

For example, many supporters of Israel have suddenly shifted their opinion when they encountered the complexity of Israel's story. When their distorted perspective that everything about Israel is "perfect" was shattered, instead of bearing the tension and seeing God's hand in history, they flipped entirely and adopted a perspective that was also distorted and incredibly harmful. They ended up rejecting God's leadership of history and His work in Israel because His leadership and work do not look the way they think they should look. To support Israel in a biblical and robust way, it is critical that we face our assumptions and come to a biblical perspective that discovers the nature of God's leadership in the messy reality of history.

There are two simplistic Christian perspectives that we need to address. The first perspective we need to address is the assumption that Zionism was primarily a religious movement. The zeal to recognize God's hand in the Modern State has caused many people to assume many of the leaders of Zionism were more religious than they actually were. Christians then defend Zionism by describing early Zionist leaders to Christian audiences as more religious than they actually were. This is especially a challenging issue because the history of the Jewish people is inseparable from the Bible, so even secular Jews still carry a connection to the biblical traditions of their people. However, the reality is that Zionism was largely a secular movement in the beginning and was initially resisted by most religious leaders.

The foundational idea of Zionism is the "right to self-determination," which is the idea that the Jewish people have the right to determine their future. As a statement that the Jewish people should not be controlled and dominated by others, this is completely legitimate. But in the context of Israel's long history with God, this statement raises issues because God is ultimately the One who determines Israel's condition and future. This is true for all the nations, but it is especially true for Israel because of her unique calling. This is the tension of Jacob: *My promise is God-given, but where is my promise?*

Why am I suffering and subject to the dominion of others? The point is that Israel's present and future are determined by Israel's God, not just Israel's people. This does *not* justify things done against the people of Israel. The Lord has very strong words for those who oppress and persecute His people.[2] But we must recognize Israel's story is led by Israel's God.[3]

To illustrate this point, let's consider the perspective of a few Jewish scholars on the foundations of Zionism. First a secular scholar:[4]

...Jews for centuries, no matter where they lived, yearned to return to this place. So on the one hand, this was a very acceptable, established idea.But it was also a very messianic wish. One day, we will return to Jerusalem. They didn't really think that next year in Jerusalem, it was an expression of messianic wish. One day the Messiah will come, and he will take us from all corners of the world, and bring us back to our homeland, to the Holy Land. So someday.

So when people in the 19th century, such as Theodor Herzl, begin to think of establishing or re-establishing the State of Israel, They're building on Jewish tradition, on the desire to return, but at the same time, it's a complete break with history, it's a revolution, it's insane...

They're saying, you know what, literally next year in Jerusalem. And more than that, they are modern people, many of them secular. They're saying, we're not going to passively wait for the Messiah anymore, we are going to be our own messiahs. Is there any more modern idea that you don't passively wait? You will be your own Messiah.

You will shape your own future. So it's a complete break with Jewish history. It rests on Jewish history and the desire to return. But it's a break with this passive notion of waiting for the Messiah and

---

2. Isaiah 34:2; Jeremiah 30:11; Obadiah 1:15; Joel 3:2; Zephaniah 3:8; Zechariah 12:9.
3. Psalm 115:3; Isaiah 46:9–10; Daniel 4:35; Ezekiel 36:24-26; Amos 9:14-15; Zechariah 8:7-8; Romans 9:20–21.
4. Einat Wilf. 2015. "The Best Explanation of Zionism and Israel." YouTube. March 30, 2015. https://www.youtube.com/watch?v=YsTJ8PXEE94.

this modern idea that we will take fate into our own hands. So this is considered a revolution....

... maybe some of you noticed, sometimes, that there are very religious looking Jews in anti Israel demonstrations. They hold signs, Jews against Israel, Jews do not support Zionism.... Even if Israel was the most perfect place on earth, they would still be against it because they conceive, and they're right, of Zionism as a rebellion against God.

I said the Zionists were secular people who said be your own messiah, shape your own future, don't passively wait. So there are those who are saying this is heresy, you're jumping the gun. We need to continue to passively wait until the Messiah will come....

And then there are people who are religious Zionists. Now I told you that Zionism was secular and even atheist and a rebellion against God. So how are there religious Zionists?... Well sometimes when I give talks and I mention that I'm an atheist people come at the end and tell me, you know what, Enoch, you might not believe in God, but God believes in you...God works in mysterious ways. For some reason, God chose those godless communists and Zionist atheists to carry out his grand plan of returning the Jewish people to their homeland. Unbeknownst to them, they were carrying out his plan. And this is, by the way, why religious Zionism really took off after the 1967 war and the 1973 war, where Israel came into possession of the West Bank... The 67 and 73 were such dramatic events that many people felt that it could not but be evidence that God is working out his plan for the Jewish people in history.

The secular elements of Zionism are why, especially before the Holocaust, Zionism was not supported by the religious community as a whole, especially by religious Jews who are ultra-orthodox (also known as the "Haredi" or "haredim."). One ultra-orthodox scholar explains:[5]

---

5. Yaffe, Nechumi. 2021. *How the Haredi Orthodox Are Changing Israel.* Jewish Tele-

Zionism as a movement started as a national endeavor that was very much aligned with European ideas about national movements at the time. Zionism was very much a secular endeavor. It wasn't a Jewish development, even though it used Jewish nostalgia and Jewish ideas. Rabbis saw it as a big threat to religious life because it was the source of a great drift away from religiousness at the time. Zionism was the first expression of Jewish identity that did not have a religious component. Zionism is still viewed by haredim as a threat to religious life. Part of the reason why the haredi community is so against the army is because it embodies the idea that Jews fighting for independence enabled the return to Zion, not the Messiah coming on a donkey. It is a big conflict for a lot of religious people that very secular people established the state. Haredim today view Zionism as an ongoing threat, even though they are stronger numerically and more religious than ever before.

While many rabbis initially resisted Zionism, there were religious Jews who participated in Zionism, and it can be argued that religious Jews were more influential in Zionism than is typically acknowledged. It must be mentioned that, after the Holocaust and the establishment of the State of Israel, there has been a significant growth in religious Zionism. Zionism is no longer as secular as it was in the beginning. But in the beginning, it largely began as a secular movement.

(For example, when Israel's Declaration of Independence was written, one of the great debates was whether to include a reference to God. Secular Jews were violently opposed to the mention of God while the religious pushed back and demanded some acknowledgment of God. In the end, a compromise was reached, and the "Rock of Israel" was mentioned with the idea that the religious could inter-

---

graphic Agency. March 10, 2021. https://www.jta.org/2021/03/10/israel/how-the-haredi-orthodox-are-changing-israel.

pret this to be God, and the secular could interpret it as they wished —to be some other foundational thing.[6])

The ideas quoted above do not give the complete perspective, but they highlight the fact that Zionism in general was a largely secular movement of national liberation (though religious Jews participated and contributed), driven by a conviction that the Jews could no longer afford to wait for their Messiah. They could not simply wait passively for God to bring them back to the land. They had to take their promise and escape their suffering and their waiting. It was a rejection of the centuries-old mindset of waiting for a deliverer. There were even some Zionists who entertained a Jewish State not located in the land of Israel.

This is the reason many of the ultra-orthodox still consider Zionism to be an affront against God to the point of refusing to serve in the army and fully integrate into Israel. They carry a conviction that God is the only One who can restore them to their land, and so they resist Zionism.

"Jacob" Returns to the Land

In Zionism, we can see all the elements of Jacob's story. After years of waiting for a divine promise, and enduring suffering, a weary people decided to secure their future.

Jacob had a God-given promise, but under pressure and gripped by the fear that the promise might never come, he ended up forming a scheme and deceiving his father to secure a blessing. Jacob accomplished God's will in his own strength, and it set into motion family conflict. The promise was his, and God was with him, but Jacob suffered in part because of how he took his promise. His life became complex, and for the rest of his life, he had to navigate family strife, first with his brother, and then with his wives, and finally with his

---

6. For more details, see https://catalog.archives.gov.il/en/chapter/the-declaration-of-independence/ and https://www.sefaria.org/sheets/311428.

children, until God met him one night, wrestled with him, and changed his name to Israel.

In the same way, the Modern State of Israel did not emerge "perfectly." The story is complex and at times messy. The early Zionists included a spectrum of very different people with varying motivations. There were atheists, communists, and religious Jews. Most early Zionists saw liberalism and European thought as the path to the future. They were not seeking to live godly lives, and they were not completely righteous in everything they did.

Like Jacob, the early Zionists used their wisdom and developed a plan, or scheme, to return to their inheritance. Like Jacob, they were desperate—in fact, they were even more desperate than Jacob because of the suffering they had endured over a long period of time. Jacob endured delay for decades. The Jewish people endured "delay" for centuries *with* persecution. Jacob seemed to face the repeated denial of his promise, while the Jewish people faced repeated attempts to destroy them and their promise. While Zionism began long before the Holocaust, the State of Israel was established in the shadow of the Holocaust, the greatest assault yet on the election of Israel. The intensity of Israel's situation in the decades before 1948 was greater than Jacob's, but the pattern is essentially the same.

Jacob's scheme created conflict and the same can be said of many of Israel's actions. And like Jacob, they have remained the chosen people regardless of their condition, and the land has remained part of their inheritance. Like Jacob, they took the promise, but that promise really was their promise. And like Jacob, they have suffered both from the nation's rejection of their promise *and* from the fruit of their own wisdom.

The mystery of Jacob is that he seized his own inheritance through his own wisdom in a way that caused conflict in his family, and yet in the end, the inheritance he took was the inheritance given to him. In a sense, Jacob accomplished the very thing God wanted. In the same way, the Modern State of Israel, though it began without faith, accomplished the very thing God desired.

God required people to respect the election of Jacob. God did not remove Jacob's election because of his sin. And He requires the same of us.

The Mystery of Divine Sovereignty

The story of Jacob and the events of 1948 bring us into the mystery of God's sovereignty. Jacob seized his divine promise in an ungodly way, and yet in the mystery of the story, Jacob accomplished what God wanted. Jacob was destined to carry the promise, and Jacob's father was resisting God's purposes. Though Jacob was a schemer who suffered for his schemes, his schemes accomplished God's will.

The same mystery is at work in 1948. Though Zionism was, to some extent, a rejection of the ongoing waiting for the Messiah and though the modern State was established on a largely secular basis, it accomplished the thing that God had promised and the prophets had long predicted. Israel would return to the land and be sovereign in the land again before the age ends. It is clearly part of God's divine process with Israel and the nations. We are not yet at the end of the promise, but it is clearly part of the plan.

We also have to acknowledge a critical fact: Israel's sins are consistently exaggerated in ways that are certainly not righteous and not even intellectually honest. Nations, media, and even organizations like the United Nations consistently exaggerate and distort Israel's national sins. It is not godly to repeat these accusations. On the contrary, we should speak against these accusations which are nothing more than thinly veiled antisemitism: a rejection of God's election.

Exaggerating Israel's sins is the most common error people make, but there is another error that some Christians perpetuate. Some Christians present Israel as a spotless, perfect people, which is an unbiblical idea. Israel is not yet the glorious people they will be. As such, like Jacob, they continue to sin and are not always righteous. This is not because the Jewish people are uniquely sinful, but simply because they are humans. Any other people group in the same situation would sin in the same ways.

Like Jacob, Israel suffers both from envy against her promise *and* from some of her own attempts to secure that promise in her strength. Jacob suffered conflict because of Esau's envy *and* the way in which Jacob tried to secure his promised inheritance. And the same is true for Israel.

A biblical view of God's sovereignty forces us to face the reality of human sin even among those chosen for a specific purpose. But it also requires us to see those sins and address those sins with a desire for the sinful to come into the fullness of their calling, not exaggerate those sins in an attempt to disqualify and accuse those who are elect.

Jacob Will Become Israel

God is committed to Jacob, but He does not overlook Jacob's condition. And He is fully committed that Jacob will become Israel. The question is are we?

The State of Israel is a conundrum to the nations. On one hand, it has obviously been miraculously preserved and helped. It should never have survived the War of Independence in 1948. Nor should it have survived subsequent wars. Some of the stories of how Israel has been preserved in battles sound like biblical stories from the past. Though it is a small country, Israel has also developed from nothing into a prosperous economy that literally affects the whole world. Nearly everyone interacts with Israeli technology in some form, and Israel's influence among the nations is only growing. There is no rational answer for Israel's survival or influence. It is obvious that God's hand is on Israel in a way that is very unusual.

At the same time, Israel is weighed down by ongoing and seemingly insolvable problems. It constantly endures conflict, threats, and accusation within its borders, in the Middle East, and among the nations. And it faces serious internal challenges—challenges some Israeli leaders believe are existential and much more serious than external threats.[7] Israel struggles under the weight of her own sin,

---

7. For examples of this see Wallach, Yair. 2024. "Israel's Greatest Threat Right Now Is Its War Within." World Politics Review. November 14, 2024. https://www.worldpolitic

the sins of others, and the accusations of others.

Israel's situation confounds the nations, but it is actually quite simple. It is the very thing the prophets predicted. Israel is still Jacob, yet called as Israel. At times, we see glimpses of "Jacob," and at other times, we see glimpses of "Israel." God preserves "Jacob" even while "Jacob" suffers from his sin and the sin of others—not because "Jacob" is any different from other humans simply because of God's election. God's glory is at stake in His ability to transform corporate Jacob into the fullness of what He predicted "Jacob" would become.

He is the God of Jacob. If you know Him as the God of Jacob, His leadership of the corporate Jacob will make sense to you.

Rage against Jacob's election causes Israel's sins to be exaggerated. We must stand *strongly* against the exaggeration of Israel's sins that is actually rooted in rage against the election of Jacob.

Toleration of Jacob's sins leads to an unbiblical view of election that simply affirms Jacob's calling without being burdened by Jacob's condition. We must confront Jacob with his sins because Jacob *must* become Israel. However, that confrontation must respect the election of Jacob because that election is not based on Jacob's condition. It is based on God's divine choice. And the way you relate to that choice is ultimately the way you relate to God.

God chooses that which does not deserve to be chosen. And in the process, He commits Himself to transform the one who does not deserve his election into someone that only God can produce.

You are called to relate to Israel in the same way. You must respect the choice *and* commit to the process of transformation so that Jacob does not remain Jacob. This includes committing to an unbreakable bond of relationship with Jacob while also having uncomfortable

---

sreview.com/israel-war-politics-democracy/ and "Former Leaders of Israel's Security Services Are Speaking out against Netanyahu's Policies." 2023. AP News. September 13, 2023. https://apnews.com/article/israel-netanyahu-mossad-military-protests-cb8742ba0b0f210953669824568eab1e and "Survey: 62% of Israelis Believe Internal Divisions Worse Threat than External Dangers." 2024. Timesofisrael.com. 2024. https://www.timesofisrael.com/survey-62-of-israelis-believe-internal-divisions-worse-threat-than-external-dangers/.

conversations with Jacob about his present condition in light of God's purposes for him.

Again, the way you relate to Jacob is, in part, the way you relate to God.

And we must remember that the story of Jacob included a full reconciliation with Esau. Their relationship was scarred by conflict, distrust, and schemes, but it ended in mutual love and inheritance. In the same way, Israel will ultimately be reconciled to her "brothers" and no longer scheming or caught up in conflicts. Accordingly, loving "Jacob" and agreeing with his election does not mean despising, avoiding, or hating others, including the Palestinians and the Arab world. Agreeing with Israel's election can and does cause tension, but being "pro-Israel" in a biblical way does not mean being "anti" other people. God's election for a redemptive purpose does not mean He rejects all others. As we saw in the beginning, election is part of a divine strategy to bring widespread blessing.

The events of 1948 and the things that have followed are a divine shout to the nations, "I have not forgotten Jacob or his inheritance."

When Jacob stole his inheritance, Isaac was ready to give it to Esau. However, Esau's leadership would not produce the family glory that God intended for Jacob *and* Esau. Jacob was chosen as the vehicle of that blessing perhaps because he seemed to be the least likely. Esau and his father thought he would be a better option, but Esau's story, which includes selling his birthright for food and his unwise marriages, also demonstrates he was not capable of leading the family, and his rage against Jacob's promise was likely based on a false sense of superiority. In the same way, while Israel is still "Jacob," God left the land in the hands of other people for nearly 2,000 years, and the blessing did not come under their leadership. God loves and will bring blessing to those who were in the land and continue to be in the land among "Jacob," but they are not more righteous than Jacob simply because of their suffering.

The issue was never that Jacob deserves it "more." Perhaps he deserves it less. The issue is that God chose a plan of blessing that would lead everyone to humility *and* bless all parties. The blessing had to come through Jacob. It could not come through Esau, not because Esau was more disqualified, but because God had chosen another one. But that blessing was for Esau's benefit. So we must bear the tension that Jacob's blessing one day is going to elevate and bring blessing to the ones who now often seem to be Jacob's enemies. As we respect Jacob, we must also speak words of hope and destiny to whoever feels they are in the place of Esau.

PART VI

A THEOLOGICAL REFORMATION

24

BIBLICALLY COMMITTED TO JACOB

THERE ARE many reasons Christians think they should support Israel. A few of these reasons include:

- Blessing Israel to be blessed.
- The righteousness of Israel.
- The State of Israel is a democracy.
- Compassion over Jewish suffering.
- Israel's end-time purpose.

Each of these reasons may contain important elements, but they are not strong enough to be the basis of support for Israel. As the basis of support for Israel, these reasons are quite superficial because none of these things are guaranteed to be true at any particular time. These reasons may produce a temporary support of the Jewish people, but they are not robust enough to sever the root of envy. These are transactional reasons to love Israel, and if any agreement is transactional, it can be broken anytime one party does not feel the agreement is beneficial for its own interests, or a party believes the other party has not upheld its side of the transaction.

We are called to honor God's *unconditional* covenant with Jacob, which means our respect for God's plan with Israel should also be unconditional. If we relate to Jacob in a transactional way on the basis of conditions, we are vulnerable to breaking our agreement when the right pressures come. The Jewish people have experienced this multiple times throughout history. They were "supported" by people for one of the reasons above or for some other reason, but then when the right pressure came, they suddenly, and shockingly, faced persecution from the very people they thought loved them.

Part of the theological reformation that has begun is realizing that, just as Paul said, God's election of Israel is *irrevocable*.[1] We cannot make appeals to Christians on the basis of Israel's condition or their own personal benefit because we have seen time and time again that this is not robust enough to sever the root of envy. When opinions change or pressure comes, Christians and others have routinely abandoned their "love" or even friendship with the Jewish people. Because of what is at stake, we must expect the satan to rage against genuine support of God's covenants, and accordingly, we must train people to love Israel on a covenantal and unconditional basis because that is how God relates to Israel. People must expect suffering if they decide to deal with the root of envy and stand with God's covenantal purpose. Obviously, not all will suffer in the same way, but we must prepare people for that. The path of following Jesus has always been an invitation to endure suffering and loving God's purposes for Israel is no different.[2]

God is committed to changing the conversation and producing a people who support His election of Israel because they love Him—a people who support Israel regardless of Israel's condition or the benefits they may receive.

Many well-meaning people have tried to change opinions about the Jewish people by appealing to Israel's "goodness" instead of boldly attacking the root of envy. The satan is quite content for this because he knows this kind of "support" does not last when trouble

---

1. Romans 11:29.
2. Matthew 16:24–26; 24:9; Mark 8:34–35; Luke 9:23–25; 14:27; John 15:18–10; 16:33.

comes. The shift that must come is a love of the Jewish people not based on conditions. This is why we must deal with well-meaning, but misguided approaches to securing support for Israel. This is more radical than it may seem. It is a true reformation—something we have not seen since the earliest days of Christianity when most of the leaders were Jewish.

We do not love Jacob out of desire for a material blessing. Yes, we have received incredible blessings from God's work through Jacob, but we need a genuine love that is deeper. We must have a love that will cut the root of envy. We need to love Jacob *and* expect it to result in temporary suffering. If we do not prepare people to suffer for their agreement with God's election, we have set them up for failure. God remained committed to His election of mankind when we were still His enemies.[3] And He demonstrated that commitment *at the cost of His own life.* He willingly suffered for the sake of His decision to elect humans instead of disqualifying humans from their assignment and leaving them in death. Jesus will be scarred forever[4] because He was willing to agree with God's election of humanity. However, the serpent was consumed by envy because he did not think mankind's election was for his benefit. He thought he deserved what was given to another. If we love Israel so we will be "blessed," it is not love, and as soon as we face pressure, we will abandon her to seek some other selfish path to "blessing."

So the question is this: Will we follow the path of Jesus or the path of the serpent?

There is no question that agreeing with Israel's election will bring great benefit because God elected Israel for the benefit of the nations, just as Jesus' serving mankind's election led to His own glorious exaltation.[5] However, we agree with God's election because we agree with God. And we know that agreeing with God's election is for our good

---

3. Romans 5:8-10; Colossians 1:21-22; Ephesians 2:1-5.
4. John 20:25-27; Revelation 5:6.
5. Philippians 2:5-11.

and transformational for us, but we do not do it merely for a transactional benefit.

We do not love Jacob because of the righteousness of Israel or the "morality" of Judaism. God chose Jacob before he had done anything.[6] When he was unrighteous and scheming to "steal" what God had already given him, God declared His commitment to Jacob.[7] Whether the Jewish people are righteous or unrighteous, God remains in covenant with them.[8] If your love of Israel is based on their moral perfection, the root of envy has not been conquered. We are only free of envy when we agree with God's election regardless of Israel's condition.

The sins of the Jews are often exaggerated, and they are presented as the "worst" of all people. We must boldly reject the demonization of the Jews, but even if all the accusations made against them were all true, it cannot change our support for God's election. When Israel sinned against God at Mount Sinai with the golden calf, Moses did not excuse Israel's sin. He interceded for Israel on the basis of God's election.[9] Our love is based on Jacob's election, not his condition. We need to shift the conversation around Israel from proving how "good" she is to confronting people with God's election and their own envy. As we have seen, the Jewish people are just like us. That means they are also sinful.

We do not support Israel because the nation is a democracy. Governmental systems are irrelevant to a biblical perspective.[10] There is no "democracy" in the biblical covenants, and we are not called to love Israel based on her current government. If you work for a government, then Israel's government is certainly a factor in how you relate to her in a diplomatic context. But as a Christian, our love for Israel

---

6. Romans 9:11.
7. Genesis 28:13–15.
8. Psalm 105:8-10; Isaiah 54:10; Jeremiah 31:35-37; 33:14–26; Ezekiel 37:26; Romans 11:1–2, 29;
9. Exodus 32:11–14.
10. Obviously, this is a factor in how governments can relate to Israel in a political sense.

has nothing to do with politics. If the State of Israel is unrighteous and sins against others, that should have no effect on whether or not we agree with God's election. We should resist accusations against the State of Israel and misinformation, but that does not mean our support of Israel is based on her political condition. Even if Israel becomes an unjust government, we are still called to support God's election.

We do not support Israel out of compassion, sympathy, or pity. Of course, we should show compassion, sympathy, and pity for Jewish suffering. It is a subject we should become familiar with to better understand the experience of the Jewish people over time. We especially need to understand the painful suffering of the Jewish people from the institutional Church. True compassion is part of our relationship to Israel, but we cannot let this become the basis of our love for Israel. The reason is simple: We love Israel because of God's election, not as a "reward" for her suffering. As an example, consider the Holocaust. In the aftermath of the Holocaust, there was an outpouring of sympathy in light of the unthinkable events of it. However, that compassion slowly evaporated. People, organizations, and countries with deep sympathy for the suffering of the Jews did not necessarily act on behalf of the Jews after the trouble was over. Instead, they quickly moved on to other agendas because their care for the Jewish people was based on sympathy and nothing else. As the decades passed, much of the support initially given to the Jews evaporated.

We must examine the Holocaust and allow it to shape our theology, but our relationship to Israel must be on the basis of what God has said, not on how much Israel has suffered. The Jewish people are not simply objects of charity to be discarded when we no longer perceive them as suffering or oppressed.

We do not support Israel simply so that Jesus will return or the end times will unfold. While the Bible deeply ties the end of the age to God's purposes for Israel, this is not a reason to support Israel. Once again, this is a transactional reason, where the Jewish people only have significance as a chess piece to bring about some other thing.

God's commitment to Israel in the context of the return of Jesus and the end times is Scriptural, but it is not there so you can see Israel as the magic chess piece or, even worse, see Israel as the "obstacle" to the return of Jesus. End-time information is there so that Gentiles from the nations will read the Scriptures and ponder: Why is God so committed to the Jewish people? Why is the end of the age so focused on their calling and inheritance?

Biblical prophecy should lead us on a journey of discovery to understand God's unbreakable, long commitment to the Jewish people. And that should lead us to agree with God's election of a people regardless of what we expect in the end times or when we expect this age to end. In that process, we should discover who God is in His relationship to the Jewish people throughout history, all the way to the end of the age and beyond.

End-time information should force us to grapple with God's unshakable, ongoing commitment to Israel, not to see Israel simply as a chess piece or, even worse, an obstacle to events that we expect to unfold. If you only support Israel on the basis of end-time beliefs, it dehumanizes the people of Israel, distorts God's leadership of history, and causes you to miss the revelation of God that is found in His commitment to Jacob as a people.

Sadly, it is true many Christians have not pondered the God of Jacob and have only seen the Jewish people and the Modern State through an end-time lens. Accordingly, their commitment to Israel is shallow and transactional. It is actually very dangerous because, if Israel is only a chess piece, then Israel can become an obstacle to God's purposes if events do not unfold according to your expectation. And when you see Israel as an obstacle to God's purposes, hostility to Israel can develop in a context that seems to begin with "support" for her. If you support Israel on this basis, what will you do if Jesus does not come when you expect? What will you do when the end times do not unfold in the way you expected or events do not happen when you expected them to happen? God's leadership of history is often unexpected, and if end-time events are the basis of your support for

Israel, then your unmet expectations can turn that support into hostility.

It is not merely important to "support" Israel, "bless" Israel, or "love" Jacob. It is critical that we support God's purposes on a biblical basis.

There is a lot of support for Israel that is sentimental and shallow, which is why so many Jews are grateful for Christian support but also are very cautious and feel uneasy about Christian interest in Israel. Many feel deep down that, when trouble comes, the support of well-meaning Christians will evaporate, and they will again be left alone. Tragically, history confirms this fear to some extent. Christians rightfully honor the Corrie ten Booms of history, but they also need to remember these kinds of stories are precious in part because they were too rare. In reality, the Holocaust should have had ten thousand or more Corrie ten Booms.

Support for Israel that is shallow, emotional, or political may seem well meaning, but it is actually dangerous because it is humanistic and humanism is not strong enough to stand against the evil that can and will come. The reasons we have examined have elements of truth, but as a basis for support for Israel's election, they are more rooted in humanism than the Scripture. Humanistic ideas sound appealing, but they are not enough to address the root of envy that is in the human heart. Nor do they endure hardship. Superficial support for Israel is perhaps more dangerous than open hostility because it is deceptive. It is something that appears to be real but is not. It not only deceives the Jewish people, it deceives the supporters who imagine their support for Israel is stronger than it actually is.

God is wise and kind, and there are many people whose support for Israel may have begun with a distorted reason but developed into something robust and more biblical. We must begin, however, to correct our errors and teach a more biblical basis for our relationship to the Jewish people. Anything less is based on faulty assumptions. When you build convictions on a faulty foundation, they lead to a distorted view of God and do not hold up under pressure.

Respecting Jacob

We have already seen from the prophets that the tests over Jacob's election are not yet over. We do not know the timing of the fulfillment of the prophecies or exactly how they will play out, but the warnings are very clear. And the prophets also indicated there will be a remnant who stand with Jacob at the cost of their own lives—something that has never happened in history.

It is time for Christians to consider the incredible blessing they have received from Jacob's election[11] and to turn our hearts back to Jacob. God looks at us and asks, "Do you care that Israel has not yet inherited her promises even though you have received incredible blessing through My story with Israel?" We are like an adopted son in God's family, a son that God delights in and has made a fully loved son with every privilege. And then He looks at us and says, "Do you care about My firstborn son?[12] Or only about your own adoption into the story?"

The satan was offended because God asked him to serve the calling of someone else. And that offense set into motion much sin and suffering. And what about us? Are we offended that God asks us to be willing to consider, support, and even serve the calling of Israel? Does that offend you? In most cases, people are not actively opposed to Israel. They simply don't care. *And God also wants to address this.*

You may not agree with God's choice. And the one God chooses is not always righteous. But God's interactions with the ones He chooses is always *for your benefit.* So it is the height of arrogance to slander, resist, or ignore the elect because they were chosen *for your benefit.* Hostility toward Jacob—typically known as "antisemitism"—is the height of arrogance. Having received blessing from Israel, we presume to be rid of Israel in our own arrogance fueled by pride and insecurity.

---

11. Genesis 12:2-3; Isaiah 49:6; Romans 11:11-12; Galatians 3:14; Ephesians 2:12-13.
12. Exodus 4:22-23; Jeremiah 31:9.

How can you receive the good from God's purpose of election but not even care about God's elect coming into their fullness?

Criticizing Jacob

None of this means we cannot have direct conversations with the people of Jacob. A small number of Christians have perpetuated the idea that Israel cannot be criticized in any way because they hold a distorted and unbiblical view of what it means to "bless" Israel. Ironically, this idea is not even shared by the Jewish people themselves.

The people of Israel, in some ways, can be their own most intense critics. Jews often joke "two Jews, three opinions," and Israelis are some of the most intense critics of their own government. More importantly, the biblical prophets were probably Israel's strongest critics. They had very direct conversations with Israel about their disobedience and injustice. Their warnings were strong. But they spoke with a deep conviction of the election of Jacob and God's commitment to save Jacob. Their criticisms were spoken not to disqualify Israel, but to provoke Israel to come into her calling. Prophecies of judgment were joined to prophecies of Israel's great and glorious destiny. The prophets did not always understand how God would do it, and they were often deeply discouraged by Israel's sin, but they spoke with a deep conviction that God would bring Israel's promises about. Even in the moments when Israel's glorious future seemed incredibly unlikely, the prophets declared God's promises.

The prophet Jeremiah is a great example. Judah had become incredibly idolatrous when Jeremiah prophesied. Ezekiel lived at the same time and described Judah's idolatry in grotesque ways:

Then he said to me, "Son of man, lift up your eyes now toward the north." So I lifted up my eyes toward the north, and behold, north of the altar gate, in the entrance, was this image of jealousy. And he said to me, "Son of man, do you see what they are doing, the great abominations that the house of Israel are committing here, to drive me far from my sanctuary? But you will see still greater abominations."...So I went in and saw. And there, engraved on the wall all around, was every form of creeping things and loathsome beasts, and all the idols of the house of Israel. And before them stood seventy men of the elders of the house of Israel, with Jaazaniah the son of Shaphan standing among them. Each had his censer in his hand, and the smoke of the cloud of incense went up. (Ezekiel 8:5–6, 10–11)

"But you trusted in your beauty and played the whore because of your renown and lavished your whorings on any passerby; your beauty became his...You also took your beautiful jewels of my gold and of my silver, which I had given you, and made for yourself images of men, and with them played the whore...You played the whore also with the Assyrians, because you were not satisfied; yes, you played the whore with them, and still you were not satisfied. You multiplied your whoring also with the trading land of Chaldea, and even with this you were not satisfied. "How sick is your heart, declares the Lord GOD, because you did all these things, the deeds of a brazen prostitute, building your vaulted chamber at the head of every street, and making your lofty place in every square. Yet you were not like a prostitute, because you scorned payment. Adulterous wife, who receives strangers instead of her husband! Men give gifts to all prostitutes, but you gave your gifts to all your lovers, bribing them to come to you from every side with your whorings. So you were different from other women in your whorings. No one solicited you to play the whore, and you gave payment, while no payment was given to you; therefore you were different. (Ezekiel 16:15, 17, 28–34)

Jeremiah was grieved over Judah's condition and persecuted by Judah's leaders. He also prophesied Judah's destruction by Babylon. In Jeremiah's day, the northern kingdom of Israel had already gone into captivity because of their gross sin, and the southern kingdom, Judah, had become so corrupt God had stirred up Babylon to destroy Jerusalem and the temple.[13] In the midst of Jeremiah's prophecies of

---

13. Jeremiah 25:8-9; 32:28-29.

judgment, he spoke some of the most profound words of hope to Judah:

> *For I know the plans I have for you, declares the LORD, plans for welfare and not for evil, to give you a future and a hope. Then you will call upon me and come and pray to me, and I will hear you. You will seek me and find me, when you seek me with all your heart. I will be found by you, declares the LORD, and I will restore your fortunes and gather you from all the nations and all the places where I have driven you, declares the LORD, and I will bring you back to the place from which I sent you into exile. (Jeremiah 29:11–14)*

> *"Thus says the LORD: Behold, I will restore the fortunes of the tents of Jacob and have compassion on his dwellings; the city shall be rebuilt on its mound, and the palace shall stand where it used to be. Out of them shall come songs of thanksgiving, and the voices of those who celebrate. I will multiply them, and they shall not be few; I will make them honored, and they shall not be small. (Jeremiah 30:18–19)*

> *And no longer shall each one teach his neighbor and each his brother, saying, 'Know the LORD,' for they shall all know me, from the least of them to the greatest, declares the LORD. For I will forgive their iniquity, and I will remember their sin no more." Thus says the LORD, who gives the sun for light by day and the fixed order of the moon and the stars for light by night, who stirs up the sea so that its waves roar— the LORD of hosts is his name: "If this fixed order departs from before me, declares the LORD, then shall the offspring of Israel cease from being a nation before me forever." Thus says the LORD: "If the heavens above can be measured, and the foundations of the earth below can be explored, then I will cast off all the offspring of Israel for all that they have done, declares the LORD." (Jeremiah 31:34–37)*

> *Thus says the LORD: If I have not established my covenant with day and night and the fixed order of heaven and earth, then I will reject the offspring of Jacob and David my servant and will not choose one of his*

offspring to rule over the offspring of Abraham, Isaac, and Jacob. For I will restore their fortunes and will have mercy on them." (Jeremiah 33:25–26)

Jeremiah even bought a piece of property when the land was being invaded as a visible statement of confidence in God's promises:

"And I bought the field at Anathoth from Hanamel my cousin, and weighed out the money to him, seventeen shekels of silver. I signed the deed, sealed it, got witnesses, and weighed the money on scales. 'Thus says the LORD of hosts, the God of Israel: Take these deeds, both this sealed deed of purchase and this open deed, and put them in an earthenware vessel, that they may last for a long time. For thus says the LORD of hosts, the God of Israel: Houses and fields and vineyards shall again be bought in this land.' (Jeremiah 32:9–10, 14–15)

Jeremiah *both* addressed Judah's sins and declared God's unbreakable commitment to Judah's future, and this is what the prophets did. They spoke on God's behalf and criticized Israel, not to disqualify Israel, but to provoke Israel to return to the Lord and come into her calling. In our time, there is much criticism of Israel, but the question is what is the agenda behind that criticism? The prophets were bold, and we should be bold on biblical issues, but their boldness was rooted in a conviction regarding Israel's ongoing election. Over the last centuries, there have been many critics of Israel who spoke from a conviction of Israel's disqualification, not her ongoing qualification. This is the spirit of accusation, and as we have seen, it is the serpent's venom.

Do you "criticize" Israel with Israel's glorious calling in mind? Are you trying to provoke Israel to come into her calling or trying to disqualify her from it?

It is not "prophetic" to criticize, declare judgment, or conclude a people are disqualified and rejected. It is prophetic to confront sin with the conviction and prediction that a people *will* come into their God-ordained destiny. The prophets spoke with Israel's election in mind.

Even when the prophet declared Israel was "no longer God's people," he predicted a different day when Israel would be received again:

> *And the LORD said, "Call his name Not My People, for you are not my people, and I am not your God." Yet the number of the children of Israel shall be like the sand of the sea, which cannot be measured or numbered. And in the place where it was said to them, "You are not my people," it shall be said to them, "Children of the living God." (Hosea 1:9–10)*

Blessing and supporting the people or the State of Israel does not mean silence regarding their sins. But it does mean that, when we speak of Israel's sins, we speak with humility and with a burden for Israel's promised future. To do otherwise is to entertain a spirit of accusation that rejects Israel's ongoing election.

It's Time for a True Christian Commitment to Israel

The Jewish people have experienced Christians who related to them and tried to influence or control them from a place of power, but God is going to produce something very different: a Christianity that stands with the election of Jacob regardless of Jacob's condition and a people who are willing to honor that election from a place of serving, not from a place of dominating, and a people who do not relate to the Jewish people only if they "convert."[14]

For centuries, wrong theologies have caused "Christians" to despise the people of Israel. But something else is coming. A company of Gentiles who love Israel and are committed to the Jewish people unto death *because* of what Jesus has done in their hearts is on the horizon.

When you read biblical history, you find that Israel repeatedly

---

14. This is a complicated word for Jews and Christians. Historically, Christians have advocated a "conversion" to believing in Jesus that erases Jewish identity. And this rightfully troubles the Jewish community.

failed for nearly 2,000 years up to the first century. And when you read the history since then, you find that the Gentiles, including many who identified as Christians, have also failed for 2,000 years. *After several thousand years of recorded history, all peoples have been humbled.* And before the end of the age, God is going to do something we can barely anticipate. He is going to produce a people among the Gentiles who love and honor Israel's election because they are followers of Jesus. This people will suffer willingly out of faithfulness to the God of Jacob and express this faithfulness by honoring God's election. They will honor that election even when Israel is sinful. They will honor that election even if they face hostility from some of the people of Israel. They will honor that election when Israel faces great trouble. And they will also honor that election when they face the rage of the serpent.

We have spoken much about Israel's election and calling, but it all comes down to this: The story of Jacob is about the revelation of the God of Jacob. So do you know this God? Do you know Him as the God of Jacob?

25

A REFORMATION HAS BEGUN

THERE WILL BE a great transition before this age is over. A Christianity will emerge that does not reject or seek to replace Israel's election, but instead takes great delight in it. Additionally, it will stand with Israel's ongoing election *regardless* of Israel's condition, and it will be committed to Israel to the point of suffering instead of merely honoring Israel for some sort of material "blessing." Many in the Jewish community may find this idea very hard to believe, but we have seen this is predicted in the Scripture and clear in the New Testament.

What's more, the God who leads history can bring it about.

We are in the beginning of a theological reformation. It will not be simple or easy. It will take hard work. But it has begun.

It is hard to anticipate how radical this reformation will be, and it is easy to overlook what is happening because the beginnings of a reformation can be overlooked. The full extent of a reformation is often only visible in hindsight. The last major shift in Christianity is typically known as the "Protestant Reformation." (And it tragically did not correct errors regarding Israel, but instead perpetuated many of them). When that reformation began, it was seen as a simple reform movement, and no one anticipated how seismic the shift would become. In the same way the reformation regarding Israel has begun, right now, very few people really understand how seismic this shift will become.

More Christians than ever in history now see Israel as significant and important. While there are still many Christians who continue to reject Israel's ongoing significance, there are already clear indicators the momentum is shifting. Committed Christians who love the Bible and are committed to living according to it are more and more asking questions about Israel. They are questioning long held beliefs and the general theological status quo about Israel. *And this is exactly how reformations and revolutions begin.*

There is a deep-seated belief that Israel is only significant to Christians so that Jesus' can return or so that "Armageddon" can unfold. And that has definitely been a factor in Christian support for Israel in the last century, particularly as various end-time theories became very prominent in the twentieth century and a State of Israel reemerged for the first time in two millennia. And the biblical narrative of the last days and the return of Jesus is important. *But something else is stirring.*

Christians are now pondering Israel and in the days ahead will be asking different questions. Israel is not simply an end-time chess piece. And the biblical relationship between gentile Christians and the people of Israel is based on covenant, not simply a transactional relationship so that end-time events can unfold or people can be blessed. The ongoing presence of the Modern State is part of God's divine provocation to the earth to reconsider Israel. And the divine invitation to consider Israel is an invitation to consider God Himself because God's relationship with Israel (Jacob) is a context in which God has chosen to reveal Himself.

The new reformation will not see Israel merely as a chess piece in a divine plan that has largely moved on from Israel or as a "problem" that must be resolved. Instead, Israel will be seen as a precious, central part of the story—a story that we have been brought into and a story that will only move forward as God continues to fulfill His purposes for Jacob and Israel. Christians who have ignored, minimized, and even despised Israel will suddenly realize that they cannot know the God of Jacob if they do not properly understand Jacob.

The story of Jacob was always about the knowledge of the God of Jacob, and Christians are already beginning to ask questions. *Why Jacob? Why is God so committed to Jacob? Why does God care so deeply about Jacob?* In the days ahead, more and more Christians are going to ask these questions because God has a burning desire to be known. And He is going to lead the nations to peer into His story with Jacob and confront them with His election of Israel and all the implications of that election.

As the nations rediscover the God of Jacob, they are going to discover Jacob in a fresh way. They will discover that Jacob is chosen, but otherwise not different from us. In fact, *we are Jacob* in so many ways. Jacob is a mirror that shows us who we are. We may not be elected in the same way, but we struggle with the same insecurities, scheming, and desire to be who we were made to be. Our arrogance toward Jacob exposes our own self-righteousness.

1948 was a thunder from heaven to the nations: *Remember I am the God of Jacob.* If we have eyes to see, it is obvious that God wants us to know Him as He *continues* His plan with Jacob. One of the challenges in life is that it can be very easy to miss the moment of history you are in. For example, if someone living one hundred years ago was told that Israel would be reborn as a state and have global influence for the first time in history and that all nations would have to deal with the crisis of Israel, they would find that unbelievable, a mere fantasy. And yet this Is the situation we live with every day. God is forcing the nations to know Him as the God of Jacob, and you cannot know the God of Jacob as He wants to be known if you do not relate to Jacob properly.

We can see the beginnings of this revolution in the realm of Christian theology and scholarship. In the last several years, there is an escalating interest and scholarly attention to the second temple period, the Jewish context Christianity emerged from, and the Jewish context of the New Testament and its teaching. There has also been significant focus on the Jewishness of Jesus and the apostle Paul.

While many theologians divorced Jesus and Paul from their Jewish context over the last 2,000 years, there is a clear momentum in academia to recover the rightful place of Israel. It is as though we are slowly realizing that the Jesus and Paul we are familiar with are in fact distortions of who they really were. They were not gentile "Christians." And if we have distorted the identity of Jesus and Paul, it is inevitable that we have distorted their message to some extent.

Most theologians probably do not see their work in context to a theological reformation, but God leads history, and it is clear He is redirecting attention to Jacob. He shocked the nations with 1948, and seventy five years later the ripple effects are beginning to show in a multitude of areas. Many people miss the connections, but there is a systematic reexamination of Christianity's relationship to its Jewish roots happening in many different contexts. Even scholars who have not yet applied their work to the Modern State of Israel are rediscovering the Jewish context of the New Testament.

Things in Academia often take a while to filter down to churches, but if you glance at scholarly efforts and the books being published, you can see a clear shift beginning to happen. God is stirring academic curiosity as one of many things he is doing to force the Christian world to recover the origin and reality of the faith. God is so merciful that He did not disqualify Israel for her many sins. And He is so kind He has not cut off Gentiles for their arrogance. Our arrogance is serious, but God is persistent in His mercy. He is confronting us and pursuing us so we can repent and change and honor His election and fully cooperate with His purposes.

We must recognize all these things as God's divine leadership. He is leading us into a revelation of Himself, His purposes, and His people that has largely been lost over the last 2,000 years.

Commitment to Jacob

There must be an unshakable commitment that God's glory is at stake in the issue of Jacob remaining a distinct people and ultimately becoming a glorious people that bring blessing to all the earth and lead to all peoples' blessing the God of Jacob and Abraham.

This does not mean there will not be strong differences or ongoing conversations that are difficult. Obviously, there are deep differences between Christians and many Jews, for example, over the person of Jesus. Loving Jacob does not mean all differences suddenly disappear. But it means the basis of our conversation and relationship to Israel must shift to become Biblical. A biblical understanding of Jacob and His God must produce an unshakable commitment to Jacob regardless of disagreements. The reason is simple: *God has an unshakeable commitment to Jacob regardless of Jacob's present condition, and if we love the God of Israel, we will become like Him and relate to Jacob the way He does.*

The apostle Paul said it clearly:

...But as regards election, they are beloved for the sake of their forefathers. For the gifts and the calling of God are irrevocable. (Romans 11:28–29)

The callings of God are *irrevocable* because they are not based on human performance or human achievement. They are made on the basis of God's desire and secured by God's ability to fulfill what He speaks. The story of Israel is not defined by Israel's failure to obey wholeheartedly. The story is defined by God's ability to perform what He promises in a full and literal way.

The theological reformation that is currently underway is going to present a Christianity that radically shifts its understanding in context to its Jewish roots. It will also produce a Christianity that honors Israel's election on the basis of God's decision. It will stand with Israel's irrevocable election if the people of Israel are righteous or unrighteous. It will stand with Israel's irrevocable election regardless of Jewish perspectives on Jesus. We can see the glimpses of this, but something much more significant is coming. There are things that still need to be addressed, but we can see the beginnings of what Jesus and the New Testament predict: a group of Gentiles who will stand with Israel's election even at the cost of suffering *because* they have been transformed with Jesus and love God's election of Israel.

The God of Israel did not use Israel to produce Christianity and then move on. The God of Israel has done tremendous things through Israel, and He remains committed to using her in a tremendous way. This does not mean we neglect or minimize God's revelation of Himself in the Person of Jesus, but it does mean we must abandon our arrogant rejection of Israel's place in the plan of God and the disastrous things that have emerged from our rejection of election and the hidden root of envy. God's ongoing relationship with Israel gives us profound insight into the nature of God and the Person of Jesus. And this is a knowledge of God we desperately need. If Christians want to know Jesus as He is and want to know the God of Israel, we must begin to know God as the God of Jacob. You cannot know Jesus or the God of Israel as He wants to be known if you do not know Him as the God of Jacob.

Have we considered how the God of Jacob feels when we ignore, belittle, harass, or persecute Jacob? The God of Jacob feels deeply about Jacob.

The prophets warn us that the controversy over Jacob's election has not yet been settled. They warn the most intense controversy is yet to come. But the New Testament predicts there will be a people who stand with God's election in that time *because* they obey Jesus. So the questions remain:

1. What will you do? Will you experience the judgment that the prophets predicted will come on Israel's behalf? Or will you stand under pressure?
2. What has your Christianity produced? In your present condition, would you survive Jesus' judgment on behalf of Israel? Or have you accepted ideas that undergird the rejection of Israel's election and the persecution of the people of Israel?

Think like Jesus

The apostle Paul told the Philippians they should "think like Jesus" because in Jesus we have been given a new way of thinking or a new "mind":

> *Let each of you look not only to his own interests, but also to the interests of others. Have this mind among yourselves, which is yours in Christ Jesus, who, though he was in the form of God, did not count equality with God a thing to be grasped, but emptied himself, by taking the form of a servant, being born in the likeness of men. And being found in human form, he humbled himself by becoming obedient to the point of death, even death on a cross. (Philippians 2:4–8)*

Paul's flow of thought is pretty simple. We should *think like Jesus* as a corporate people. And thinking like Jesus is demonstrated in the life of Jesus. As humans we were elected and chosen by God to bear His image and rule in His creation. But we were corrupted by sin, not walking in our election, and we had no way to change our situation. However, Jesus had the ability to do what no one else could do. As God, He could become a human and give His life to secure our redemption so we could walk in our divine election.

Jesus gave His life and embraced our suffering so we can walk in the fullness of our election.

Paul continued to say this is why God has highly exalted Jesus:

> *Therefore God has highly exalted him and bestowed on him the name that is above every name, so that at the name of Jesus every knee should bow, in heaven and on earth and under the earth, and every tongue confess that Jesus Christ is Lord, to the glory of God the Father. (Philippians 2:9–11)*

Jesus is exalted because He leveraged His life to secure our election. Notice He is not exalted simply because He is God. He is exalted as a human because of what He did. The implications are obvious. We should think like Jesus because God wants to exalt us as well so we can rule in His Kingdom. And God exalts those who follow the pattern of Jesus. When we see those who are chosen and elect by God but not walking in the fullness of their calling, we should give our lives to see them walking in the fullness of their election. *This is the way of Jesus.* The way of Jesus is not offended at someone else's election. Nor do we remain settled with someone's disqualification. The way of Jesus is to leverage our gifts and our abilities to see *other people* walk into the fullness of their calling.

Our biggest problem is apathy over Jacob's calling. Behind that is our rejection of Jacob because he has "failed." But God is going to produce a people who do not reject or overlook Jacob but instead choose the path of Jesus and give their lives so that Jacob may walk in the fullness of his calling. The question is will you be among this people? And this will not be limited to the calling of Jacob. We must become a people who fight for the calling of all people, especially when those people seem "disqualified."

Will you follow the way of Jesus where God's election is concerned?